PREFERRED
LIES

PREFERRED LIES

AND OTHER
TRUE GOLF STORIES

CHARLES HAPPELL AND **MIKE CLAYTON**

Hardie Grant

PUBLISHING

Published in 2018 by Hardie Grant Books,
an imprint of Hardie Grant Publishing

Hardie Grant Books (Melbourne)
Building 1, 658 Church Street
Richmond, Victoria 3121

Hardie Grant Books (London)
5th & 6th Floors
52–54 Southwark Street
London SE1 1UN

hardiegrantbooks.com

 A catalogue record for this
book is available from the
National Library of Australia

Preferred Lies
ISBN 978 1 74379 467 8

Cover design by Josh Durham
Typeset in 11/16 pt Sabon by Kirby Jones
Printed by McPherson's Printing Group, Maryborough, Victoria

 The paper this book is printed on is certified against the
Forest Stewardship Council® Standards. FSC® promotes
environmentally responsible, socially beneficial and
economically viable management of the world's forests.

'Jack Nicklaus in Hobart' (Charles Happell) originally published by *The Age* as 'Open's
glory days are gone' (2010); 'Jason Day Rises' (Charles Happell) originally published by
Guardian Australia as 'Jason Day not only killed off "the wicked witch", he did so in
grand style' (2015); 'What the Masters Means' (Charles Happell) – a version of this story
was published by *Golf Digest* (2013); 'His Masters' Choices' (Charles Happell) originally
published by *The Age* as '10 things you (probably) didn't know about the US Masters'
(2017); 'Sawgrass 17th: Golf's Treasure Island' (Charles Happell) – a version of this story
was published by iseekgolf.com.au as '17th at Sawgrass – Great or Gimmick?' (2017);
'Ian Baker-Finch: a Rare Bird' (Charles Happell) – a version of this story was published
by iseekgolf.com.au as 'Baker-Finch: a Notable Absentee at Birkdale' (2017); 'Viva
Mexico' (Charles Happell) – a version of this story was published by iseekgolf.com.au as
'WGC-Mexico Is Only A Good Start' (2017).

 For Trevor Grant

CONTENTS

INTRODUCTION

I first came across Mike sometime in the early 1980s when a few mates drove to Metropolitan GC one weekend to watch a Victorian Open. (I can't remember whether we jumped the fence or paid the entry fee; given we were students, probably the former.)

Anyway, Mike's reputation as a young firebrand had preceded him. Somehow we knew not just of his prodigious talent – he had won the Australian Amateur in 1978 and was being spoken of by esteemed golf writer Don Lawrence and others as one of the country's brightest prospects – but also the fact he had something of a temper.

And no sooner did we begin wandering around the course than we came across Mike in trouble to the left of the 18th hole. His drive had finished perilously close to a tree and he wasn't looking happy. Clearly, if he took a big swish at the ball, he was going to damage his club on the follow through – which is exactly what happened; his club bent beyond recognition after a full, lusty swing. The air was then full of the fruitiest language, which gave us all a chuckle.

From that rather inauspicious beginning, I've come to know Mike well over the ensuing 35-odd years, watching him go on to win tournaments in Australia and overseas, appreciating his insightful golf columns in *The Sunday Age*, then coming to work alongside him at tournaments when I became *The Age*'s golf writer in 1995. He has taught me much in the past 20 or so years, and disabused me of several of the 'bullshit' views that I'd held.

He loved nothing more than talking about golf and swapping stories after a day's play with his fellow pros. His encyclopaedic knowledge of the game, especially the professional game in Australia, was extraordinary. And his opinions generally didn't carry many shades of grey; they were all black and white, and full of certainty.

That self-belief has served him well in his most recent incarnation, as a course architect, a job that necessarily attracts the intense scrutiny – and, inevitably, criticism – of hundreds of club members, some of whom wouldn't know a revetted bunker even if they fell into one but are happy to freely dispense their views anyway.

So when looking for a co-author for this book of essays, there was only one choice, really. It was the polymath golfer, writer and architect who could have written 100 essays blindfolded but, after much persuasion, confined himself to 22 – and excellent, thought-provoking pieces they are.

– Charles Happell, April 2018

* * *

In an era long past, newspapers wrote seriously about golf on a weekly basis and covered not only top professional golf but the best amateurs as well. Australian writers would travel to all the local tour events as well as at least two of the major championships, often reporting on the play from Wimbledon while they covered The Open Championship. The players got to know them well, and if a writer didn't know their golf, the players would quickly pick out an imposter.

The Age always had terrific writers and journalists who knew the game and how best to cover it, and alongside them all was the remarkable Peter Thomson, who was equally as good at writing about the game as they were but who could spot them more than a few shots a side. Charlie, a long-time member at Royal Melbourne and a good player, very quickly established a reputation among the players as one who both knew the game and could be trusted.

Today's players, especially in the United States, have lost some trust in the media and the game is less interesting for it, simply because they are so guarded with their real opinions. Geoff Ogilvy is one of the very few who is not, and as a consequence is a player writers gravitate to for a reasoned quote or a reasoned opinion. That he grew up playing at Victoria, the club of Thomson, and at the same time Charlie was *The Age*'s golf writer, is likely why he understands better than any of his contemporaries how the relationship between player and journalist ought to work.

Charlie took over from Brendan Moloney, who'd taken over from Trevor Grant, who'd replaced Peter Stone, and before him was the legendary Don Lawrence, who'd controversially gone over to the *Herald Sun*. It's hard to believe now but Charlie and the others were household names, certainly among anybody who played golf or tennis. The job as the golf writer at *The Age* was a prized and privileged position, especially in the era when Greg Norman was making headlines most weeks – and if he wasn't making them, he was making them up.

I'd been lucky enough to be offered some space in *The Sunday Age* by Steve Perkin, and my time writing at *The Age* coincided with Charlie's time as the main golf correspondent. We got to know each other well.

I remember chiding Charlie gently in an *Age* column for believing Craig Parry's tale of putting woes one particular day at Huntingdale and reminding him never to believe a player moaning about the putter, especially one who putted as brilliantly as Parry.

'Just remember, Charlie,' I told him, 'we mostly all lie about our putting.'

– Mike Clayton, May 2018

PART 1
PLAYERS

IN THE BEGINNING, ADAM

His reputation as a gifted prodigy reached the pro ranks some time before he did. But when the teenage Adam Scott teed up in one of his first big tournaments, playing partner **Mike Clayton** got a first-hand glimpse of what all the fuss was about.

'Have you heard of this kid?' asked my playing partner, Mark Allen, on Cranbourne's first tee just before we teed off in the 2000 Victorian Open.

I had heard of him and seen a picture of his swing in a magazine. 'Yeah, I think he's a pretty good player,' I remember saying.

Adam Scott was 19, an amateur and presumably a little nervous. We were probably less nervous because we had done it all before and were in the old and cynical stage of our professional careers.

The opening hole at Cranbourne is a par five but it was barely playing as a long par four, easily reached with a drive and a middle, or even a short, iron. The kid was playing with a set of Bullet irons, a set so uncommon the only other player I ever saw use them was Simon Hobday, the extravagantly talented South African and one of the game's real characters. Hobday must have been paid to use them, but Scott presumably was not.

I don't remember the driver he was using but his opening tee shot came out of the toe, started out at the right tree line before hooking far to the left and finishing in the trees.

Mark and I looked at each other, thinking the same thing: not very impressive.

We all just went about our own business, neither of us offering any words of encouragement as Adam made a mess of his chip out of the trees. He got his third shot far enough up the fairway to reach the green with an eight iron but it missed, although he did manage from the back of the green to get it down in two more for a six.

I distinctly remember saying to Mark, 'I guess he's not that good' as we walked to the second tee.

The kid then hit a massive drive down the long par-four second and pitched a wedge into a few feet. Birdie.

The third isn't so strenuous – a short hole, and an eight iron to 6 feet made it look even easier. Birdie.

The fourth is a short par four: an iron and a pitch and Adam knocked his second to a foot. Birdie.

The par five to follow he covered with another great drive, a beautiful long iron into the right bunker, from where he flipped a little splash shot out to a foot. Birdie.

The sixth is one of the more difficult holes, oddly bending from left to right around a curious copse of trees on the inside of the dogleg, yet the green is best approached from the outside of the dogleg. Design faults aside, Adam blasted another long drive, put his six iron on the green and made it from 20 feet. Birdie.

As we walked to the seventh, I well remember saying to Mark: 'Can you believe how good this kid is?'

Oddly, I barely recall a shot he hit from there until the end, but he finished with a 64 and finished up losing on Sunday to another up-and-comer at the time, Brad Lamb, thanks to a three-putt on the 17th green and a misdirected iron into the last.

A couple of weeks later, the tour was in Perth and Ken Brown, the British five-time Ryder Cup player, was doing the television commentary. We caught up on the range and I told him about this kid I'd played with in Melbourne.

'He's playing next week in Sydney at The Lakes in Greg Norman's tournament,' I said. 'Check him out.'

The next Friday I was on the range at The Lakes warming up for my afternoon round when Brown walked up.

'I just watched Adam Scott play the back nine. It was some of the best golf I've ever seen – one of the easiest 63s you ever saw,' he said.

From someone who had played Ryder Cups with Seve Ballesteros, Sandy Lyle, Bernhard Langer and Nick Faldo – and who is not easily impressed – it was worthwhile praise.

Occasionally it's obvious from the very first shots you see that someone is going to be a brilliant and successful player. Whether they turn into truly great players is another thing, but it hardly took a clairvoyant to see Adam had the skills to be something special.

A couple of months later, sponsors invited Adam to play in the Moroccan Open and the Benson & Hedges (it was still a time when cigarette companies were allowed to attach their miserable product to healthy pursuits) in England.

He finished fifth in Morocco, sixth in the Benson & Hedges, turned pro almost immediately and in eight European Tour events earned enough to win his player's card for the following season.

His great play since has been entirely predictable. He drives the ball far and accurately, moving it both ways and setting up the rest of the game. The irons have always been beautifully flighted and he's a decent enough putter.

Some think Adam a bad putter, but there are no bad putters on the PGA Tour – and certainly no bad putters ever win at Augusta. Three putts stick in my mind and should be used as evidence against the prosecutors of the 'Adam Scott is a bad putter' argument.

In 2004, he was in contention to win the Players Championship, which delivers the game's biggest paycheque, the promise of endorsements and a five-year exemption. It's a huge deal, and even bigger for a 23-year-old just getting started in the United States. Adam needed only a bogey on Sawgrass's 18th to win. After a perfect drive on the most intimidating tee shot which isn't the 15th at New South Wales (try that one into a stiff northerly), he inexplicably pulled a six iron into the water on the left. Adam dropped from the Florida lake, pitched to 10 feet and holed a putt he had every excuse to miss, to make that bogey.

The other putts are obvious – and came within minutes of each other. On the 72nd green at Augusta at the 2013 Masters he had 25 feet across the hill (almost the exact same putt Greg Norman had so barely missed in the Larry Mize 1987 Masters) to be the first Australian to win the Masters – barring an Ángel Cabrera birdie.

The brilliant Argentinian – every Argentinian who is any good is brilliant, it's just the way they learn to play – did make his birdie, so the pair then headed back to the 73rd tee for a sudden-death playoff.

After relatively uneventful pars on the 18th they went down the 10th, where Adam hit a beautiful iron pin high to the right, again about 25 feet from the hole.

It was a putt caddie Steve Williams knew so well (*Ed: as he himself explains later in this book*). He suggested giving the ball plenty of air on the right – and the long anchored putter did the rest. The matter of becoming the first Australian to win the Masters must have weighed as heavily, if not more so, than the pressure all those years earlier at the Players Championship – but the result was the same. Bad putters don't sink those.

Adam is not a great putter in the fashion of Jordan Spieth or Ben Crenshaw or Bob Charles, but he has what I'd call a 'comfortably reliable' method. And given how good he is from tee to green, he doesn't have to be a great putter to make an awfully good career.

But it's not yet a great career. To put it in perspective, six-time major champion Lee Trevino described his career as being 'on the edge of greatness'. Six majors is about the point where the vastly overused word 'great' applies – Adam has one to his name. And if Scott is to get to six, he will need to make a lot of great putts. More than he has made in the past.

Almost two decades on from that day at Cranbourne, I wonder if Adam has achieved what he thought he might and what that day promised. He has the perfect life, at least from the outside, with houses in all sorts of exotic places, a lovely wife, two kids, all the money he will ever need – and he's managed it while still keeping a modicum of his privacy.

I'd have guessed there would be more than a single major championship, and there should have been at least one more. (Eight years later, the exact same shot that almost cost him the Players Championship – a pulled six iron into the left rubbish – on the 71st hole at Lytham would cost him The Open Championship in 2012. And in fairness to the 'bad putter' argument prosecutors, he three-putted the 70th hole from 35 feet for a second consecutive bogey – a harbinger of what was to follow.)

But his successes have not surprised me one bit. And in his time, no-one has made the game look easier or more elegant than Adam. Style may not win trophies but it sure adds so much to the game.

IAN BAKER-FINCH: A RARE BIRD

Ian Baker-Finch produced one of the great final rounds
in British Open history to claim the 1991 championship at
Royal Birkdale. His next visit to the Southport links seven
years later provided for quite a different experience,
as **Charles Happell** explains.

When the British Open rolled around in July 2017, Ian Baker-Finch was not there. Instead, he was back home at Palm Beach, Florida, having skin cancers burnt off – an annual ritual brought about by too many years in the Queensland sun. Now a successful golf analyst with the CBS network in the US, Baker-Finch has one week's holiday between early April and September and it's always the same week, when the British Open features the game's elite and the PGA Tour stages the Barbasol Championship for those left behind.

Rather than make the pilgrimage across the Atlantic, the popular Australian kicked back to watch the tournament with his family and friends, with the final groups teeing off on the weekend about the same time the Baker-Finches were cooking up their waffles for breakfast.

But this is always a bittersweet time of year, for when the Open comes around each July, and especially when those Opens are hosted at Royal Birkdale, Baker-Finch knows he will be hounded with requests for interviews and reminiscences.

Of course, he loves re-living that magical Sunday in 1991 when he went out in 29 shots, on the way to a final-round 66, and became just the fourth Australian to hold aloft the championship's famous trophy, the Claret Jug. But he also understands that the interest in that triumph has a slightly perverse edge: it only serves to highlight his sudden and extraordinary loss of form over the ensuing years that prematurely ended his career.

It's a story that's been well told: Baker-Finch was ranked in the world's top 10 after his two-stroke win at Birkdale, then, three years later, he couldn't hit the side of a barn. His game and his confidence deserted him, just like that. After mid 1994, he did not make the cut in 32 PGA Tour events, and just one in 55-odd tournaments around the world. He went through 30 coaches, not to mention psychologists, hypnotists, nutritionists, healers, gurus, swing doctors and spiritualists. And from a sea of wellwishers, he received more than 4500 letters containing maps, prescriptions, poems, mantras, gadgets, potions, recipes and lucky charms. All to no avail.

When the Open was next played at Royal Birkdale, in 1998, Baker-Finch had hoped he could rediscover enough form to just allow him to take his place in the field. But his game was in such poor shape – and the memory of his horror first round at the previous year's Open at Royal Troon still vivid – that he opted not to enter.

But he did visit the fabled links in the days prior to the Open, having agreed to an interview with a Japanese television network about his 1991 win, and, as part of that program, he played a practice round. It was the first time he'd been back at Birkdale since the greatest week of his career.

The grandstands had already been erected for the Open, giving it the feel of British golf's biggest week, and the course from the back tees was playing devilishly hard in biting wind and rain. As he was walking up the final hole, with the Japanese journalist and camera crew trailing behind him, Baker-Finch heard a noise – faint at first then building to a crescendo – coming from around the green.

Unbeknown to him, the club's general manager, Norman Crewe, had made a tape of the broadcast of Baker-Finch's win as he walked to the 18th green in 1991. Crewe and some of his staff had rigged up large speakers in the grandstands, so when Baker-Finch appeared up the 18th fairway, they let him have it, full blast, through the makeshift sound system. All of a sudden the Merseyside air was full of the sound of cheers, clapping, roars and whistling. All for the beleaguered Australian who had forgotten what it was like to be applauded.

Surrounded by this wall of sound, Baker-Finch walked up to the green and momentarily felt as if the clock had been turned back to a time when he was one of the world's best players. If he closed his eyes, it was 1991 all over again and he was walking up to the 72nd green, waving to the crowd, acknowledging their applause, receiving a bottle of French champagne from his old Queensland mate, Wayne Grady, kissing his wife, Jennie, then, in that timeless pose, kissing the Claret Jug.

As Baker-Finch drank in the scene, he looked up to the clubhouse and saw Crewe, the club captain, members, staff and barmen lining the windows and balconies, standing up to applaud him, the last Open champion at Birkdale and one of the most popular names to grace its trophy.

The gesture overwhelmed the Australian, who struggled to maintain his composure. 'They played the tape and it was unbelievable. Just unbelievable. Norman Crewe had apparently walked into the clubhouse – and there had been a big members' competition on that day, so it was busy – and announced to everyone that I was playing the course. He said: it would be nice if you all stepped out as he walks up the last and showed him your appreciation. So everyone stood in the clubhouse and outside on the balconies – and they were all up there cheering and clapping as I came up the 18th.

'I'd always had a good relationship with the club – and still do – and made a point after winning in 1991 of meeting the volunteers and the members, and doing photos with them, and then singing "Waltzing Matilda" with them afterwards. Perhaps they saw me as a decent, down-to-earth guy. But what they did was unbelievably generous. I was fighting back the tears that were welling up in my eyes; it was an amazing experience, very special.'

Seven years after his scintillating final two rounds at Birkdale, Baker-Finch couldn't fathom how he had played so well around such a demanding layout. 'I can't believe I was such a good player to shoot 64, 66 on the weekend around such a hard course,' he said. 'It's bloody tough, the rough was unbelievable.'

In July 2017, somewhere in suburban North Palm Beach, a widescreen television was tuned in to NBC's telecast of the British Open and the tallest Australian in the room allowed himself a quiet smile as he remembered that wonderful week 20 years earlier, a time when he was among the game's best players and no course was ever too tough for him.

BEN HOGAN'S LONG SHADOW

Ben Hogan was a feisty perfectionist who might have flunked charm school, but he played golf in the 1940s and 1950s with a machine-like precision that few, if any, have matched since. **Mike Clayton** recounts his visits to Hogan's home club, Shady Oaks in Texas, to get a better understanding of the man whom few knew well.

Ben Hogan was a golfing genius. No-one before or since hit shots so precisely or so accurately and only a few before or since dominated the game as he did in his prime years, an era so maddeningly altered by a horrific car accident.

The modern players hit the ball farther than he ever did, of course, but he'd be shocked to see most of the top ones, including Dustin Johnson, Adam Scott, Brooks Koepka, Justin Thomas, Rory McIlroy, Phil Mickelson and Jason Day, aren't among the straightest 140 drivers on the tour.

I never saw 'Mr Hogan', as he is still reverently referred to by many, play but in 1987 David Frost (the South African golfer) and I drove to his club, Shady Oaks in Fort Worth, Texas, in the hope he might be around.

Thirty years later I was back at Shady Oaks again, this time with my business partners, Mike Cocking, Ashley Mead and

Geoff Ogilvy. The club had commissioned our design company to rebuild the course.

Architect Robert Trent Jones designed the course at Shady Oaks in the late 1950s for Hogan's much older friend, Marvin Leonard, a big department store owner in Fort Worth. Leonard thought that a city with a very marginal climate should have a course with bent grass greens. When the club he was a member at rebuffed his suggestion to convert their Bermuda greens to bent, he went off and founded two other clubs, first Colonial Country Club and then, when it got too busy, Shady Oaks. Hogan followed his friend across from Colonial to set up camp at Shady Oaks in the late 1950s and stayed there for the rest of his life.

Although he's been gone for years now, having passed away in 1997 aged 84, Hogan's presence is everywhere at Shady Oaks. His two lockers, sitting in the corner of an alcove between the pro shop and the main locker room, remain as they were when he died. There are the perfectly polished London-made shoes with the extra spike in the middle of the sole, the equally perfectly pressed pants, golf balls, the famous hats and all manner of things you might find in a chemist shop to lessen the pain in his legs from that car wreck. His left ankle, pelvis and collarbone had been fractured when his car met with a Greyhound bus one foggy Texan morning in 1949, but it did not stop him winning the US Open the next year, the so-called 'Miracle at Merion'.

On his death, Hogan left 900 of his clubs to Mike Wright, the Shady Oaks club pro. (It was Hogan who suggested to the board that they hire Mike when, as Mike says, 'I was only twenty-four and, at best, barely qualified to take the position.' Hogan told the board, 'If he's no good you can fire him after a year, but I think he'll turn out fine.' That he did; indeed, if there were a world ranking of club pros, Mike Wright would be right at the top.)

The room next to Mike's office has an indoor training net where the walls are lined with Hogan's old clubs, drivers, putters, wedges, irons and assorted wonders, including a belly-putter with two grips, plus a metal hybrid club he made in the 1960s.

His black persimmon drivers are everywhere, all identical looking, which reminds me of Bob Charles, the great putter, who had a collection of identical and perfect Acushnet centre-shafted putters. The irons are all four degrees flat, meaning the heel sits off the ground for most people, and the five irons look like a five iron used to look before manufacturers started making four irons and stamping '5' on them to have gullible amateurs think their new clubs were going further. The putters are an array of ungainly-looking implements befitting a man uninterested in putting and who ended up fighting a war with the yips.

'See that practice green out there,' Mike told Geoff, Mike, Ashley and me, pointing to the club's practice green right outside the pro shop. 'I saw him on that green one time in forty years.'

Every element of Hogan's drivers seemed to be arranged to make it all but impossible to hook the ball. He had grown up with the destructive shot ducking low and left – and he detested it, once referring to the fear of hooking as 'like walking around with a rattle-snake in your pocket'. The cord grip on each driver is thick, with the 'reminder' at the back turned to the right to encourage the weak grip he employed and advocated in his book, *Five Lessons: The Modern Fundamentals of Golf.* There is no roll or bulge on the face because he didn't believe in it and the last step on the shaft is only a few inches from the binding. It's pretty much a barge pole.

Mike sent us out to play with some of Mr Hogan's clubs: 'He'd want you to be out there playing with them – there is no use them just sitting here.'

I'd heard the stories of the driver slicing wildly to the right but surely it couldn't be that hard to hit straight? I went first and hit the predicted wild slice to the right. And then another and another before one went straight.

Mike Cocking, a good enough player to win the Victorian Amateur and finish fourth in the Australian Masters as an amateur, went next and the same thing happened – only his went a little longer and a little further to the right. Geoff smirked and said, 'There's no way I'm doing that.'

But he did – sliced wildly to the right.

Geoff is usually very good at picking up old clubs – hickory or persimmon – and quickly getting a feel for what the shaft and the head are doing. Within a hole or two, he was ripping the driver far and straight but, try as he might, he could not make it hook. 'How much better would golf be if we played with this stuff,' was Geoff's predictable (if you know him) comment.

People generally think the game is more fun when it's easier (or at least the clubs are more forgiving). But when you're playing for amusement – not for your living – it's often way more fun when it's made harder, with the clubs a little more difficult to hit with, the sweet spot not so easy to find. The 'old stuff' is also a more reliable lie detector than modern clubs, which better disguise mishits.

Hogan was famed for a swing born of utter contempt for the hook; it was also part of his reason for making a club that wouldn't hook. With his own factory in Fort Worth making some of the best clubs in the world, he had the means and the time to experiment with his equipment just as he patiently refined every move in his swing. His process with both swing and clubs was to throw out the things that didn't work, keep the ones that did and then test them in the crucible of championship golf.

There are lots of things that work on the practice fairway but not the course. There are lots of things that work on the course but not in a tournament. Then there are lots of things that work for the first 70 holes of a tournament but not the last two holes. Finally, there are lots of things that work for all 72 holes of a tour event but not on the 72nd hole of a major championship. All the great players drove their games to the ultimate destination, the 72nd hole of a major championship, and proved to themselves what they were doing worked – and worked and worked.

In another part of the Shady Oaks clubhouse is a basement room with racks of sets of old irons, enough clubs for golf nerds to pore over for days. Almost all of them were Hogan irons, but there was one set of old Wilson Haig Ultras. I asked Mike about them. 'Oh, he'd come into the pro shop, and if he saw a set he liked he'd buy them and try them out, just to see what his opposition was making,' he said.

Hogan used to practise on the 'Little Course', a rudimentary par-three layout (with one par four) wedged between the 10th, 11th and 18th holes on the main course. The greens were really basic and the few bunkers little more than round holes in the ground.

Mike Cocking started our redesign by rebuilding the Little Course, making proper greens and bunkers and a course where anyone could spend hours practising every shot you might care to try. Kids can go out there and play the holes in order or they can let their imaginations run wild and play from wherever to wherever. The long shot from the third tee to the fifth green is a beauty and you can go to the far side of the fourth fairway and play a great medium-length par four to the ninth green. It's a simple concept but one golf needs more of. Obviously it takes some space but less than you might think, and if there isn't room for nine holes, three, five or seven is fine. It doesn't matter.

The big course at Shady Oaks isn't really very big but it's a perfect length for members and for a club with no need to stay relevant for big professional tournaments. It's a 1950s Trent Jones course with huge runway tees, massive sloping greens and flat, sprawling bunkers. It has ambience, interesting hilly land, beautiful trees and, of course, history, but the architecture could be better – and we are hoping to improve it. The third is a decent enough hole, requiring just a three wood and a wedge, but it could be an amazing, driveable par four for the long hitters, and an equally vexing drive-and-pitch hole for the rest. The 14th is a par five with the second shot playing around a small river, but it's lined on the fairway side with trees so you can't see the green from back on the fairway. That's two black marks: one, it's a bad shot, and two, it should be a great-looking shot. It's a day with a chainsaw away from being a really good hole.

In many ways I wish 'Mr Hogan' was still around to have him see what we have planned. Then again, he was such an intimidating man you'd want to make sure he was on your side. And you knew what you were doing. After Hogan signed the contract to sell his club-manufacturing company to a Japanese conglomerate, he said to the conglomerate boss, 'You've just bought the crown jewels. Don't screw it up.'

We feel the same pressure working on his course.

KARRIE ON

Karrie Webb is Australia's most successful golfer in terms
of major championships won: seven. And as **Charles
Happell** reveals, she has done it the hard way, ever since
she left the small Queensland town of Ayr as a 20-year-old
with her childhood sweetheart at her side.

In 1995, armed with little more than a set of clubs and burning
ambition, Karrie Webb set off from her home town of Ayr in north
Queensland (population 8885) to conquer the world. At her side
was childhood sweetheart Todd Haller, who had also grown up in
the small sugar town south-east of Townsville.

This was not a simple matter of a young couple setting out on a
global adventure together, backpacks on their shoulders and stars
in their eyes. Webb, aged 20 and a professional golfer for all of
three months, was going to try her luck on the Ladies European
Tour, and Haller was to be her caddie.

As if the task ahead of them wasn't hard enough – trying to
make a living against the best women players in the world – they
were adding this other level of complexity to their relationship:
Webb would be Haller's boss in their workplace, on the golf course.

As any professional golfer will tell you, the player-caddie
relationship is fraught at the best of times. One of the immutable
laws of golf is that when life is going swimmingly, and the
prizemoney is flowing, it is the golfer's skill and clever play that has
brought about this happy state of affairs. Likewise, when things

take a turn for the worse, and the golfer is suddenly spraying them all over the place, it is the caddie's fault. This was the dynamic that awaited Webb and Haller as they set off together on their grand enterprise.

Webb had performed so well in her second tournament as a professional, the 1994 Australian Ladies Masters at Royal Pines in Queensland, finishing a close second to then world number one Laura Davies, that tournament promoter Bob Tuohy threw in two return airfares to Europe alongside the $25,000 runner's-up cheque.

Webb had played in Europe before, representing Australia in the Espirito Santo world amateur teams event in Paris in late 1994, but this was a world away from Ayr's canefields, the Burdekin River and Sugar Loaf café, which her parents ran in the main street.

The British Open at Woburn Golf Club in 1995 was to be Webb's 10th appearance on the tour and, as events would transpire, by far the most important. She announced herself with an opening 69 then took the tournament lead with a second-round 70. Despite the widespread belief that the Australian rookie would collapse under the pressure of the final 36 holes, she showed barely any sign of nerves and actually pulled away from the world-class field, winning in the end by six shots from Annika Sörenstam and Jill McGill. Laura Davies finished 19 shots further adrift.

Webb – a shy 20-year-old – had become the youngest winner of the biggest tournament in European women's golf.

Yet it was the nature of Webb's relationship with Haller, as much as her golf, that fascinated some onlookers. Reporting on the championship for *The Independent*, Richard Edmondson was one who couldn't help remarking on the dynamic: 'The celebrations around the 18th green were conducted mainly with Todd Haller, Karrie's fiancé and caddie, who rewarded his partner with a kiss each time she made a birdie. The prurient in the crowd may have wondered what would follow an eagle or albatross, perhaps a deliberate drive into the woods the following hole.'

Proving it was no fluke, Webb went on finish second in the LPGA Tour School later that year, despite playing with a broken bone in her wrist. The result guaranteed her playing rights on the world's richest circuit.

In keeping with her stunning impact on the European Tour, Webb made a similar splash in the US, finishing second in her opening LPGA tournament, then taking out the HealthSouth Inaugural event in Orlando at her second start. That took her earnings after a fortnight to US$192,000, a dizzying figure for a young couple not accustomed to such riches. 'We're very conservative people,' Haller said at the time. 'Karrie hasn't even bought herself a car yet. We put the minimum deposit down on the house [in Orlando].' Webb seemed equally nonplussed: 'I'm not used to having this much money; I guess I'll have to sit down and figure out how to spend it.'

As her profile grew, Webb began fielding questions about her coach, of whom there seemed to be no sign. And it's true that Kelvin Haller, who came into her life when she was in primary school and also happened to be Todd's uncle, was back in Ayr, monitoring Webb's progress from a distance. The reason he wasn't alongside his most famous charge is that he was a paraplegic, confined for the past decade to a wheelchair, after a terrible electrical accident and complications in surgery. When Webb ran into the occasional problem with her swing, she'd get Todd to film her hitting balls on the practice range then send the images back to Ayr. Kelvin would then ring up Webb to discuss any glitches he'd been able to identify.

Of all the player-coach relationships in top-line sport, it had to rank among the most unconventional.

'He can move his right arm,' Webb explained to the incredulous media. 'He just can't walk. He's all right mentally. He knows my swing, so he doesn't have to demonstrate anything to me. Kel has taught me everything I know, and I've honed those skills. He has taught me a lot about discipline and determination, too … but maybe the biggest thing he taught me was about the will to live.'

So not only were Webb and Haller alone together in the US, they had none of the support – coach, family, trainer, dietician, physio and so on – that are mandatory among all the top players these days.

While Webb was embarking on her barnstorming run through the early part of the 1996 LPGA season, Haller stayed pretty much in the background, being a dutiful support for his fiancée but never hogging the limelight. Webb had earlier hinted at tensions, but no more than those experienced by any young couple in a new environment. 'We argue, but not for long,' she said.

The childhood sweethearts were featured on the front of *USA Today*'s sports section about this time, sharing a loving embrace.

Haller was a handy player himself, playing off a handicap of three at Ayr, and the pair had friendly bets whenever they played, although the stakes did not involve money – rather who'd do the laundry or dishwashing.

But at the Sprint Titleholders tournament in May, which Webb claimed as her second victory of the year, Haller spoke for one of the few times about the strain of being a caddie, fiancé, friend, emotional support, club cleaner, yardage measurer and bag-lugger. 'Oh my God, it's the hardest thing I've ever done,' he said. 'We've been together 24 hours a day, on the course, travelling, at hotels on the tour. There's an incredible strain on the relationship. Karrie's so intense and competitive. We try to leave the game on the course but she's got to let off steam at someone.'

A short time later, the first serious cracks began to appear in their relationship when Haller abandoned Webb in the middle of a tournament in Japan. The following week, at the LPGA Corning Classic in New York, he wasn't on the bag at all. Nor was he to be seen at the US Open the week after that.

After the second round of the Open, Webb was quizzed by journalists about Haller's absence; the persistent questioning eventually brought her to tears.

As Steve Williams, perhaps the best-known caddie of all, observed of the extraordinary pressures in any such relationship: 'It's a very delicate situation when you're a player and caddie. At the end of the day, despite how well you might have played, that break and time apart – when you go back to your hotel and chill out – is very refreshing and much needed. So I can't imagine how difficult that would be to not be able to have any time apart. You'd have to be two very special people to make the dynamics of that work. Sharon Funk caddied for Fred Funk on the PGA Tour for a while, and that was successful, but they were married and older. Sheryl Calcavecchia carried Mark's bag for a while, and Nicki Stricker worked with Steve, but there haven't been a lot of relationships that can handle that strain.'

Finally, after four years together, Haller packed his bags and headed back to Ayr, leaving Webb on her own and trying to keep her career on track.

Players from outside the US trying to make a mark on the PGA and LPGA tours are often faced with these kinds of challenges. The degree of difficulty in trying to master myriad logistical issues when away from home and forge a successful career with very little support is enormous. Despite being made of stern stuff, Webb faltered over the next few months and in the six tournaments after the split she finished 41st, 75th, 19th, Missed Cut, 18th and 12th, her worst sequence of results (until two decades later) on the LPGA Tour.

As she told me in an interview at the time, 'It was a very tough time and it's been hard getting over, but I wasn't very happy with myself even though I was having so much success on the golf course. Things just didn't work out how we planned them ... I guess I'm very intense on the golf course so it was very hard on both of us.'

Yet, slowly, through the back half of the year, and with a new caddie – South African Evan Minster – on her bag, Webb began to rediscover her groove. In September, she won the Safeco Classic then, settling into her rhythm, took out the Tour Championship two months later, closing with a 65 to win by four strokes.

Capping off an emotional year, Webb made a tearful acceptance speech by the 18th green, acknowledging the personal turmoil in her life and paying tribute to the work Kelvin Haller had done with her swing. In the end, she won four times that year to become the first LPGA player to surpass $1 million in a season.

In the years to come, Webb just kept racking up the victories – six in 1999, then seven in 2000. She cracked her first major at the 1999 du Maurier Classic – played in Alberta, Canada – in grand style, with four birdies in the last five holes to complete a pair of 66s on the weekend. Comparisons were soon being made with Tiger Woods, and they weren't frivolous ones. She won the Nabisco Championship, her second major, by 10 shots in 2000 and the US Open by eight strokes the following year, echoing similarly dominant performances by Woods at that time.

Webb captured the career Grand Slam faster than any other player – seven years – and is the only woman to win all five of the LPGA Tour majors.

Such was her early success, the Australian qualified for entry to the World Golf Hall of Fame in 2000, having reach the required 27 points – one point for a tour victory, two points for majors – after just five seasons. But she had to wait another five years before being officially inducted because she had not fulfilled another requirement – playing 10 years on the LPGA Tour. She did this in June 2005 when she completed the first round of the LPGA Championship – and at the age of 30, just one decade after setting out from her sleepy home town of Ayr, she became the youngest person ever to enter golf's Hall of Fame.

During her induction, Webb told of Sunday mornings at Ayr Golf Club as a four-year-old with plastic clubs playing one hole before her grandfather put her on his golf bag and pulled her the rest of the way on his buggy. Her grandparents bought her real clubs on her eighth birthday, she said.

'It seems like a big jump from that memory to be standing before you tonight,' she told the audience. 'It's hard to believe I'm here. I still feel like a little girl with big dreams from a small town called Ayr.'

To complete her extraordinary journey, in 2011 Webb was elected by her peers to serve on the LPGA Board of Directors – the same Karrie from small-town Queensland who set out in 1995 to take on the world, and was once so shy that she hid behind wraparound sunglasses and only let her clubs do the talking. Now the grand dame and elder stateswoman, she was to be the voice of her generation of golfers.

FILLETED SHARK

It's a day that still causes anguish among Australian golf fans. Greg Norman took a six-shot lead into the final round of the 1996 Masters and ended up losing by five. **Charles Happell**, who covered the tournament as a journalist, was there on the course when Norman fell apart, and there on his yacht when he tried to put the pieces back together.

Greg Norman was due to tee off at 2.49 pm on that sunny Sunday in Georgia. On the practice fairway warming up, the Australian appeared the picture of relaxation. He chatted with Kiwi Frank Nobilo, then worked his way through half a dozen irons and woods, pausing now and then to joke with his caddie, Tony Navarro, and coach, Butch Harmon.

Not far away, his playing partner, and nemesis, Nick Faldo – who hadn't played well in his third-round 73 – was all business.

The previous day, late in the third round, the Englishman understood as he surveyed the leaderboard beside the 18th fairway that he needed to make a birdie at the final hole to break out of the tie with Phil Mickelson and earn himself the right to feature in the last pair, alongside Norman, on Sunday. Only then would he be able to stare down the Australian. Birdie it he duly did, holing a nervewracking side-hiller to finish at seven-under 209, with Mickelson at 210 and Norman lengths in front on 13-under 203.

Now, at practice before the final round, there was no by-play with his caddie, Fanny Sunesson, and coach, David Leadbetter, as he warmed up: it was down to work as he tried to iron out glitches in his swing. It seemed Faldo was wrestling with some inner demons, while Norman had not a care in the world.

As a first-time visitor to Augusta National, where I was covering the year's first major for *The Age* and *The Sydney Morning Herald*, I was quietly chuffed on the Saturday night, thinking: Here I am at my first major, and Greg Norman is about to become the first Australian to win the Masters ... The story will play so well back in Australia that maybe, surely, it will lead to more trips to Augusta. So as I jauntily set off with 'the Shark' on that Sunday, who could have possibly guessed what was about to happen over the next four hours?

Norman strode to the first tee, a par four. After a few deep breaths and a tightening of his jaw muscles, he made the first mistake of his day, pulling his opening drive left into the trees separating the first and ninth fairways. From a tricky position, he found the greenside bunker with his second shot – and a bogey resulted. Off the tee, the inscrutable Faldo hit the middle of the fairway and made a solid par. The Australian's six-shot lead suddenly became five – a bad start for a player occasionally prone to nerves.

The first thing apparent to any moderately observant golf watcher on that fateful day was Norman's pre-shot routine. It had suddenly become a jittery, twitchy mess. The natural, fluid brilliance that had taken him to a first-round 63 in that Masters – tying the major-championship record low score – and a six-shot lead after three rounds had deserted him.

Whether it was because of the weight of history on his shoulders – no Australian had won the green jacket before – or the steely, unflinching play of Faldo, Norman slowly started to fall apart on the biggest day of his life.

As he stood over the ball for the rest of his round, Norman gripped and re-gripped his club, seemingly unable to get comfortable. It often took him 10 or 15 seconds before he felt ready to pull the trigger and begin his backswing. Over the other side of the fairway, Faldo didn't need to be a great student of body language to understand that his great rival was in trouble.

Up in the CBS commentary tower, golf analyst Peter Kostis was not the least bit surprised by what he was seeing. At the beginning of the week, Kostis observed Norman experimenting with a stronger grip on the Augusta practice range.

The day after Norman's record opening round of 63, Kostis noticed his grip on the club had slightly weakened, and he didn't hit the ball as precisely on Friday but still shot 69 to increase his lead to four. The trend continued in the third round. To the swing guru's trained eye, Norman's grip was back to where it was before the week began, and he was missing shots to both sides of the fairway. Thanks to his chipping and putting, he managed to shoot 71 on Saturday.

'Were it not for some phenomenal short-game work, he could have shot 78 or 80 but, as it was, he left the golf course on Saturday night with a six-shot lead,' Kostis said in a *Sports Illustrated* article dissecting Norman's performance that week. 'Everybody thought he was playing better, yet I saw someone ... who was in trouble. You can't play any golf course with a two-way miss, especially not Augusta National.'

Every golf fan in Australia knows how this story ends, and how Norman's dreams of winning his first major in the US and being the first Australian to leave Augusta with the green jacket draped over his shoulders were dashed in the harshest, most public way. Even when it is mentioned now, more than 20 years on, it elicits the same groan of disbelief among Australian golfers and fans.

It seemed like half of Australia had set their alarms on that Monday morning, full of hope and not a little expectation, only to trudge off to work several hours later, cursing Norman for making them sit through another Masters horror show and perhaps kicking the cat on the way out the door.

First came the bogey at number one, then a birdie at the par-five second, followed by a terribly unlucky bogey at number four, the long par three, where Norman's four iron floated high and straight towards a pin on the far right edge of the green, tucked behind the front bunker. But then it somehow stabbed into the hill of grass between the green and bunker, took a hop, and rolled back into the sand. Norman recoiled as if he'd taken a blow to the chest then leaned forward and put his hands on his knees, shaking his head. That image ended up adorning the next cover of *Sports Illustrated*.

From that moment on, everything started to head south: Faldo's birdies at number six and number seven piled pressure on the Australian and narrowed the gap to three shots. Norman then bogeyed the ninth, 10th and 11th – the latter after a nervy short-range three putt – so that when the pair stood on the tee of Golden Bell, the devilish par-three 12th, they were on level terms. His six-shot lead had dried up in not much more than two hours.

When Norman's tee shot at the 12th splashed into Rae's Creek, I turned and headed back up the hill to the media centre. I'd seen enough. Norman, so buoyant on the practice fairway hours earlier, now looked utterly forlorn. His close friend Nick Price had a similar reaction to me. Watching the telecast in the players' locker room, he turned away after Norman's tee shot on 12. 'I can't watch this,' the Zimbabwean said. 'It's making me feel sick.'

Augusta had done it again. It was the scene of so much heartache for Norman over the years – seven top-six finishes, including the desperate near-misses in 1986 (to Jack Nicklaus), 1987 (to Larry Mize) and 1989 (to Nick Faldo) – and it had once again mugged him in broad daylight.

For Steve Williams, who caddied at Augusta that year for Ray Floyd, the problem was clear: Norman simply played too cautiously and showed none of the derring-do that had marked most of his tournament play. 'People say he choked but I don't believe in that word. He lost because after three days of playing aggressively he started to go into his shell and play conservatively, trying to protect his six-shot lead. It's an easy mistake to make with a lead that big,' Williams told me.

When Faldo and Norman had hugged on the 18th green, the Englishman seemed to tower over his vanquished opponent. Looking for a fresh angle, I bolted up to Augusta's clubhouse hoping to find someone who could help put this performance into some context. Propped up by the bar, drinking a lemon squash, was Faldo's coach, Leadbetter, looking flushed after just walking the 18 holes. He was as baffled as anyone: 'I don't know what happened to Greg's pre-shot routine. I've never seen him grip and re-grip the club like that before.'

After I'd filed my final story and began to think about the Monday flight back to Australia, via Atlanta and Los Angeles, I received a call from Patrick Smithers, the sports editor of *The Age*. Smithers – who always had a good nose for a news story – suggested that I follow Norman to Hilton Head in South Carolina, where he'd entered to play the Heritage Classic the following week. The task was simple, said Patrick: get a one-on-one interview with Norman.

I rearranged my flights back to Australia, hitched a ride to Hilton Head with the esteemed Australian golf writer Bernie McGuire, and found a room in a cheap hotel. On the Tuesday, Bernie and I knew Norman would make his first appearance at the Harbor Town course for a practice.

We knew he'd try to sneak in and out without being noticed, and, after playing just nine holes, he did indeed try to scarper from the ninth green, but three or four of us managed to head him off at the pass. Norman could have put his head down and marched straight to his courtesy car, but – as he invariably did – he looked his questioners in the eye and answered everything that was put to him.

'Okay, so people realise he does screw up, he does make mistakes, he is a human being, he does take seventy-eight on the final day of a major,' Norman said of himself. He looked gaunt and tired. 'But I'm stronger than that. It will take a lot more to lay me out – like a bullet here between the eyes.'

He said his spirits had been lifted by the messages of sympathy he had received. Davis Love and South Africa's Fulton Allem had both put an arm around Norman when he arrived on the practice fairway earlier that day. The public was also caught up in the mood: when he appeared on the practice tee, the gallery of 150 or so burst into applause.

'There's been a flood of commiserations from all around the world, to tell you the truth,' he told us. 'It's been phenomenal. I really can't describe the support I've had – from friends I knew I had, and some I didn't know about. There hasn't been a player who hasn't come up and said something, which means a lot.'

Norman said that, only minutes after returning to his rented Atlanta home from Augusta National on Sunday night, he'd received an emotional call from the American player Freddie Couples, which had greatly moved him. After flying back to Florida later that night, Norman, his wife, Laura, daughter, Morgan-Leigh, and manager, Frank Williams, were met at the airport by three close friends. The group stayed in the plane on the tarmac for the next hour and a half, drinking beer and talking.

Norman's parents, Merv and Toini, were among the first to call on Monday morning, from Queensland. The Australian prime minister, Bob Hawke, followed soon afterwards.

It was around then that it really hit home what a golden opportunity he had let slip. 'I woke up angry, only angry at myself because I realised I had let myself down, which you don't like doing but sometimes it happens in life,' he said.

After less than four hours' sleep, Norman took his children to school, then, still tired and hungover, went to his office for an early meeting. There, he found the fax machine awash with messages from all parts of the globe.

'This wave of faxes started from Australia, because we're a day ahead right, first from the east coast as people started getting into their offices at nine o'clock, then they started up again at midday as people got into their offices on the west coast. It was an amazing sequence of events,' he told us. 'I started reading some of them and it breaks you up, some of the responses. I'm going to keep every single one of them; I'm not going to throw them away.'

After our brief interview beside Harbor Town's ninth green, Norman mentioned to McGuire and me that he was having a party that night aboard his boat, *Aussie Rules*, which was moored in Hilton Head harbour. Would the two of us like to come? Sure, we said. So that's how two scruffily-dressed Australian journalists found themselves aboard *Aussie Rules* that night.

At 29 metres, *Aussie Rules* was more a luxury liner than a boat, panelled inside with Australian silky oak and filled with enough television sets, bars, chairs and exotic trimmings to equip a small hotel. Dwarfing almost every other vessel in this well-to-do part of the world, it attracted crowds who first marvelled at it, then noticed the distinctive great white shark logo on its stern and peered inside trying to glimpse one of the world's most recognisable sportsmen.

Among the first to arrive for the party were Nick Price and his wife, Sue. Then came Frank Chirkinian, producer of CBS television's golf telecasts, followed by Jeff Sluman, Davis Love, Peter Jacobsen, Frank Nobilo and a host of other golfers. Navy blazers with gold buttons were the order of the day. Navarro was playing barman.

Norman welcomed each guest with a smile and warm handshake that appeared heartfelt. If he had suffered a tragedy in the past 48 hours, he wasn't letting it show. And he still found time to give Bernie and me a guided tour of the boat, through the bridal suite and beyond, proudly pointing out all its bells and whistles. But we felt out of place, as though we had just gate-crashed a wake.

For beneath Norman's stoic façade, there was a palpable sadness. You sensed that he'd have traded in his boat – and any of his other million-dollar toys besides – for the one prize he most coveted: a garish green jacket (55 per cent polyester, 45 per cent wool blend) that he'd struggle to sell at the local op shop and certainly never think of wearing to a cocktail party on a yacht.

People complain that golf, especially amateur golf, isn't covered in the newspapers anymore. It's true. Newspapers do a woeful job covering golf. *The Times* of London doesn't even have a full-time golf writer, an extraordinary fact considering Bernard Darwin once wrote golf for them. Nor does *The Age*, the paper for which Peter Thomson wrote uniquely eloquent and opinionated columns for decades. When *The Age*'s managing director Ranald Macdonald was playing for Royal Melbourne it helped get the pennant scores all the way down to Division 5 in the paper. But golf has never been better covered with all the blogs and podcasts discussing the game. And then there is Twitter and Instagram. But the days of papers employing golf and tennis journalists like Don Lawrence are long gone and they are not coming back.

– Mike Clayton

WHEN TIGER BURNED BRIGHT

Steve Williams carried Tiger Woods' bag for 12 years, helping him to 13 major titles, which gave him a ringside seat to some of the great moments in the sport. He looks back at his time with Tiger and their glorious decade together. And regrets? He has one or two.

What made Tiger so good? It's a question I'm often asked and the answer is simple: his mental strength and his unquenchable, uncompromising desire to be the best. I've not seen any professional golfer in all my time caddying who had that complete focus to be number one.

In his decade or so at the top, Tiger got his game to a level where he had complete faith in it. He knew he could perform under the fiercest pressure – and that's not something a lot of players can say hand on heart. His scoring average was better on Sundays than it was on Thursdays, unlike just about every other player. He just thrived on those tense situations in tournaments, those big moments when it meant the most. That's a hallmark of the greatest athletes – Michael Jordan, Wayne Gretzky and the like.

Tiger's self-belief was extraordinary. He stared down other players as if to say: I know I'm going to win, you know I'm going to win, and we both know you're not going to win. And he hated losing more than just about anyone I've met. That all made for a pretty formidable combination.

Some guys weren't fazed by going head-to-head with Tiger; they were chomping at the bit. They wanted to test themselves against the best, and Tiger was the best. But a lot of players found it very difficult playing alongside Tiger, not just because of how good he was, but because part of the challenge was actually playing in the same group as him. Wherever Tiger played, for 10 or 12 years, there were extra television people following him, extra media people inside the ropes, extra marshals, extra security; the galleries were bigger; there was more noise, more distractions. Tiger also drew a lot of new fans to the game, who perhaps didn't know the on-course etiquette. And often these people weren't there to see the other guys play, they were only interested in Tiger. That can be daunting.

As Rory McIlroy said after playing the first two rounds of the Genesis Open with Tiger in 2018, 'It's tiring … I need a couple of Advil, I've got a headache after all that.'

On Sundays, when Tiger put that red shirt on, I saw him as Superman. He was bulletproof: so poised, so calm and in such control. That can be unnerving for his rivals on the final day of a major.

Tiger had certain tactics that were designed to make opponents feel uneasy. He would always let other players go to the first tee first, for example. Always. So that when he arrived on the tee, he'd invariably get a huge reception and those players would well and truly know what they were up against. That was a bit of intimidation right there.

He also wasn't averse to indulging in a bit of gamesmanship if he had to, either. Not often, but sometimes.

Playing in the singles against Scotland's Andrew Coltart at the 1999 Ryder Cup, for example, Tiger was well aware that Coltart hadn't been picked to play in any of the first four matches. The European captain, Mark James, had made him sit out the first two days so his first appearance at Brookline was in the singles on the final day – against Tiger. Which is a tall order for anyone. As they were waiting to hit off on the first tee, Tiger said to him, 'This is a dogleg left, in case you've forgotten.'

Later on, Tiger and Andrew hit great approaches into a par four. They were both about a metre from the hole, and Andrew said, 'Good, good', meaning both putts were to be given and the hole halved. Tiger wasn't having any of that. 'No, Andrew, I'll make my putt and then see if you can make yours.' (Both holed their putts, thankfully.)

That kind of byplay is not so unusual: every player when the opportunity arises is going to indulge in a bit of banter that's going to make their opponent think about their game. And having said all that, one thing I admired about Tiger was that he was always sporting and professional towards his opponent. When praise was due he'd always give it. He'd always say 'good shot' to another player, even in the final day of a major when there was so much on the line.

Another thing that always impressed me about Tiger was that when he was being paid to play in a tournament, he seemed to try even harder to win. He prided himself on doing the absolute best he could. Often these weren't the biggest tournaments going around, but that didn't matter to him. To the best of my knowledge, in the entire time I caddied for Tiger, he never finished outside the top 10 in an event where he was being paid. I've caddied for some guys who've been paid to appear and they haven't put in much effort at all; with Tiger, it was 11 out of 10 for effort. I admired that.

He had a long memory, too. Like an elephant. Once you crossed him, he never forgot.

At the Presidents Cup in Virginia in 2000, Tiger was playing against Vijay Singh in a foursomes match. When he arrived on the first tee, there was Vijay's caddie, Paul Tesori, wearing a cap that said 'Tiger Who?' Such disrespect to someone who takes an extraordinary amount of pride in his performance is only going to make him play his best.

Same with Stephen Ames, who made a derogatory remark about Tiger's wayward driving ahead of their match in the 2006 WGC Match Play event. The result? A nine and eight whupping. It was comical: you can't piss off someone like Tiger when he is a far better player than you are. I'd never seen Tiger as determined to win. He told me before that round that his goal that day was to wipe this guy off the planet, 10 and eight. It's a pretty tough goal to win the first 10 holes, but he almost did it. He won nine and halved another.

Yet what Stephen said was actually true: Tiger was a little wild off the tee. That had always been the case, since he was a junior. In every age group he played, he was always longer than every other player he was up against. That meant his misses ended wider of the fairway than everyone else's. He just had total acceptance of this. Many other players would get down on themselves if they kept hitting wides. Not Tiger: he would accept the challenge and see the best he could do. His mindset was: I'm over here in the rubbish; now how can I make a birdie from this position? And he would make some bizarre birdies. I gave up being amazed; he could make them from anywhere.

Tiger's mental strength set him apart. It was something many other players – Ernie Els, Sergio Garcia, Davis Love, Lee Westwood, and even Phil Mickelson for a while – struggled to come to terms with. Tiger often psyched them out. (Unlike some of the others, Phil worked it out in the end and turned that negative into a positive.)

If you look at the two greatest players of all time – Jack Nicklaus and Tiger Woods – they both had that unbelievable mental strength. In his prime, Tiger won an awful number of events due to the intimidation factor. Same with Nicklaus. As their records got better and better, and the years progressed, the aura around them grew, making them even more intimidating.

I believe Tiger had the same practice routine as Nicklaus; it never changed in all the time I worked for him. He'd start with a chip or putt just to get the feel in his hands. Then he'd go to the driving range and go to work with a sand wedge, then eight iron, then four iron and then into his woods. If he wasn't hitting his eight iron right, for example, he wasn't afraid of going back to the beginning and starting all over again. The last thing he did before leaving the range – and this happened every single time before a tournament round – was hit the shot he needed to hit from the first tee. He'd stay there until he nailed that shot.

I'd caddied for Greg Norman and Ray Floyd before Tiger and they were two guys who knew how to relax when the time was right. But Tiger had no off switch – or at least not when I was around.

When I look back at the 12 years I worked with Tiger, I know I bought into all his goals to keep breaking records and win as many majors as possible. His one overriding ambition was to pass Nicklaus's record of 18 majors. So that became a goal of mine too. In that whole period from 1999 to 2011, it was very intense.

We'd win an event, but rather than take some time to sit back and appreciate it, we'd be packing up our hotel room, catching a plane and thinking about the next tournament. We'd win the Masters, tick that off, and then immediately our attention would turn to the US Open in June: where's that being played this year? Let's focus on that course. What sort of shots are going to be required around there? Okay, then it's on to the British Open in July. We'll need to practise our long irons and low ball flight.

Tiger's focus was only on what was happening next – the next obstacle to overcome. At the time, I thought that was great – but it might have been more enjoyable if we'd done things a bit differently. Looking back, the only sad thing for me in our working relationship was that there was no time to enjoy our successes; it was all work and very little play.

Contrary to what many people think, we didn't spend much time together off the course. He wasn't a big drinker at all – he occasionally might have one or two drinks and that would be it.

Despite all the success, we rarely had a wild celebration into the wee small hours after a notable win.

That's why, when all those revelations hit the news in 2009 and 2010, I couldn't really comprehend them. Really? Was this the same guy I'd worked alongside for so long? The fallout from that whole episode marked the beginning of the end of our relationship. That, and his injuries, which meant he was often sidelined after surgery.

The player-caddie relationship is unusual in many respects. The caddie spends more time with the player than anybody, even his family. It's 25–30 weeks a year, five or six days a week, 10 hours a day, side by side – and there are no guarantees. You can be fired on the spot – there's no appeal, no union you can turn to. It sometimes even happens on the golf course, in the middle of a round. So you're living in the moment; it's a day-by-day thing. You can't afford to look too far ahead. In the back of your mind, you know it's going to come to an end one day. Nothing lasts forever – and that's as true on the golf tour as it is everywhere else. When the day comes that you're fired, you're never too surprised.

That day came for me when Tiger pulled out of the 2011 US Open, and I caddied for Adam Scott instead – against Tiger's wishes. I can't sit still, so when Tiger wasn't playing, I found it very hard to do nothing and be away from the game. But it was a sad way to end the relationship.

Now that I'm retired, when I sit back and reflect on the success we had together, I take an enormous amount of pride in what we achieved. To have the opportunity to work alongside someone like that is very special. To be the closest one to him on the course, and play some part in his success, is something I take great satisfaction in.

I know Tiger made his first appearance back on the PGA Tour in the 2018 Farmers Insurance Open. And I only know that because someone texted me saying he'd made the cut (some people will find this strange but I don't watch golf on television, period).

Tiger's had multiple operations on his back and he's 42 years old now. Given that, it would be difficult to consistently hit the ball perfectly, like he did when he was 25. But the way the ball came off the club when he was in his prime – it was an amazing thing to watch. Every player who stood behind him on the practice fairway and watched him would have felt nervous. The ball just flew off the clubface.

But he doesn't have that intimidation factor anymore, so he'll find that aspect of the game very different. No longer can he just turn up and expect other players to wilt in his company. These young guys in the top 10 now like Jon Rahm, Justin Thomas, Jordan Spieth, Patrick Reed, Jason Day and Rickie Fowler – they don't have any baggage or bad memories from playing alongside Tiger at his best. He is just like any other player to them.

There was a time from late 1999 to 2002 when Tiger won seven of 11 major championships, including four in a row. That's an astonishing figure. It shows how dominant he was in the game. But every golden era comes to an end, and that's almost two decades ago now. Then again, I suspect Tiger hates losing as much as he ever did, and he will do all he can to get back to the top. It would be very difficult for him to win on the PGA Tour again – but what a fairytale it would be if he could return to the winners' circle one more time. I'd stand and applaud that.

The distances Tiger would hit each club in his prime (early 2000s)	
Driver – 305 yards	Seven iron – 175 yards
Three wood – 270 yards	Eight iron – 160 yards
Two iron – 240 yards	Nine iron – 145 yards
Three iron – 225 yards	Pitching wedge – 130 yards
Four iron – 215 yards	56° wedge – 110 yards
Five iron – 205 yards	60° wedge – 85 yards
Six iron – 190 yards	

SHARK v TIGER

For reasons no-one can readily explain, former world number one players Greg Norman and Tiger Woods have barely been on speaking terms for 20 years. They are neighbours in the small Florida community of Jupiter Island yet have shared, by Norman's estimation, one word in 10 years. **Charles Happell** charts the spat that started in 1996 – and is still going strong.

Greg Norman sidled into Queensland's Coolum resort in 2012, ahead of a rare playing appearance on the home tour he once dominated, and wasted no time in doing what he has done so effectively for the past three decades: stir up a controversy.

At the official tournament dinner before the Australian PGA Championship, Norman warmed up by declaring that new world number one Rory McIlroy had a psychological hold over Tiger Woods and the US superstar couldn't 'keep up' with the Ulsterman.

Invited into the media centre the following day – as he always is, for few players give greater value for money behind the mic than ol' Sharky – Norman continued in that vein. The Australian, then 57, said McIlroy was best placed to overhaul Jack Nicklaus's mark of 18 major titles.

'If anybody can break Nicklaus's record I think he could, because he is young, he is ahead of the game, he is ahead of the curve on a lot of things and he has a very balanced life across the board,' Norman said. 'So I will keep my fingers crossed for him 'cause I would love to see that happen because somebody will do it one day and it could be Rory. I am a big fan of Rory's, I think he's really the tip of the iceberg. He can be as big as he wants to be.'

On the surface, those statements amount to nothing terribly significant, just one pro's unabashed admiration for another. But in saying that McIlroy, whose major tally then sat at two, had a greater chance of reaching golf's Everest figure of 18 than Woods, who has won 14 of the things, Norman was being deliberately provocative and mischievous. It was a calculated slight.

And Norman's gushing praise of the Northern Irishman, and all that he stood for, amounted to yet another backhander, another cuff around the ears, for Woods.

The comments continued the fraught and testy relationship between the two players who dominated the world number one ranking over the past quarter of a century. Norman was top dog for a total of 331 weeks before handing the mantle over to Woods on 11 January 1998, which marked the start of the American's 623 weeks at the helm – until that reign was infamously and salaciously derailed in 2010.

Carbon-dating the source of their dispute is difficult but it is generally accepted that the trouble began in 1996 when Norman's long-time coach, Butch Harmon, began to spend more and more time with Woods.

Norman had been working with Harmon since 1992 and won the 1993 British Open during their partnership; they were still working together at the 1996 Masters where Harmon's tutelage was unable to prevent that horror last-day collapse. Woods became a Harmon student after his third US Amateur victory four months later, in August 1996.

There were two big egos there, two men used to getting their own way, two bulls in the one paddock and something had to give. There was also the issue of Norman feeling as though he hadn't been paid due respect by the precocious prodigy; that Woods hadn't sought out Norman for advice in the same way that the

Australian had regularly sought counsel from Jack Nicklaus when he first arrived in the US in the early 1980s.

Norman ended up leaving Harmon later in that year, 1996.

Soon afterwards, in late November, Woods made his first trip overseas as a professional – to The Australian Golf Club in Sydney where he competed in the Australian Open (which happened to be run by his management firm, IMG). This was a championship previously won by, among others, Gary Player, Arnold Palmer, Jack Nicklaus and Norman himself.

The American was just 20 and had been a pro for two months but the hype reached Australia a long time before he did and the crowds that turned up to The Australian that week were enormous.

In that opening round, Woods drew a late tee time, late enough for the wind to have sprung up around Sydney's eastern suburbs and for the smallish greens to suddenly take on the aspect of a medium-sized picnic rug. He couldn't tame the gusts, tight layout, deep bunkers and slick greens and shot a seven-over 79, a score that was to remain his worst as a professional for almost six years – until his 81 in a howling gale at the 2002 British Open.

Norman won that week – the Australian had an early tee time on the Thursday – and afterwards couldn't resist a gentle dig at his much-hyped young adversary: 'At least he got the flavour of Australian courses,' Norman said. 'Perhaps he will appreciate why Australians play so well when they leave home. The first time you play here, you get a deep appreciation of how difficult they can be.'

That snipe pretty much set the tone for their relationship from that day to this.

In January the following year, 1997, Norman was in Melbourne for a tournament launch and took time out afterwards to speak to a couple of local reporters, including your correspondent. The subject inevitably turned to Woods, who was reportedly becoming irritated with the constant media and public attention he was attracting since turning pro.

Norman said that while he had not read the newspaper reports, it came as no surprise to him that golf's wonderchild was becoming increasingly disenchanted with his life in the spotlight. 'I feel sorry for him in lots of ways because he doesn't have a life,' Norman said. 'He's a kid who's twenty-one years old and he's got all this stuff he's got to do. I know what I was doing at twenty-one, and that was being out there enjoying my bachelorhood and experiencing the fruits of life. To be successful in business, in golf or in any field, you've got to trim the fat now and then and maybe he's got to start trimming some of that ancillary stuff that's becoming a bit of a burden on him.'

Norman obviously couldn't imagine how much Woods would go on to 'experience the fruits of life' with a series of mistresses later in his career but, at this time, the Australian's observations were probably accurate.

Norman said Woods needed to learn how to cope with the attention and accept that it was part of the whole package of being a top-line sportsman. 'He can't run away from the attention, there's no way in the world he can run away from it,' Norman said. 'His responsibilities now are huge because of the position he's in – he has responsibilities for the minorities of America, responsibilities for Thailand – he really has got a lot on his plate for a twenty-one-year-old. He's got to accept responsibility for who he is and what he represents ... and it will be interesting to see how he handles it.'

The pair's relationship, and Norman's mood, hit a new low at the Presidents Cup at Royal Melbourne in 1998, coincidentally the one and only time the International team has beaten the US in 12 instalments of the competition. Such was the International team's dominance in the first two days of competition that they led the US by the impregnable margin of 14.5 points to 5.5 going into Sunday's singles.

The rout had the unintended consequence of making the final day's play a complete washout for the US television broadcaster, CBS. But the network quickly realised the one singles match that might help maintain the ratings was Woods v Norman. And once CBS decided this was the match-up it needed to enliven an otherwise moribund telecast, it was no surprise that, as soon as International team captain Peter Thomson put up Norman's name for the 11th pairing on that Saturday night, Jack Nicklaus immediately countered with Woods. The American won a close match on the final hole – but Norman was furious at what he saw as his manipulation by television execs, that he was being used as a pawn to boost their ratings figures.

As Norman slipped into retirement from golf in the new millennium, and Woods began the most dominant run of success in the history of the game, the spat lay dormant. But it didn't stay that way for long.

In November 2011, having been almost silent on the Woods question for ages, Norman told a US golf magazine that Woods now had too many distractions to maintain the focus he had when he won 14 major championships. Because of that, Norman thought it unlikely that Tiger would win another one – leaving him stranded four short of Nicklaus's record.

'Tiger, when he dominated, had a single-shot approach,' said Norman. 'It was only about the golf. Tiger can still play, and I think he'll win again. But he's not going to do what he did before.'

In the interview, Norman also took note of Woods' body language on the course since being engulfed by that embarrassing sex scandal in 2009, saying, 'He doesn't keep his head up anymore. He's got his eyes down. He's trying to keep his eyes away from the camera, right?'

Then, while promoting his Shark Shootout tournament in Florida late in 2011, Norman said if he were the US Presidents Cup captain, instead of Freddie Couples, he would have chosen PGA Championship winner Keegan Bradley, not Woods, to play for the Americans at Royal Melbourne. 'I can understand the name of a Tiger Woods and his history of what he's done on the golf course,' Norman told the *Naples Daily News*. 'But I pick the guys who I think are ready to get in there and play and have performed to the highest levels leading up to it.'

To drive home his point, Norman added, 'I just don't think he's swinging the golf club the way he used to, when he won all those major championships. He's a different player out there nowadays.'

Woods has, by and large, not bought into the spat, maintaining a dignified silence. But when he scored the point that delivered the US victory in the 2011 Presidents Cup at Royal Melbourne – beating Australian Aaron Baddeley four and three in the singles – he could not help himself. At the US team's victorious press conference, while surrounded by his 11 celebrating teammates, Woods smirked into the microphone: 'Greg's probably not happy with it ... me closing out the Cup.' Another harpoon into the Shark's hide.

One American golf writer about this time – quoting an unnamed source – said, 'Tiger and Greg don't speak. There's a lot of animosity between them.' The writer contended that one reason Woods wanted the word spread about the course-record 62 he shot in 2011 at the Medalist course in Jupiter, Florida, is that Norman's best score on the course he co-designed is 64.

Underlining the weirdness of their relationship, Woods and Norman live maybe a kilometre away from each other on Jupiter Island, their extravagant mega-homes among the largest in a celebrity-laden community that numbers just 864 people. So you'd imagine they must bump into each other occasionally down at the shops, or walking the dog. But apparently not.

In an online interview with Graham Bensinger in the middle of 2017, Norman was asked his opinion of Woods, both personally and professionally. He replied, 'Personally, I don't know him, even though we live half a mile from each other on Jupiter. I wouldn't have said one word to Tiger Woods in ten years.

'At the Presidents Cup at Royal Melbourne, we probably said four words and that's about it. So it's kind of strange ... kind of surprising given how close we live [to each other], but I don't have anything against Tiger Woods.

'I haven't had a conversation with Tiger Woods to know whether there's a barrier there. I'm willing to [talk], I'm happy to, but that's his choice. People have their choice in life. It's not going to take any skin off my nose.'

The ill will continues a tradition of top-line golfers not quite seeing eye to eye: Hogan v Snead, Palmer v Nicklaus, Faldo v Lyle and Mickelson v Woods. This one hasn't had the publicity of those rivalries but, in terms of longevity – two decades and counting – it might just be the daddy of them all.

John Daly once ran into Tiger Woods coming
out of a gym after a serious workout.
　'I can't believe you do all that stuff, Tiger.'
　'John, if I had your talent, I wouldn't
have to.'

– Mike Clayton

LYDIA KO, THE PUPUKE PIPSQUEAK

At the age of 17 years and nine months, Lydia Ko became the number one player in women's golf, the youngest player of either gender to achieve that ranking. That was in early 2015. But then, as **Charles Happell** writes, she tempted fate by sacking her coach and caddie, then tinkering with her swing.

When Bon Suk Hyon and her six-year-old daughter, Lydia, walked into the pro shop at Auckland's Pupuke Golf Club in 2004, so began one of golf's more remarkable journeys.

Bon Suk and her husband, Gil Hong Ko, had emigrated from South Korea a month earlier. Having tossed up between Canada and New Zealand as the place to start their new life, they eventually plumped for the Antipodes, where the climate was more temperate and golf could be played 12 months a year. The family moved into a house right behind Pupuke's first green.

Although Lydia didn't know it, her parents had big plans for her in this game, which had exploded in popularity in Korea following Se-ri Pak's early LPGA success.

The first person they bumped into at the Pupuke pro shop on that fateful day was a 22-year-old rookie teaching pro by the name of Guy Wilson, who'd only just finished his apprenticeship. In her halting English, Bon Suk explained that she wanted her daughter, whom Wilson could barely see above the counter, to learn golf.

Wilson knew how tough it was getting young children to stay focused on such a difficult sport, but agreed to take her on. 'I saw her three times a week to start off with after school,' he told me. 'That was challenging enough. It's difficult to coach anyone three times a week, let alone a six-year-old girl who hardly spoke any English. So a lot of our work revolved around games and competition to start off with because that was the thing that was enjoyable for her. She had a good ability to hit the ball straight for a six-year-old, but there was nothing there to indicate what a talent she'd become.'

As she became more proficient, and with her parents' urgings, Ko spent six hours a day practising, a couple of hours before school and then three or four more after she'd put away her exercise books. She joined Pupuke as a member, got a handicap and began to play in club competitions and then amateur tournaments.

And when, aged 12, the pint-sized prodigy – who was now driving the ball 185 yards – finished seventh (just four shots behind Laura Davies) in her first professional event, the New Zealand Open, Wilson knew he had a special talent on his hands. One who was not just technically proficient but showed extraordinary poise under tournament pressure.

In the ensuing three years, Ko played 14 professional events and won three of them: the 2012 New South Wales Open in Australia as a 14-year-old (becoming the youngest person ever to win a pro golf tour event); the Canadian Open in August of that same year against a full LPGA Tour field, shooting a 67 on the final day to prevail by three shots and become the youngest winner on that tour (at 15 years and four months) and the first amateur champion since JoAnne Carner in 1969; and, early in 2013, the European Tour's New Zealand Open – even though, at 15, Ko had to cope with being the face of the tournament and headline act on all the billboards.

The week after securing her national Open, Ko scorched around Royal Canberra with an opening-round 63 and led the Australian

Open going into the final day. Such was the interest she'd created in attempting back-to-back victories as a 15-year-old, the US Golf Channel chose to telecast live the final round. Alas, she faded to finish third.

In that whirlwind 14 months, Ko, the world's number one amateur, forwent about US$650,000 in prizemoney. But Wilson insisted at the time she was in no hurry to turn pro – against the advice of Steve Williams, a fellow Kiwi who had taken a close interest in her career – saying the family had a clear plan for the years ahead. That involved Ko completing the final two years of high school before taking the plunge into pro golf's shark pool sometime after that.

'She could turn pro now – she hasn't missed the cut once in fourteen pro events – but it'd be a bigger mistake going too early than going too late,' Wilson told me in 2013. 'Also she may find it different when golf is no longer a game but a job.'

Ko travelled everywhere with her mother, Tina, as she's known, while her father controlled pretty much every aspect of her career back in Auckland. Wilson said he and Gil had developed, unintentionally, a good cop–bad cop routine, where her father was the hard taskmaster while he liked to keep things light and laidback.

As a fun way to motivate Ko ahead of the Australian amateur title in 2012, Wilson vowed to jump into a lake fully clothed if she won. Soon enough, he was emailing her a video clip of him plunging into the water. Before the final round of the NSW Open, Wilson made a similar promise – this time wearing golf shoes, golf cap and a golf bag over his shoulder. Again, he was forced to make good on his dare via an iPhone clip. He still hasn't gone bungee jumping yet – his 'prize' to her for the Canadian Open win. 'It's those sort of silly things that help motivate her at the moment; anything that makes me look stupid,' said Wilson, who was only 31 himself.

At that time, Ko was leading a kind of double life: at school and kicking around with friends, she was Kiwi through and through (which naturally meant becoming an All Blacks supporter).

Her accent was pure New Zealand, complete with local slang, and she wasn't afraid to give a bit of cheek to her coach and sometimes even the media.

At home, though, her parents still held their Korean values dear and there wasn't much tolerance for frivolity or backchat. The family spoke Korean at home, and Tina and Gil imbued in their daughter a strong work ethic. 'Many other kids her age have it their own way and do what they want,' Wilson said. 'There's probably not much discipline there, or focus or drive. So I think her parents are trying to guard against that.'

As an amateur, Ko didn't miss a cut in 25 professional tournaments and, by September 2013, had risen to fifth in the world rankings as a 16-year-old.

A month later, the riches on the professional tours finally tempted her. Via the unconventional method of a YouTube clip, she announced she was ready to abandon her amateur career in golf's wading pool and begin swimming with the sharks.

Having made the call to move to the US fulltime, Team Ko then made the dramatic decision to sack Wilson as her coach and move to David Leadbetter's academy in Florida, where she'd work with both Leadbetter and his assistant, Sean Hogan. Ko's father apparently admired the swing of Hee Young Park, a student at the academy, and that was the basis for the move.

It was a devastating development for Wilson, who had been Ko's only tutor over the past decade and helped her develop from Pupuke pipsqueak into precocious world-beater.

By being sacked, he obviously lost the kudos of being associated with the game's greatest woman player but also the handsome remuneration package that came with such an association. Wilson might not be in the same league as Tiger Woods' former coach Hank Haney, say, who charges upwards of US$17,000 for a day's tuition at his academy in Lewisville, Texas, but his deal with Team Ko would surely have been well into six figures if he'd remained her coach during her early days as a professional.

Some were outraged on his behalf; Steve Williams, for one, called the move 'unethical'. But in spite of the shock, the young Kiwi put on a brave face.

'It's been an honour to help develop Lydia into the number four golfer in the world,' Williams said in a statement at the time. 'When I first met her the golf clubs were taller than she was and she didn't know the first thing about a driver or a putter, but now she has one of the most envied swings in the women's golf world. Lydia's consistent and outstanding performance is the ultimate payback for any coach and it has been truly wonderful working with someone with her talent, dedication and focus.'

Ko was granted a special exemption to join the LPGA Tour by Commissioner Mike Whan, who waived the usual requirement that members be at least 18. A short time later, *Time* magazine chose the teenage golfer as one of its 100 Most Influential People in the world, giving her a truly global profile. Alongside Hillary Clinton, Beyoncé, Serena Williams and various other A-listers, there was Lydia, wearing large glasses and standing 1.52 metres in her spikes.

At her ninth start as a professional, the teenager notched her first win, at the Swinging Skirts LPGA Classic, one of 53 consecutive cuts she would make on the LPGA Tour through to the middle of 2015. In claiming The Evian Championship in France later that year, Ko became the youngest woman, at age 18 years, four months and 20 days, to win a major championship. She backed up at the next major, the ANA Inspiration in early 2016, and won that as well, becoming the youngest player to claim two women's major titles.

No-one in golf had seen anything like it. Ko just kept going from strength to strength, her career formline inexorably heading north, her star permanently in the ascendant. Or so it seemed.

But then something strange happened. Ko and her team, which included a manager and her parents, decided on a series of changes that trashed the old maxim 'if it ain't broke, don't fix it'.

Lydia's game most certainly wasn't broke; in fact it was purring along like a recently serviced Lexus, yet they decided it needed some fixing.

On top of the decision to sack Wilson and move to Florida, Ko also changed her caddie, her swing and equipment manufacturer (moving from Callaway to PXG clubs in a lucrative deal) in quick succession. Even a game as solidly grounded as Ko's couldn't withstand that kind of shaking to its foundations. In fact, she began going through caddies like golf gloves, discarding them every few months and taking on a new one. There was Jason Hamilton, then Peter Godfrey, then Gary Matthews and several others, and now there's Jonny Scott, who took the job at the start of 2018. That made him Ko's 11th caddie since she turned pro in late 2013.

From a position of harmony, happiness and effortless success, Team Ko opted to change a proven formula and, in doing so, damaged the delicate ecosystem that produced such sustained brilliance.

It would be wrong, however, to portray her time with Leadbetter as anything other than a success. She won 12 LPGA titles, two majors and an Olympic silver medal in her first three years as a pro; she also became the tour's youngest Rookie of the Year in 2014 and its youngest Player of the Year in 2015. But given the trajectory her career was already on, many have suggested that she was going to succeed on the LPGA no matter who her coach was. In the first half of 2016, Ko won three times, including her second major championship, and appeared on her way to a second straight season as player of the year.

But after taking the title at the Marathon Classic in July, her game began to slip – not dramatically but noticeably – as she managed just one top-five finish in her next 15 LPGA starts, a sequence of results that, to her, amounted to a form slump.

Over time, her swing – a natural, rhythmic motion – had been remodelled into a loopier version to encourage a distance-increasing draw. But rather than produce longer shots, the new swing began to affect her distance and also, tellingly, her biggest weapon, her accuracy. New Zealand's most famous golfer, Sir Bob Charles, the winner of the 1963 British Open and World Golf Hall of Fame inductee, weighed into the debate, intimating she'd made a mistake in changing coaches. Her old swing was not perfect, he said, it had definite flaws. But it had an intrinsic beauty. The Leadbetter swing was neither pleasing to the eye, nor graceful, he felt.

All Ko's numbers were down in 2016. She went from second in greens in regulation in 2015 to 32nd, while dropping from 60th to 126th in rankings for distance. Her results were also heading south, the relationship with Leadbetter was souring and soon enough he, too, was sacked late in 2016.

Ko then went to Gary Gilchrist, another teacher with a history of working with good players, including former number one Yani Tseng. But that relationship lasted about a year – a winless 2017 – before she took up with the California-based Ted Oh.

After missing just one cut in her first 94 LPGA starts, Ko missed three in quick succession. Early in 2018, her world ranking dropped to number 18, falling outside the top 10 for the first time since her amateur days. She remains without a victory since the Marathon Classic triumph of July 2016 – a drought that would have been unthinkable two years ago when she just had to turn up to win, and collected trophies for fun.

An eternal optimist, Ko conceded that for the first time in her career she was suffering a mini crisis of confidence. 'I think it would be a lie to say I've been positive all the way through,' Ko said. 'There have been times when I have said: man, I don't know why I have not been playing as well. It's a big learning curve where it's not always going to be a high. Fortunately, for me, the last few years I've had so many highs.'

Sir Bob Charles was the first to raise the idea of a reconciliation with her childhood mentor, Wilson, saying she needed to stop looking 'outside her environment' for inspiration and instead seek advice from the person who knows her game best. 'Please, please don't go out looking for another David Leadbetter or whatever, just go back to Guy,' Charles told a local media outlet when she left the Floridian. 'Just have casual conversations with him and I think she would be a lot happier.'

But there is no sign of a reunion or rapprochement. Wilson, now one of the senior coaches at New Zealand's Institute of Golf, seems happy enough in his post-Ko career – and understands that the notion of some kind of get-together is probably just romantic nonsense.

For all that, though, he is still thanking the patron saint of golf for the fortuitous series of events 15 years ago that delivered the pig-tailed prodigy to his pro shop counter – a piece of serendipity that changed his life.

'I wouldn't be anywhere near where I am now without that relationship,' he said. 'I don't think anyone else in the world has taken a little kid, a six-year-old, to [eventually] world number one so I know I'm very lucky.'

THE SPANISH MAESTRO

He might have been errant but his artistry was unmatched. Few have played the game in the way Seve Ballesteros did – with panache and dash – and fewer still have brought such excitement and theatre to golf. **John Huggan** offers an appreciation of the Spaniard.

The exact year is unimportant, but one-time Masters champion Ray Floyd is in the media centre at Augusta National to discuss his just-completed round. Or so he thought.

'Ray,' said the first questioner, 'can you explain the shot your playing partner hit at the fourth hole today?'

A pause.

'I can,' said Floyd, a four-time major winner and one of the premier short game practitioners of his or anyone else's generation. 'But it's going to take me a while.'

The stroke in question, a massively high, softly floated pitch feathered off the barest of lies right and short of the deep bunker that fronts the severely sloping green, finished within a few feet of the cup, which was cut less than four yards from the sand – a feat that left even the great 'Raymondo' all but breathless. It was ever thus with Seve Ballesteros. Bringing off the virtually impossible was, to this golfing genius, an almost everyday event.

He wasn't just about the short game, either.

'I was on a range beside him once,' says two-time Masters champion José María Olazábal. 'The weather had been very dry so the ground was very dusty. Clouds would fly up after every shot. Except for Seve. I stopped to watch him hit one irons that barely made a noise, never mind sent up a puff of dust. The quality of strike was so high. He was incredible.'

That he was – right from the start of his career, which, like the character of the man, had a little bit of everything.

It is late March 1974 and Manuel Piñero has just won the Spanish National Professional Championship at the Sant Cugat Club in Barcelona. Celebrating afterwards with compatriot and future Ryder Cup teammate Antonio Garrido, Piñero is asked if he has seen anything of the youngster who finished 20th, a remarkable 16-year-old from the small fishing village of Pedreña on Spain's windswept northern coast. He has not. But, curiosity piqued, Piñero goes in search of the teenager to congratulate him on a fine performance in what was his professional debut. He didn't have to look for long.

'He was sitting quite near me behind a high row of lockers,' Piñero recalls, smiling. 'And he was crying. I asked him what was wrong and he told me he had come to win the tournament but now he had failed. He expected to win. That was the first sign for me that Seve Ballesteros was special.'

'I only played with Seve once, near the end of his career,' says US Open winner Geoff Ogilvy. 'Whenever he went to the chipping green, I went with him. Just to watch. For me, he is maybe the most talented player ever.'

It was at Carnoustie during the 2007 Open, racked with pain from a back he first injured in a friendly boxing match as a 14-year-old, that Ballesteros finally drew a line under a career that, between his maiden victory at the 1976 Dutch Open and his last, the '95 Spanish Open, produced a record 50 European Tour victories. Around the world he won another 33 times, including five World Match Play titles at Wentworth. He played in eight Ryder Cups for Europe, finishing on the winning side three times. And, most impressively, he finished first in five major championships:

three Opens and two Masters. Between 1976 and 1992, he was never out of the top 20 on the Order of Merit

Mere statistics, however, do not begin to sum up the overall contribution of a man who lifted the Old World and carried it to what amounted to the Promised Land. It wasn't so much that he was a trailblazer for a new generation of world-class European players. He was. It wasn't so much that he went to the US and won against the very best. He did. It wasn't even that he almost singlehandedly resurrected the Ryder Cup as a living, breathing golfing entity. He did that, too.

No, as Ogilvy and Piñero intimate, it was the *way* he did all of those things. Perhaps only Arnold Palmer has ever played a simple ball-and-stick game with as much panache and verve.

Just how special the disconsolate teenager comforted by Piñero would be did not remain a mystery to the rest of the golfing world for long. By October of 1974, the then 17-year-old Ballesteros – whose uncle, Ramón Sota, placed sixth in the 1965 Masters – had finished fifth in the Italian Open. One year later, he had recorded a handful of top-10 finishes in European Tour events – the highlight third place behind Gary Player at the Lancôme Trophy in Paris – and topped the Continental Order of Merit, a distinction that offered with it an exemption into the 1976 Open Championship at Royal Birkdale.

Even now, more than four decades on, the performance put in by the teenage Ballesteros over the famous Southport links resonates with all those who marvelled at his instinctive play and natural charisma. It was an arrival upon the world's stage that has since been matched only by that of Tiger Woods for sheer impact.

Ballesteros didn't win; that honour went to Johnny Miller by an ultimately comfortable margin. But even now it is Ballesteros who captures the mind's eye. With all hope of victory long gone, he struck an audacious chip-and-run through the narrow gap separating two greenside bunkers to set up an 18th hole birdie and tie Jack Nicklaus for second place. Far away, at home in Dallas, no less a shot-maker than six-time major champion Lee Trevino leapt whooping from his chair in instinctive tribute.

Ballesteros even impressed the 'Golden Bear'. The three wood Ballesteros struck from a distant fairway bunker to the edge of the final green at PGA National during the 1983 Ryder Cup remains the greatest shot Nicklaus, the game's greatest player, ever saw. As accolades go, that is hard to beat.

For Ballesteros though, such feats were commonplace, mere extensions of an artistic temperament ideally suited to the creation rather than the mere execution of shots. Those skills still had to be learned and the young Seve's classroom was the beach at Pedreña. The product of a modest family background – his father was a sometime farmer, sometime fisherman whose home, significantly, backed onto the Club de Golf de Pedreña – Ballesteros learned the game armed only with a rusty old three iron. The pre-teen manufactured all kinds of shots: high, low, slice and hook and everything in between.

For all that Ballesteros eventually achieved, his contribution to the game is perhaps summed up best by the passion he brought to the Ryder Cup. His partnership with Olazábal alone is the stuff of legend. In 15 matches together, the two amigos combined for 12 points, losing only twice. 'The great thing about Seve was that I knew all I had to do was put the ball somewhere near the green,' says Olazábal. 'If I did that, we were in with a chance. That gave me a lot of strength.'

It was ever thus for Ballesteros. Every time out – and in his winning role as non-playing Ryder Cup captain at Valderrama in 1997 – he wanted to show the world how good Europe could be at golf, a point he was determined to make to the many naysayers across the Atlantic.

No-one who was present will ever forget the iconic fist-pumping celebration that followed the 12-foot putt that beat Tom Watson and won the 1984 Open Championship at St Andrews. 'That was my most exciting shot,' said Ballesteros. 'Because I won at the birthplace of golf.'

Sadly, it was not to last. None of it. The brain tumour that was first diagnosed in October 2008 brought Seve's life to a premature close on 7 May 2011, aged 54. Typically, he went down fighting. Friends and family said he battled his condition with a singleminded determination rarely seen in someone so debilitated. He rests now in Pedreña, where he learned to play.

As you'd expect, many other tributes have since been paid to the great man, even from players a generation younger than him, such as Ogilvy. 'Seve was the coolest golfer ever,' says the native Melburnian. 'Ask anyone from his generation and he's still the best. Anyone and everyone who played in Europe between 1975 and 1995 still thinks Seve was the best. They don't care as much about Tiger or anyone else. They won't even discuss it. Seve was the best.'

The last word, however, must go to Ernie Els. The big South African battled Ballesteros many times, most notably in an epic encounter in the 1994 World Match Play Championship at Wentworth. Ballesteros made 14 birdies over the course of the 35 holes – seven of them at short holes – and still lost.

'Seve was my hero,' says Els. 'I always wanted to swing like him, putt like him, chip like him. He was always the picture in my mind when I was practising. You can talk all you want about Arnold Palmer – and Arnie was great – but Seve was golf outside America. He was the European Tour. He was Tiger before Tiger was Tiger.'

MAXIMUM CONTRAST: GRAHAM AND OGILVY

They grew up in Melbourne, 30 years apart, and came from very different backgrounds, yet David Graham and Geoff Ogilvy are the only two Australians to have won the US Open. **Mike Clayton** charts their compelling stories – and different paths to the top.

It constantly amazes me how many teenagers determined to be good players have no interest in the history of the game. It would be unimaginable for one aspiring to be a great novelist or a great playwright not to have read and understood the great novels or great plays, yet so it is in golf.

Golfers can be very good without understanding, or having any interest in, the sport's history, but maybe it helps to know Ben Hogan wasn't very good for a long time or to read Bobby Jones or Byron Nelson to learn they were so emotionally worn down by the stress of championship golf they retired at 28 and 35, respectively. Or maybe just to have an interest in the game outside of their swings, TrackMan numbers, scores and results.

I met a really nice kid who was doing some work experience for Kathie Shearer in the press tent during the 2011 Australian Open. He'd made the semifinal of the Australian Amateur the previous year and we were talking about Bob Shearer when it dawned on me he had no clue who Bob was, and certainly no idea that he had beaten Jack Nicklaus to win the 1982 championship.

'Never heard of him.'

You know who Peter Thomson is, right?

'Yes – he's the golf-course designer.'

I didn't think there was much point asking if he knew of Norman Von Nida, the best bunker player ever and the first Australian to really make a living travelling and playing golf around the world.

Personally, I've always enjoyed reading about the old players, what they did and the different pathways they took to the top of the game. It's my problem, not theirs, but it has always seemed to me there is a something to learn from those who have come before and how they achieved what they did.

David Graham and Geoff Ogilvy grew up in Melbourne three decades apart but both managed to win the US Open, the only Australians to climb the ultimate narrow-fairway, high-rough, USGA-made mountain where, as Ogilvy once said, every hole seems like the hardest hole you've ever played.

Their history, though, is perhaps illuminating as they took remarkably different roads to their respective triumphs at Merion and Winged Foot.

* * *

Graham has written about his parents' difficult relationship, both with him and each other. His father told him they would never speak again if he turned pro but he did anyway, as a 15-year-old left-hander. While his father's threat was inexcusable, he probably had good reason to be concerned. The elder Graham did turn up unexpectedly at the US Open in 1970 but by all accounts he pretty much kept to his word.

Graham learned to play at Wattle Park, a little nine-hole public course – one that never caught the attention of Alister MacKenzie. George Naismith was the old pro at Melbourne's second-oldest club, Riversdale, and Graham's first boss. On the youngster's first day at work Naismith watched the left-hander hit some shots and announced he would, henceforth, play right handed.

'Could you have ever won the US Open as a left-hander?' Graham was asked later.

'Not a chance.'

Much is made of Graham's early struggles. While other young pros mocked him and his apparently fruitless efforts to play the game well enough to feed himself, he just quietly pounded balls in a desperate attempt to make a life for himself, one where he wouldn't have to rely on other people. He took a club job at Seabrook in northern Tasmania but was soon bankrupted and paying off his debts to Precision Golf Forgings the great Australian golf company, by working in the Sydney factory and playing pro-ams.

Still, by February 1970, he was good enough to win the Victorian Open at Riversdale, and at the end of the year he and Bruce Devlin won the World Cup for Australia in Argentina.

Eighteen months later, he beat Devlin, a friend and mentor, in a playoff for the PGA Tour's Cleveland Open, and with it came the precious exemption from Monday qualifying. If you asked most young pros playing today what Monday qualifying was, they probably wouldn't know what you were talking about. In one way it was a terrible system because there was no way to plan a schedule but in another it was brilliant. If you made the cut you were in the next week and if you kept making cuts and played some good golf you could play your way into the coveted elite 60, earning your exemption from qualifying.

By the mid 1970s Graham was ensconced in the top echelon and winning tournaments both in the US and elsewhere, including the 1976 World Match Play at Wentworth and the 1977 Australian Open.

Then he won the 1979 US PGA Championship at Oakland Hills, but not before making a complete mess of the 18th hole. Needing a five to win, he blocked a drive so far right it finished on the first fairway, blew an iron over the green, whiffed a chip then eventually missed from 5 feet for a bogey. Ultimately, he holed two long putts he could very reasonably have been expected to miss to tie the opening two holes of a playoff with Ben Crenshaw before he hit a typically accurate long iron to 10 feet at the par three to set up a winning birdie.

Two years later at Merion, another of Hogan's Open courses, Graham won his US Open after putting on one of the great ball-striking clinics over the final 18 holes.

He missed the opening fairway by a few inches but hit every green in regulation and made a couple of decisive putts, one on the first green to get within two shots of the leader George Burns, and another across the hill at the 15th to move two ahead. By day's end a three-stroke deficit had become a three-stroke victory, thanks to his round of 67.

The lesson of Graham's career is hard work and perseverance pay off; all that dedication to practise made him a great ball-striker. But hard work on its own, however, is no guarantee a player will be any good – there are legions of players you've never heard of who worked hard. His success was a triumph of belief and the overcoming of obstacles that would have derailed most players.

* * *

Ogilvy's parents couldn't have been more supportive of their son's early days playing around Victoria, always encouraging (Mum a little more loudly than Dad) but without ever pressuring.

Ogilvy began part-time work as a caddie at Royal Melbourne, being the last generation of the soon-to-die-out club caddie, who was allowed to play the course in the evening after the members' rounds and after school during the week. He was also a member at Cheltenham, another of the city's nine-hole courses open to the public and across the fence next to Victoria GC, the club he would join as, very quickly, his game improved.

MAXIMUM CONTRAST: GRAHAM AND OGILVY | 65

Unlike Graham, he was never a figure of amusement to contemporaries. He was slow to grow tall but once he did he was good enough at 17 to hold the 54-hole lead in the 1995 Victorian Open and later in the year he finished in the top 25 at Kingston Heath in the Australian Open.

It was obvious from the beautiful flow to his swing, the power and the towering flight of his irons he was going to be a player. And he could putt: 'In my best years, I hardly ever missed from six feet.' He wasn't going to get to the US Tour and have someone tear his game apart and put it back together as Bruce Devlin had done for Graham in 1971.

By the time Ogilvy got there in 2001 he was ready to play. He'd played in Europe, as Graham had, for a couple of seasons and went to the tour school with no pressure in him: 'I knew if I missed it didn't matter. I could just go back to Europe.'

His father, as Graham's had almost 40 years earlier, understandably worried about his son's prospects in the US. 'Do you think he will be all right?' he asked me at the South Australian Open just before he went to the US to play.

'Don't worry, he will be just fine,' I replied.

Amazingly to me, 20 years on, so many young pros dismiss Europe as an option, instead seeing the United States as the only worthwhile place to play. Ogilvy is one who has another opinion, saying, 'Any card is better than a Web.com card.'

Ogilvy's US Open highlighted the game's astonishing capability of asking the most uncomfortable questions at the very worst time. For Doug Sanders, Sam Snead and Scott Hoch, it was a tiny putt to achieve a dream and had each of those putts been 6 or 8 inches closer the hole they'd have been gimmes – but they weren't and, once missed, they left scars for a lifetime.

On that 72nd hole at Winged Foot, Phil Mickelson was asked to hit a fairway with a driver. After he'd failed that test, he was asked to make a sensible decision but he chose the reckless path and lost. Colin Montgomerie, a man Ogilvy himself has described as the 'best ball-striker I've played with', had made a living hitting seven irons to 10 feet, yet when it absolutely mattered he chunked one short and right of the green and took another four shots to get in from there.

Both lost by one to Ogilvy, but the Australian, too, faced his moment of truth. Those who think him lucky fail to understand he was the only one capable of answering the uncomfortable question when his moment came.

Most Australians learn to chip with the ball back in the stance, the shaft angled forward and with the leading (front) edge of the club contacting the ground. Terry Gale was a master at it.

Ogilvy's coach, Dale Lynch, told him he'd need to learn a different shot in the US, one where the ball was forward, the shaft level and the whole of the sole of the club contacting the ground at the same time, not just the front edge. It's more popularly known as 'using the bounce' and 'at first I was terrible at it but Lynchy had kept insisting one day I'd need the shot'.

Sure enough, on the 72nd hole at Winged Foot after a perfect drive (which ended in a divot) and what he thought was a perfect iron, but which came up a yard or two short and tumbled back down the steep bank of the green, he was faced with the exact shot Lynch had told him he would have to play when it was important.

He flipped a lofted wedge up to 5 or 6 feet and, as he said, 'I hardly ever missed from six feet.'

Ogilvy had to overcome a temper, hardly something unusual – golf is a game likely to uncover a bad one. Bobby Jones, like Ogilvy, had been a reformed club thrower. George Walker, the USGA president (and great-grandfather of George W Bush) told a young Jones: 'You will never play in a USGA event again unless you can control your temper.' Both Ogilvy and Jones managed to keep the outward displays of displeasure from the spectators – and for those into their golf history, both made hugely important putts on that 18th green at Winged Foot – Ogilvy in 2006; Jones at the US Open in 1929 when he needed to make a swinging 12-

foot putt to tie Al Espinosa. The next day he won the 36-hole playoff by 23 shots.

* * *

The biggest difference between Ogilvy and Graham traces perhaps all the way back to their beginnings in golf. Graham grew up at Wattle Park and Riversdale where the fairways are narrow and tree lined, promoting straight driving. Ogilvy in contrast learned at Royal Melbourne and Victoria, where there is space from the tee, especially at Royal Melbourne, where accurate driving to a point of a wide fairway is a different test altogether. Unsurprisingly Ogilvy was a less precise driver – he would admit the US Open was hardly the major championship he was likely to win. His game, one clearly influenced by the type of golf Royal Melbourne encouraged, was far more suited to Augusta.

That they both won the US Open and Australian Open double by following wildly different paths proves there are many ways of successfully playing the game. Those who study the history will know that, and those who don't miss an important brick in the wall.

JASON DAY RISES

Jason Day cracked his first major tournament win at the 2015 US PGA Championship after a series of heartbreaking losses. That mountain climbed, Day would reach golf's number one ranking a month later. **Charles Happell** charts Day's victory, and extraordinary backstory.

After six near-misses in golf's major championships from 2011 to 2015, Jason Day began to doubt himself: was he just a good player out of luck – or did he in fact lack that indefinable quality, the intestinal fortitude and true grit, which marks all champion athletes?

The 27-year-old Australian took a share of the lead into the final round of the US Open and British Open in 2015 yet came up short both times. In 2011, Day had also come close in the first two majors, finishing runner-up in the US Masters and US Open. He might have been young and precociously talented, but suddenly the naysayers and doom merchants could be heard mumbling: did he actually have the right stuff to compete with Rory McIlroy and Jordan Spieth, golf's established twentysomething stars?

But that all changed when the Queenslander – whose background is a truly remarkable one in the bourgeois world of US Tour golf – finally clinched one of the game's big four tournaments, the 2015 US PGA Championship, with a display of such poise that all those demons and doubts were banished for good.

Cradling the trophy later, the famously assured Day let slip his inner feelings about what another narrow defeat might have meant for his self-confidence. 'Knowing that I had the fifty-four-hole lead for the last three majors and not being able to finish, it would have been tough for me mentally to really kind of come back from that,' Day said at his winner's media conference. 'Even though I feel like I'm a positive person, I think that kind of in the back of my mind, something would have triggered, and I would have gone: maybe I can't really finish it off.' But finish it off he did – and in what grand style.

His final score of 20 under par at Whistling Straits set a new record in major championships, in terms of a score against par, and in carding his near-flawless final round of five-under 67, Day saw off the challenge of golf's hottest player, Spieth, and two other hardened pros who featured large in 2015's majors, Justin Rose and Branden Grace. The win validated all the hype about Day's game over the previous five years, since he finished 10th in the 2010 US PGA at just his second start in a major.

He took to Twitter soon after his media commitments had finished, posting a photograph of himself with the Wanamaker Trophy above the telling message: 'Ding dong the witch is dead'. The wicked witch – the one whose voice he heard cackling at him at Augusta, St Andrews and Chambers Bay – had been slayed. Now the Australian could legitimately take his place at the forefront of golf's new order – alongside McIlroy and the new world number one, Spieth, with Japan's Hideki Matsuyama and American Rickie Fowler sitting just off their shoulder.

Day's story is not a typical one in the world of pro golf, especially not in the US, where most players seem to have graduated from one elite college golf program or another. The Queenslander's tale is a grittier one and the more inspirational for it.

He grew up in the small Queensland town of Beaudesert, whose population was barely nudging 4000 when Day was born in 1987. His father, Alvin, worked at the local abattoir while his mum, Dening, who hailed from the Philippines, kept accounts in the office at the same meat-packing plant. The meat works were one of the only longstanding industries in a town prone to both droughts and floods.

Money was always tight and it is said the Days would often forage for useful items at the town dump. On one trip, Alvin found an old three wood and brought it home to his son. And so began the boy's introduction to the game.

Alvin died of stomach cancer when Day was 12, a tragedy which sent his life careering off the rails. He began drinking, staying out late, and getting into trouble at school. Dening, worried her son might be lost to a life of petty crime, sold the family's home when he was a teenager and borrowed money from relatives to send Day to Kooralbyn International School as a boarder. The school was barely a half hour's drive from home, but Dening sent him there to grow up. Amazingly, Adam Scott was leaving the small school just as Day was arriving, and Olympic 400-metre gold medallist Cathy Freeman had preceded them both.

It was there Day met Col Swatton, the school's golf coach. Swatton was won over by his young student early on when Day disobeyed him one day, then showed up on the practice ground soon afterwards to admit he'd behaved badly and apologised.

'We had that little disagreement initially, but from that day forward, we have become a really good team,' Swatton said. 'After that, if you gave him something to do, he would just do it. He wouldn't question why, he wouldn't just do it for a day or two, and move onto something else. It was just: I'll do it until you tell me to stop and just tell me what you want me to do.'

Swatton spent most of the next 10 years not just fine-tuning Day's enormous talent, but knocking the rough edges off his headstrong young charge.

Never has an embrace between player and caddie been as tight, and emotion-charged, as the one shared by Day and Swatton that mid-August Sunday on Whistling Straits' final green.

There have been plenty of trying times in recent years as Swatton has straddled the roles of father figure, coach and caddie – and dealt with the disappointments of Day's near-misses at the 2013 Masters, then the US and British opens earlier in 2015 – but forged by that hardship over a decade, their bond is now unbreakable. When Day relieved Swatton of his caddying duties in 2017, it was to save their friendship – and his role as swing coach.

In the many interviews he gave at Whistling Straits immediately after Day's triumph, Swatton revealed the depth and complexity of their relationship: 'It's pretty well documented that Jason could have ended up on the wrong side of the tracks when he was twelve and that's true; he could easily have gone the other way. He would have wound up in a totally different spot. He wouldn't have been standing on the eighteenth green at Whistling Straits.'

Back in Queensland, Day's mother watched the PGA Championship telecast from home, as proud as any mum could be. Had he not become a professional golfer, Day figured he would 'be working at a meat processing plant, like he [his father] did'.

Day has spoken candidly of his childhood and modest upbringing. 'I'm going to be honest here,' he said in 2014 at the winner's press conference after the WGC World Match Play event in Arizona. 'I came from a very poor family. So it wasn't winning that was on my mind when I first came out on the PGA Tour. It was money. I wanted to play for money, because I'd never had it before.'

And now he's got a pile of the stuff he couldn't jump over – more than US$40 million in prizemoney, with years and years to add to it. But more importantly, he is now a major championship winner. And that, in the rarefied air of professional golf, where majors are the only currency that really matters, is the most valued prize of all.

CASINO GAMBLE COST TIGER EVERYTHING

Charles Happell pieces together the events that unfolded in Melbourne in November 2009 that led to Tiger Woods' extraordinary fall from grace, and helped derail perhaps the greatest career the game has seen.

The unremarkable outer Melbourne suburb of Heatherton, dotted as it is with market gardens, rubbish tips, parks and golf courses, seems an unlikely place for Tiger Woods' glorious career to flame out so spectacularly but, late in 2009, that is precisely what happened.

Woods, the world's number one player, had accepted a US$3 million appearance fee to play in the Australian Masters tournament at Kingston Heath that November, a decision that set in train a sequence of events that, two weeks later, would culminate in him losing his marriage, his reputation and, for all intents and purposes, his career.

Woods had not played in Australia for 11 years, since the late 1990s when the prodigy teed up in three events in short succession: the 1996 Australian Open at The Australian GC in Sydney, the 1997 Australian Masters at Huntingdale and the 1998 Presidents Cup at Royal Melbourne.

So the galleries in the sports-mad town were out in force, waiting to catch a glimpse of perhaps the world's greatest sportsman at that time, a 14-time major winner who seemed destined to eclipse Jack Nicklaus's record of 18.

On the Monday of that week, 9 November, Woods and his entourage checked in to Crown Towers casino resort on the banks of the Yarra River. And it was quite a retinue: his mother, Kultida, was with him, as was his longtime caddie, Steve Williams, his manager from International Management Group, Mark Steinberg, and some childhood friends from the US, including Bryon Bell, the president of Tiger Woods Design.

Unbeknown to anyone, another friend, this one by the name of Rachel Uchitel, had also checked in to Crown. Who knows what possessed Woods to include Uchitel in his entourage? Perhaps he thought, in the southernmost city on Australia's mainland, he'd be so far from his other life in Florida as husband, father, celebrity and paparazzi target, that no-one would notice.

The Australian golfer Craig Parry had phoned Woods before the Masters and asked the American if he'd like a personal crash-course in how to play the tricky nuances of Kingston Heath, rated among the best couple of courses in the country. The pair had played together many times since being grouped with each other in the first two rounds of the 1995 Scottish Open at Carnoustie, when Woods was still an amateur, and had become friends.

Parry happened to be the architect of the International team's 1998 Presidents Cup victory over the Woods-led Americans at Royal Melbourne – holing a chip shot from the rough by the 18th green to steal, with Japan's Shigeki Maruyama, a memorable foursomes victory from underneath the nose of Woods and Fred Couples. Coincidentally, in the 2002 New Zealand Open it was Parry who outshone the master, taking the title at Paraparaumu, while relegating the tournament drawcard to sixth place.

So it was that Parry became Woods' local guide in Tuesday's practice round, showing him the subtleties of a hard, fast sandbelt course in the middle of a mini heatwave – the sort of layout that Woods might get to play once or twice a year, at most. As fate would have it, they were picked to play in the same group – along with Queenslander Rod Pampling, who also got on well with Woods – for the first two rounds of the tournament proper on Thursday and Friday.

So Parry spent the best part of three days by Woods' side, never once having an inkling of the double life the world's greatest golfer was living while in Melbourne.

Well, perhaps one small inkling. As they strode around Kingston Heath together, the roly-poly Australian and the lean, dapper American got talking about all sorts of things outside golf. Woods mentioned that his mother had been to the theatre at least twice while in Melbourne and had urged her son to join her. But Parry said Tiger had told his mum: thanks but no thanks; I have more fun staying in.

When you combine that mundane snippet of information with reports from tournament organisers, sponsors from JBWere and even Australian IMG officials that Woods was very hard to get hold of that week after dark – even leaving the official tournament dinner at Crown early on Tuesday night so he could try his luck on the casino tables – then the ensuing revelations began to make some sense.

Out on the course, in the heart of suburban Heatherton, though, Woods smiled his way through Wednesday's pro-am, alongside three local players, and gave the appearance of not having a care in the world. A contented family man whose career was at its zenith, he seemed at peace with himself and doing what he loved best.

Williams remembers the week well: 'I recall the incredible atmosphere surrounding the event – it had a major-like buzz to it. The fans were very appreciative of Tiger playing in Melbourne – they hadn't seen him since 1998 and he'd won thirteen majors since then.

'Tiger was so excited to be at Kingston Heath. I rate that golf course as the best in the world. Architecturally, that's the number one for me, and I had told Tiger so much about it. He was super excited to be there, and just fell in love with the course.'

In Thursday's opening round, Woods shot a blistering six-under-par 66, followed by a 68 on Friday to open up a three-shot lead at the half-way mark of the tournament. For Parry, his friend seemed no different to the person he'd played alongside for many years on the US PGA Tour and against in two Presidents Cups. 'He was the same old Tiger,' Parry told me later. 'The same guy I'd played with many times before. He seemed very relaxed and it probably helped that he was playing with two guys he knew quite well, Rod Pampling and me.

'He was picking my brains about the sea breezes and prevailing winds. He was doing his homework. At one point on the ninth hole on the Friday – which was our last hole that day – we were waiting for Pamps to hit and I remarked on the beautiful bunkering down both sides of the fairway. He said that was one of the main reasons he came down to Melbourne: to look at Alister MacKenzie's bunkering and get inspiration for his course designs.

'There are not many times in a year where he'd play hard, fast conditions like we get in Melbourne. Maybe sometimes in Texas and at the British Open, but not often. Still, he understands how to play golf courses in that condition. He respected the golf course. He didn't go around blasting drivers off the tee like some players would; he took four irons off the tee sometimes and carefully negotiated his way around the course. Not many overseas players who come here show the sandbelt courses that sort of respect.'

But on Sunday morning, ahead of the final round, Williams sensed that all was not well when he called by Woods' hotel room to pick up his gear. Williams repeatedly knocked on the locked door but got no answer – something that was totally out of character for Woods, who was a stickler for punctuality and routine.

After waiting out in the hotel corridor for 10 minutes, the Kiwi began to get slightly panicky, fearing they might end up being late to the course. He rang security and asked if Tiger was waiting down in the lobby, but they hadn't seen him.

Five minutes later, the door opened and Williams immediately knew something was wrong. He could see Tiger's friends in the room, dressed as if they'd just stumbled in after a night on the town. Woods himself appeared distracted and preoccupied and, Williams thought, not ready to play golf. Woods told his longtime caddie there had been a change of plans and he would be packing up now and heading straight to the airport from Kingston Heath that evening.

That's weird, thought Williams.

If there was something on Woods' mind in that final round, it didn't show as he pieced together another clinical 68. From midafternoon, his renowned ability as a frontrunner made the tournament result a formality and he coasted to a two-shot win over Western Australia's Greg Chalmers.

After being presented with the trophy, having the gaudy Masters gold jacket slipped over his shoulders then fulfilling his media commitments, Woods and his team got on a chopper – skipping a shower back at the hotel – and headed straight to the airport to board a private plane.

As Williams drove back to the hotel on his own, he got a text from Steinberg, Woods' long-serving agent, which read: 'There is a story coming out tomorrow. Absolutely no truth to it. Don't speak to anybody.'

Despite their incredibly close relationship at work, on the practice range and golf course, Williams and his employer did very little socialising together. When they'd finished their shift at the course, they'd often go their separate ways and not meet up again until the following morning. It was quite a different relationship to the one Williams had with Greg Norman in the 1980s, for example, when socialising was part of the deal.

That's why the revelations about his boss's private life, when they finally began to emerge a week or so later, came as a shock to the Kiwi.

'It was an unusual text that I got from Steinberg on the Sunday but I thought nothing of it,' Williams remembers. 'But a few days later, I'm back on the farm in New Zealand and I'm listening to the radio, riding along on a tractor, when I hear this news about what had happened with Tiger. I couldn't believe it.'

The US tabloid *National Enquirer* and celebrity website TMZ revealed the story of Uchitel's presence in Melbourne – and Woods' double life. Soon enough the tawdry detail of his affairs with not just Uchitel but a dozen or more women were being uncovered and published almost daily.

The frenzy of horrendous publicity killed off Woods' career temporarily, and his marriage permanently. That closing 68 at Kingston Heath was to be his last round of competitive golf for more than four months. He lost his number one ranking the following year and didn't win another tournament until 2012, when he had a brief mid-career resurgence, claiming three Tour titles that year and another five the following season. But since the end of 2013, knee, Achilles tendon and back injuries and an increasingly frail short game – his chipping and putting lost the foolproof brilliance from his heyday – have served to produce a winless drought extending into its fifth year.

Like Williams, Parry was blown away when the first stories broke about Woods, smashing his image as a doting, clean-living father to smithereens. 'I thought like everyone that he was a great role model and family man,' he said. 'I couldn't believe it. Most players, as far as I'm aware, had the same view of Tiger as the public: that he was a great thing for golf for all the right reasons.'

Nine years on from that visit to Melbourne, Woods has not added to his 14 major wins, his world ranking plummeting at one point in 2017 to number 899.

Aged 42, he headed into the 2018 PGA Tour season attempting another comeback to regular tournament play. If anyone can overcome the sort of setbacks he has had to deal with since 2009, it's Woods – but even the most miserly bookmaker would be offering long odds on that.

When golf historians come to carbon date the end of the Woods era, they'll look at that week in November 2009 as the defining moment. When the outer suburb of Heatherton, Victoria, provided him with one final week of glory, success and adulation, before hubris spectacularly brought him undone.

WHAT THE MASTERS MEANS

Writing for an American golf magazine, **Charles Happell** attempts to place Adam Scott's victory at the 2013 Masters in the pantheon of Australian sporting achievements.

On Australian talkback radio and internet forums, one question kept recurring the day after Adam Scott became the first local to win the Masters: where does his feat rank in the pantheon of great Aussie sporting achievements?

There are five or six moments that always get mentioned when the 'pantheon' question arises, among them Cadel Evans' victory in cycling's Tour de France in 2011, Rod Laver twice winning tennis's Grand Slam, in 1962 and '69, Cathy Freeman, an Indigenous Australian who lit the Olympic flame at the Sydney Games, claiming the 400-metre gold medal days later, and Australia in 1983 wrenching the America's Cup out of the grip of the New York Yacht Club for the first time in 132 years, ending the longest winning streak in sports history.

Now, though, they had a challenger. Several respected commentators thought Scott was not only worthy of a place in the national shrine of sport but his effort in conquering Augusta surpassed all those world-beating feats that had gone before him.

When Australia won that America's Cup, incidentally, the then prime minister, the garrulous Bob Hawke (who once had an entry in the *Guinness Book of Records* for downing a yard of ale – 1.4 litres – in world-record time of 11 seconds) jubilantly declared: 'Any boss who sacks anyone for not turning up today is a bum.'

The same problem of tardy, sleep-deprived workers reared its head 30 years later. For any Australian with a serious interest in sport – and in the wide, brown land that means a fair slice of the population – the Monday of the Masters is a day when you arrive to work late. The telecast from Augusta begins about 5 am on the eastern seaboard. People start staggering out of bed sometime after that – drawn like zombies to the glow of the television – and there they stay, on the couch, until the final putt is holed sometime after 9 am. The real tragics stay in their place for the Butler Cabin presentation ... and then think about having a shower.

Part of the reason for the fascination with the championship is Australia's notable lack of success in the event – until 2013, eight runner-up finishes, but no cigar. That run of misery was exemplified by the much-loved Greg Norman, who turned his six-shot final-round lead in 1996, in golf's greatest case of reverse alchemy, into a steaming pile of vegetable matter.

But in 2013 the final stages of the tournament attracted even greater Australian interest than before. With two Queenslanders, Adam Scott and Jason Day, and a Victorian, Marc Leishman, all in contention after 54 holes, local electricity companies would have reported a power surge sometime before dawn on Monday as televisions, then kettles, were turned on in unison.

And when Scott holed that 5-metre curler across the hill at the 10th, the second playoff hole, the roar from Australia's living rooms could have been heard all the way down Magnolia Drive, while the Twittersphere in this part of the world revved into overdrive as everyone from the then prime minister, Julia Gillard, down joined in the nationwide high-fiving. 'Huge congratulations to Adam Scott – the first Australian ever to win the Masters,' tweeted Gillard.

Greg Norman admitted to watching with a tear in his eye. Ogilvy simply tweeted: 'Yes!!! I reckon it's time for a beer.' Steve Elkington was more jingoistic, tweeting: 'Waltzing Matilda ... Waltzing Matilda ... you'll go a Waltzing Matilda with me ...' A host of other sporting, business and political figures lauded the win; even US surfing champion Kelly Slater and UK boy band One Direction got in on the act.

Melbourne's *Herald-Sun* newspaper, a Murdoch tabloid with a deep-seated passion for the local football code but only a seasonal interest in golf, devoted a four-page wraparound to Scott's victory.

But amid the euphoria, there were some hard-luck stories as well.

For 25 years or more, Fairfax – Australia's second-biggest newspaper publisher, and Murdoch's local competitor – had sent a golf reporter to Augusta. It's a long trip – Sydney–LA–Atlanta–Augusta in one 24-hour session, all wedged up the back end of the plane – but has always been considered worth the pain. In 2013, the publishers of Melbourne's *Age* and *The Sydney Morning Herald* chose not to send anyone.

Of course an Australian was finally going to win after fate had been tempted in such a blatant way.

And so it proved, Scott not just becoming the first Australian in 77 years to slip his arms into the famous bottle-green jacket, but confirming that nice guys do occasionally finish first.

PART 2
TOURS AND TOURNAMENTS

Graham Marsh played a lot and advised everyone else to do the same.

Vijay Singh hit more balls than any man ever and played 35-plus tournaments a year for years.

Bruce Crampton was a 38-a-season man for years in the US.

But no-one has ever played more competitive professional rounds than Peter Fowler. He started competing in assistant professional events in Sydney in the late 1970s and 40 years later he's still playing Senior events all over the world. For six years from 1979 to 1984 he played 43 tournaments a year. 'How do you get better if you don't play?' he'd ask.

When professional players now say that all they can manage is four or five tournament weeks in a row, the pros of the past must just laugh.

– Mike Clayton

HIS MASTERS CHOICES

Golf-course preparation ahead of big tournaments is now
a sophisticated, hi-tech business. And no course is
prepared more lavishly and expertly than Augusta National,
home of the Masters. **Charles Happell**, who covered five
Masters, explains how the tournament committee leaves
nothing to chance.

Augusta National Golf Club is the most manicured, primped, preened and fussed over tournament venue in the world. It's possible, in fact, that no other 140-hectare plot anywhere receives quite the level of attention that's lavished on this verdant landscape in the otherwise unremarkable city of Augusta, Georgia.

Nothing is left to chance in the preparation of the course in the lead-up to Augusta's fabled tournament, the Masters, each April. And that applies to every aspect of the club's operation. Such is the level of sophistication of the club's equipment and technology, the Masters' tournament committee is able to exert control over not only the set-up of the course, but also the elements – and even the winner's score.

Here's how they do it:

1. Shot data has been taken at Augusta since 2002, recording the precise details of every stroke played in every Masters since. All hole positions have been pinpointed by GPS and the scoring data recorded,

factoring in firmness, speed and wind. Based on this information, each hole location has a scoring average. So the organisers know, for example, that a certain pin position at the par-three 12th, a certain wind direction and strength as well as a certain green speed will produce an average score over the day of, say, 3.25 strokes.

2. The committee's desired winning score, after 72 holes, is between 8 and 10 under par. The daily set-up – including pin and tee positions – is then manipulated to produce something close to that desired score. Patrick Reed's 15 under to win in 2018 was an outlier, as was Jordan Spieth's 18 under in 2015, but the nine under of (playoff winner) Sergio Garcia and Justin Rose in 2017 was within the range, as was Bubba Watson's eight under aggregate in 2014. Adam Scott and Angel Cabrera scored nine under in 2013, and Watson and Louis Oosthuizen finished at 10 under in 2012.

3. Green-surface firmness is measured each morning and afternoon of the tournament, and stimpmeter readings taken. The data is used to plan preparation of each green. Some greens are mown twice or three times a day. A heavy or light roller is used according to the data, to achieve uniformity across all 18 greens. Target stimpmeter readings are in the 13–14 range. Some watering is occasionally done on the Saturday afternoon to improve scoring for Sunday.

4. All of the greens at Augusta have been equipped with an underground Sub-Air hydronic fan system, with pipe network, that can warm the greens in winter, blow cool air into the root system during a humid summer, and suck moisture from the turf after heavy rain.

5. During Masters week, plug marks on the greens are repaired and filled with green sand by eight staff walking over each surface after every day's play.

6. Special hole placements are created to enhance drama. The funnelling towards the left pin on the par-three 16th green, for example, is designed to increase the chances of a hole in one on Sunday and help build excitement over the closing holes. This green was resurfaced in recent years to accentuate the funnelling, and the Sunday pin position adjusted slightly. The strategy worked a treat in 2016: Shane Lowry, Louis Oosthuizen and Davis Love all made aces at the 16th on the final day, as did Matt Kuchar the following year, and Charley Hoffman in 2018.

7. Fairways are mown in one direction from the green back towards the tee to create into-the-grain growth, reduce ball roll and produce a uniform colour, rather than the more common two-tone stripes.

8. Extreme measures ensure all the bunkers drain well. Underneath the sand in each bunker face, a cloth material is placed to stop the underlying 'dirty' sand migrating into the vivid white sand – which is imported from South Carolina. It also assists in stopping any balls from plugging in the face.

9. Black colourant is dripped into the water at Rae's Creek and other ponds to give a made-for-television, clean-water appearance. To maintain that pristine look, a staff member is stationed upstream during Masters week to intercept any rubbish flowing down into the course waterways.

10. Given the idyllic parkland surrounds, perhaps it is not
    surprising that Herman and Elizabeth Thacker, who
    live in a brick house at 1112 Stanley Drive, have resisted
    all Augusta's attempts to buy their property, which is
    earmarked for demolition so the club can expand its car
    park. Augusta's grandees have managed to persuade all
    their other neighbours to sell, but the Thackers continue
    to reside happily inside Augusta's grounds, near Gate 6-A.
    They've lived there since 1959 – and aren't planning
    to move anytime soon. Sure, the cars are a problem in
    Masters week but, hey, for the other 51 weeks of the year
    who's complaining?

EUROPEAN TOUR, 1980s: THAT WAS THEN

Mike Clayton played his second full year on the European Tour in 1984, when capless players endured the rigours of Monday qualifying, wooden drivers and balata balls were the order of the day, cigarette companies sponsored tournaments – and metal-spiked shoes were leather, attractive, and long-lasting.

Starting in April

The first tournament of the 1984 season was in Tunisia in April, the week after Augusta. The opening event of the 2018 season was the Hong Kong Open in the third week of November. 2017. It's a world tour now, something resembling the vision Peter Thomson articulated in the 1960s.

Practice ball bags

Caddies used to 'fox' their player's practice shots until Titleist started providing brand-new range balls each week. Luxury. Previously caddies weren't averse to impressing upon their players, often right around the 16th hole, just how well they were playing and it was hardly necessary to pound balls on the range for a couple of hours. Occasionally caddies would be hit by balls – it was amazing no-one was seriously hurt. Caddies can now make a living if they work for a good player. In 1984 very few were doing more than surviving from week to week.

Wooden drivers
They had character, personality, and every single one of them looked and felt just a little different. Players were always searching for the magical club – and once found it'd stay in the bag for years. Drivers are much more effective now, much more forgiving of a missed shot, but they are utterly without soul.

Sunningdale
We played the European Open at Sunningdale in the 1980s and in 1990 (Peter Senior won that week) but that was the end of it. It was all class, just like playing a tournament at Royal Melbourne.

Ping one irons
Karsten Solheim, the first to weight up the perimeter of the irons, was the transformative genius of club-making via his company, Ping. Almost every putter now is just a counterfeit of his original Ping Anser. His long irons were the easiest to hit and the best exponent of the Ping one iron was Sandy Lyle. It was a brilliant club on the windy links, one many saw as an essential part of their arsenal. No-one carries one irons now. This is partly because the ball is easier (better?) to use in the wind and partly because of the invention of the hybrid cross between a one iron and a four wood.

Balata balls
Compared with the modern ball, the balata covers were soft and easily damaged, but they were high-quality golf balls. Opponents of rolling back the ball would have you think it would be like going back to gutta-percha – but no-one in 1984 thought there was a problem with the ball.

Cigarette sponsors
In 1970, Mark McCormack (founder of IMG) was writing in his annual review of the professional game about the impending ban of

cigarette advertisements on television. He felt much of that money would soon find its way onto television screens another way. He was right: cigarette companies bought the naming rights to big golf tournaments, among other sports. For years one of the biggest events in England was the Benson & Hedges in York. Cigarette sponsorship was tolerated for about 25 years until the inevitable happened and tobacco company sponsorship was banned. A good thing, too.

Monday qualifying

1984 was the last year of the dreaded Monday qualifying, as the tour went all-exempt with the top 125 money winners given full playing rights for the 1985 season. Previously, only the top 60 players were exempt from the rigours of shooting a good enough round on Monday to win the right to play come Thursday.

Monte Carlo Open

Nice city with a golf course not quite up to it. It was so foggy on top of the mountain we would sit around for hours barely able to see 5 or 10 yards ahead while our wives were happily sunbaking on the beach below.

So many Australians

Wayne Grady, Rodger Davis, Graham Marsh, Jamie Crow, Ian Baker-Finch, Noel Ratcliffe, Ossie Moore, Gerry Taylor, Peter Fowler, Mike Harwood, Wayne Riley, Vaughan Somers, Peter Senior. I don't understand many of this generation's reluctance to play in Europe, eschewing it for the Web.com tour and its promise of the top 25 earning a card to the PGA Tour. It's been a professional graveyard for many.

Three over par cuts

Those days are long gone. Well, long gone unless they take the Scottish Open back to Carnoustie.

Bare-headed players

All players now have logos on their caps – and you thought the caps were to keep the sun off. Companies used to pay the most to have their names on the golf bag but in time they came to realise the most valuable space was right on the front of the player's head. Robert Rock is the lone hold-out.

Footjoy Classics

Footjoy made the best shoes. Leather soles, beautifully crafted, heavy and with a wide variety of styles and colours. Shoes are lighter now, more 'athletic' and probably 'better'. They are also mostly ugly and disposable, looking good only for a few months. Given players don't pay for them I suppose it doesn't matter for them. At least the greens are better now for the new plastic spikes, instead of the metal ones we had.

Randy Fox

Randy was an American travel agent who somehow arranged for everybody to get from week to week. His most stressful time was on Friday afternoons, when annoyed players who'd missed the cut just wanted him to 'get me out of this dump'. He was very good at it.

Ivor Robson

Ivor was the starter famed for his Open Championship introductions: 'This is match number thirty-four. On the tee ...' He did all the tournaments in England and was very good at a very simple job. Which doesn't mean it wasn't important. He had a terrific rapport with the players.

English reporters

People in England bought newspapers in 1984 to read golf writers like Peter Dobereiner, Michael Williams, Dai Davies and Mitchell Platts. Not anymore. At the BBC, Henry Longhurst was gone by

1984 but Peter Alliss was an admirably good replacement. They covered all the British tournaments until pay television bought the rights and started covering the European Tour 50 weeks a year.

Seven tournaments in England
Now there are four tournaments in South Africa and just two in England – not counting The Open when it goes south of the border. Amazing how the tables have turned. We've also lost the German Open, and the Spanish Open was resurrected in 2018 after a year's absence, which seems unimaginable given what Bernhard Langer did for golf in Germany, and Seve Ballesteros and José María Olazábal for Spain.

A club pro in the Ryder Cup team
At the end of 1983 Brian Waites, the club pro at Notts, played in the Ryder Cup in Florida. The Europeans almost won and in the midst of their despondency Ballesteros reminded them it was a triumph. 'Next time we win.' But it would be without Waites.

Seve
The lives of everyone who played on the Tour in his time were enriched for watching him play golf. Charisma is a very over-used word but no-one lit up a room or a fairway like Severiano Ballesteros.

Peter Fowler's daughter was maybe three or four when her dad went through a miserable run of missed cuts on the European Tour. In their London house, there was a selection of his golf photos on the wall and one Friday, after another missed cut, 'Chook' was so disgusted with himself he took them all down. A few weeks later, his wife, Kim, and their two young daughters were at Heathrow on Sunday night instead of the all-too-frequent Friday night pick-up. Georgia already knew enough about golf to know coming home on Sunday was good. In the car on the way home, she asked: 'Does this mean we can put the photos back on the wall?'

– Mike Clayton

JACK NICKLAUS IN HOBART

The Australian Open was once a prestigious event, its trophy adorned by the names of the game's greatest players, including Nicklaus, Palmer and Player. But in the 21st century it is struggling, under threat from other sports, encroaching US PGA Tour dates and golf's dowdy image, as **Charles Happell** writes.

When he was at the peak of his considerable powers, Jack Nicklaus chose in 1971 to forgo the season-ending US PGA Tour event in Las Vegas – which was vital in determining who'd win that season's money-list title – and instead make the 13,000-kilometre trip to Tasmania to play in the Australian Open.

The national championship was being held for the first (and last) time at Royal Hobart Golf Club – no-one's idea of a goat track but, then again, a course no-one has confused with Pine Valley either. In fact, it has on occasion dropped out of the top 100 courses in Australia.

So Nicklaus teed up his Slazenger B51 ball at this rather unremarkable layout on Hobart's outskirts and shot rounds of 68, 65, 66 and 70 to beat Bruce Crampton and the rest of the field by eight shots. Oh, and collect the first-prize cheque of $4320, not to mention his third Stonehaven Cup.

Back in Las Vegas, he'd left Lee Trevino and Arnold Palmer

to fight over his slender lead on the Tour moneylist at the Sahara
International. Trevino ended up profiting most from the great
man's absence, winning the event and, thanks to the $27,000 first
prize – more than six times what Nicklaus came to Australia to
play for – overhauling Nicklaus's earnings lead. But that didn't
seem to perturb the Golden Bear (a nickname, incidentally,
bestowed upon him by an Australian sportswriter, Don Lawrence,
during one of Nicklaus's many visits Down Under) one bit.

After collecting his winner's trophy by the 18th green at
Royal Hobart, Nicklaus said, 'I'm still interested in being at the
top of the money stakes, but only if it doesn't interfere with my
competing in what I consider to be prestige events. I've won [the
money title] three times so it's no longer a case of "I've got to
do it." Besides, it's far more important to win a national title like
this.' (As it happened, Nicklaus went back to the US and claimed
the title anyway.)

Australian golf officials standing nearby puffed out their chests
and beamed with pride. Here was the game's greatest player,
who earlier that year at the PGA Championship in Florida had
won his ninth of (what would become) eighteen majors, spurning
an important week back home to compete in their very own
Australian Open, playing at an obscure course at the end of the
earth, where if you hit out of bounds on the wrong hole, your
nearest point of relief was an Antarctic ice floe.

Nicklaus even referred to the event as golf's 'fifth major' –
although some suspect this was simply a bit of PR spin to
schmooze local golf writers and officials – and his name adorned
the Stonehaven Cup alongside those of Gary Player, Arnold Palmer
and Gene Sarazen. What greater vote of confidence, what more
significant imprimatur and seal of approval could there be for
their national championship?

But what we have witnessed in recent years is a pale and
anaemic version of an event that was once a leading fixture on
the Australian sporting calendar. Now, the 'fifth major' reference

is uttered only ironically. And all that golfing administrators in Australia can do is shake their heads ruefully and wonder what the heck happened to their once-great tournament.

The answer is complex: Australia's tournament dates now invariably clash with the lucrative and ever-expanding US Tour, and sometimes the Tour qualifying schools; golf is not regarded as a sexy vehicle to promote non-golf products; A-League soccer and Big Bash cricket have emerged as competition and sponsorship money as a consequence has slowed to a trickle; *Golf Australia* can't afford to pay appearance money to more than a couple of top-line players; Australia's golfers are by and large a fairly beige lot ... and Greg Norman has retired. That's a pretty potent mix of factors.

Even 20 years ago, few could have predicted how dire the situation would become. At the 1997 championship played at Metropolitan GC in Melbourne, Lee Westwood beat Greg Norman in a playoff. A handful of shots behind that pair were, among others, Vijay Singh, Phil Mickelson, Mark Calcavecchia, Darren Clarke and Ryder Cupper Andrew Coltart. These days, the fields for Australia's national title feature most – but never all – of our leading players, plus a handful of internationals. After that, they have little more depth than a footpath puddle.

At the 2012 Australian Open, which was played at The Lakes in Sydney (the scene, incidentally, of Nicklaus's first Open victory, in 1964), the cast was headlined by many of the best Australians. Then the marquee names were Justin Rose, who was major-less to that point in his career, a 63-year-old Tom Watson and the 14-year-old Chinese prodigy, Guan Tianlang. In 2017, the tournament again boasted Jordan Spieth as its marquee signing – and a welcome four-time visitor and two-time champion he has been, adding much-needed star power to proceedings, spurred on by his longtime Australian swing coach Cameron McCormick. Jason Day made a rare appearance, along with the likes of Matt Jones, Cam Smith and the Canadian former major winner Mike

Weir, but there was, tellingly, no Adam Scott – for the first time in years – and no Marc Leishman, both supposedly miffed at the carve-up of appearance money.

Emirates Airlines remains the tournament's naming-rights sponsor but, in truth, they're a pretty minor major backer. Total prizemoney in 2017 was A$1.25 million, which is not to be sniffed at – but when you consider that the 1996 Australian Open (Tiger Woods' first tournament appearance in Australia, on his first overseas trip as a professional) offered a purse of A$1 million, you can see that things haven't come very far in the two decades since. In fact, the tournament has just been treading water. And the challenge to stay afloat has never been greater.

In 2017, former world number one Vijay Singh highlighted how ridiculous it was that the Fijian national championship carried a greater prize purse than the Australian one. The three-time major winner made his telling observations after the opening round of the Fiji International, worth $1.5 million. 'The economy of Fiji compared to Australia is worlds apart, yet we have the biggest golf tournament in this part of the world,' Singh said. 'I think Australia should take a hint from that and come up with a tournament that is better.'

The 2018 Australian Open will be staged at The Lakes from 15 to 18 November. That very same week, the PGA Tour stops off in Georgia for the RSM Classic – hardly one of the biggies on the US circuit but still worth about A$7.8 million, more than six times what's on offer in Sydney.

We are left to wonder how many players will be brave enough to invoke the spirit of Nicklaus and turn their back on that pile of greenbacks in favour of playing golf's 'fifth major', a time-honoured national championship and 'prestige event' that was first contested in 1904. The last time we looked, Australian golf officials weren't holding their breath in anticipation.

I once asked Tom Weiskopf: 'Who is the best putter you have ever seen?'

'Jack Nicklaus,' he said without any hesitation. 'Did you ever see him miss a putt he had to make?'

'What about Ben Crenshaw and Bob Charles?' I ventured.

'They had to be.'

— Mike Clayton

NOT SO EASY RYDER CUP

Once little more than a glorified teams exhibition that was routinely won by the Americans, the Ryder Cup has developed into one of the most popular events in golf, and a lucrative one too – just not for the competing players. **John Huggan** charts the cup's remarkable evolution.

Today, the biennial contest between the best golfers from the United States and the continent of Europe is perhaps the most anticipated event in the world of golf. But not so long ago, the Ryder Cup wasn't important at all. Not even a little bit.

When the Cup began, a bunch of guys from the US would get together with a group of gentlemen from Great Britain and Ireland every two years and everyone would have a jolly nice time. And every two years, the little trophy with the figure of Abe Mitchell on top – the former Irish Open champion was the swing coach of event founder Samuel Ryder – would invariably make its way 'home' with Uncle Sam's nephews. Barely competitive, it was the sporting equivalent of a garden party.

'We had cars parked around the eighteenth green at Royal Birkdale in 1969, so that we could putt out by the glare from the headlights,' laughs Open and US Open winner Tony Jacklin. 'Lee Trevino, Neil Coles and I all had putts from about five feet that were impossible it was so dark. The Ryder Cup wasn't such a big deal back then.'

The nadir came in 1977. What for so long had been merely inconsequential made its final descent into almost total irrelevancy, at least as far as one American player was concerned. Instead of travelling to Royal Lytham and St Anne's with his compatriots, Tom Weiskopf opted to go elk hunting in Alaska. It was an indication that the Ryder Cup's perennial winners were losing interest – since the end of the Second World War, the team from Great Britain and Ireland had won only once.

For Jack Nicklaus at least, it was the final straw. Writing to Lord Derby, president of the Professional Golfers Association, the game's most successful player suggested that continental Europeans be added to the opposition in the hope that the matches might become more competitive.

Sure enough, they did. In 1983 at PGA National in Florida, the European team lost only by a single point. Two years later, armed with a side containing Seve Ballesteros, Nick Faldo, Sandy Lyle, Ian Woosnam and Bernhard Langer – the so-called 'Big Five' of European golf – the Old World won convincingly at The Belfry in England. And in 1987 they triumphed again, for the first time on US soil, at Muirfield Village in Ohio. Ironically, Nicklaus was the American captain on his home course.

In less than 10 years, the 'garden party' became one of the most anticipated and entertaining events in all of golf. At last, a real and sometimes cut-throat rivalry had been added to the building of friendships on which the event had been founded.

The 1980s represented the beginning of a new Ryder Cup. Golf fans around the world and particularly in the US began to take notice. After 1985, the next eight Ryder Cups were closely contested, producing four one-point matches, two decided by two points and one by three, as well as a tie in 1989. In giving the average fan a level of intensity and pressure greater than any other, the event has established itself as one of the premier events in modern golf. Instead of playing as individuals for prizemoney, this is playing for pride and one's country. That unique combination means fans have been treated to some of the most memorable match-play battles ever seen, the quality of golf truly outstanding.

In turn, the players themselves have embraced the matches as something special and – alongside the four major championships – career-defining occasions.

'Playing in the Ryder Cup was the greatest experience in my career,' says four-time major champion Ray Floyd, one of the toughest competitors in all of golf. 'I got to play on eight teams and captain one more. My wife, Maria, and I loved the matches. Representing your country is the ultimate in any sport. It is very special.

'Some of my great friendships in the game have come from the Ryder Cup. When you compete at the highest level and represent your country, there is a tremendous amount of respect between opponents. That creates an unbreakable bond between you and the other guy. I look back on matches with Brian Barnes, Bernard Gallacher and Tony Jacklin with great affection. They are buddies of mine and it all started at the Ryder Cup.'

Indeed, watching highly paid individuals playing for nothing more than an intangible point in an event from which they will derive no direct financial benefit is an intriguing thing. Even the hardiest and most durable competitors have been reduced to the golfing equivalent of babbling fools over the closing holes of crucial Ryder Cup matches.

'The Ryder Cup brings with it a different level of pressure,' acknowledges five-time Open champion Tom Watson. 'I experienced more strain playing for my country than I ever did in any major championship.'

'It's all to do with pride,' agrees Jacklin, four times the European skipper. 'It's all to do with answering the ultimate question: How good am I really? Players are naked in the Ryder Cup, totally exposed. And all they care about is beating the other guy. There is no hiding place. It's a lonely spot if you don't have the equipment or have fudged your way in.'

Watson and Jacklin speak the truth. The mind goes immediately to Fred Couples and what should have been a routine nine iron to the final green at The Belfry in 1993. Good enough to win the Masters two years earlier, Couples missed the putting surface by more than 30 yards to the right.

Scotsman Sam Torrance – who holed the winning putt in 1985 at The Belfry and skippered Europe to victory at the same venue in 2002 – can even trace the genesis of his long-term battle with putting yips to the Ryder Cup. 'I know exactly where they started,' he says with a shudder. 'At the 1987 Ryder Cup I played Larry Mize in the singles. I had two putts ... from maybe fifteen feet to win the last hole and halve the match. It felt like my hands were shaking so badly. I had no idea when I hit the ball whether it was going to be stone dead or ten feet short or ten feet past.'

Then there was Jay Haas and Philip Walton on the last hole of their match at Oak Hill in 1995. By the end, both could barely walk in a straight line, never mind hit a straight shot, such is the effect of Ryder Cup pressure. And four years earlier, one-time Open champion Mark Calcavecchia was physically ill as he wandered aimlessly on the beach at Kiawah Island after losing the last four holes to Colin Montgomerie.

There is nothing professional golfers with large egos hate more than having to announce: 'I lost.' That word is anathema to pampered individuals reared on the weird notion that top-10 finishes in 72-hole stroke play events are somehow laudable.

Almost inevitably, with such competitiveness has come some nastiness. Sadly, the 1991, 1999 and 2016 Ryder Cups provoked unruly crowd scenes, with players on both sides routinely abused.

'The best and worst Ryder Cup match I was ever part of took place at Kiawah Island in 1991,' sighs Floyd. 'Fred Couples and I took on José María Olazábal and Seve. It was just so exciting. The aura around it all was amazing. They were an incredible team.

But that was also the year that the matches took a nasty turn … That is not what golf is about. And it certainly isn't what the Ryder Cup is about. The matches should be about goodwill and camaraderie, not what we saw that year.'

With the rise of the matches has come money. Huge money. A fact that has made the Ryder Cup the straw that stirs the European Tour's drink. The financial success of every home game cannot be overstated when it comes to golf's second-largest circuit.

'The reality is that the Ryder Cup is a commercial juggernaut, a business that produces upward of £100 million,' points out Paul McGinley, who holed the winning putt for Europe at The Belfry in 2002, then skippered the side to victory at Gleneagles 12 years later. 'It's massive and a lifeline for the European Tour. We – the players and the executives – all know that. In these tough economic times we need all the Ryder Cup revenues to be re-invested into the tour. It underpins so much of what we do over the four years between home matches.'

Still, it is what happens on the course that fans all across the globe surely remember most vividly. All golfers love the Ryder Cup, even the best in the game. Today, it is that important.

PRESIDENTS CUP: A POISONED CHALICE?

In its 24 years, the Presidents Cup has struggled to achieve any of the passion, rivalry or competitiveness that has been a hallmark of the modern Ryder Cup. **Charles Happell** wonders whether golf's various tours should put more effort instead into resurrecting the World Cup, a teams event with a rich history.

You can be sure that Royal Melbourne Golf Club will put on a spectacular show when it hosts the 2019 Presidents Cup, that crowds will line the gallery ropes in their droves – as Australians do when a big sports event comes to town – and that PGA Tour officials will go home happy, their coffers overflowing.

But the elephant in the room is the relevance of the tournament itself.

The truth is that the results since the Presidents Cup's inception in 1994 have been so lopsided – the Internationals winning just once in 12 outings – that the Cup risks becoming a glorified exhibition rather than a genuine competition.

This is what the Ryder Cup felt like in the mid 1970s when the matches between the US and Great Britain and Ireland became such a procession – the latter team winning just three of 22 contests between 1927 and 1977 – that the event almost ceased to exist as a bona fide contest. Europe was added to the mix in

1979 and, voila, golf's administrators realised they had, almost by accident, hit on a Michelin-starred recipe for sporting success.

Of course, the Presidents Cup gives golf followers in Australia, Canada, South Korea and South Africa a chance to see many of the greatest players in the world every once in a while. And that's got to be a good thing for the game.

The announcement that Tiger Woods and Ernie Els will captain the 2019 US and International teams, respectively, can only help to build interest in the contest too. For Woods, the appointment will mark his ascension to golf statesman and grandee, surely something that not even he could possibly have envisaged at the start of the decade, when his reputation was so shredded that the idea of him captaining even an American tiddlywinks team would have been dismissed as absurd.

Yet until we get some of those vital ingredients added to the Presidents Cup – passion, drama, excitement and intense rivalry – it will remain an artifice, a contrivance, a biennial sporting fixture desperately in search of an identity.

The Cup's premise is illogical. The International team is the sum of many disparate parts – Australians, Japanese, Koreans, Indians, New Zealanders, South Africans, Fijians and Paraguayans – and these players, who often don't know each other well, are expected to bond together for one week every two years and develop a team spirit while playing under a strange-looking blue-and-yellow flag with 12 stars on it.

I get the feeling players couldn't much care whether the Presidents Cup appeared on the tour calendar or not. When the tournament was last played in Melbourne, in 2011, Japan's boy wonder Ryo Ishikawa inexplicably turned up a day late, and half asleep, irritating the hell out of team captain Greg Norman. For reasons never properly explained, Ishikawa chose to arrive in Melbourne on Tuesday night, thereby missing the team dinner on Monday night and team practice on Tuesday. That left him with one day's practice and familiarisation at the idiosyncratic Alister

MacKenzie layout, a course that over the years has made fools of much better players than him. Unsurprisingly, the Japanese lost his first two matches.

The lopsided results between the two teams over 12 Cups have also put pressure on the concept. Since 1994, the US has won 10 editions, drawn one and lost one – in 1998, at Royal Melbourne as it happens.

The International team captain at the 2015 Presidents Cup in South Korea, Zimbabwean Nick Price, acknowledged the pachyderm's presence, expressing exasperation at the lopsided scoreline and saying the Internationals really needed to win that week to inject some life into the competition. 'I will tell you guys, this is a really important Presidents Cup,' Price told a pre-event press conference. 'I'm not going to say, What if? But this better be closely contested. I'll let you guys figure out the repercussions [if it isn't].'

One of those repercussions could be players not wanting to take part at the end of a busy season, with Price, a three-time major winner, admitting, 'It's hard for these guys. You ask these guys to give up a week and to play in an event that is not competitive. Any one of these guys can go play anywhere around the world and receive money and they can easily dump this event if they wanted to.'

His top-ranked player at the time, Australia's Jason Day, agreed with his captain, adding, 'This is a huge deal for us right now. If it doesn't happen and we keep losing, guys won't get interested in it and won't want to play in it and won't want to travel.'

Four days later, the Americans triumphed again, if only just.

Then, in 2017, at Liberty National in New Jersey, the tournament became another US procession, with a scoreline of 19–11, taking their winning streak to seven – redolent of the early days of the Ryder Cup when the Americans barely broke sweat in compiling success after success.

The PGA Tour continues to support the concept because the Cup makes a good deal of money. It pays Royal Melbourne a peppercorn rent to host the tournament, yet rakes in a small fortune from ticket sales and merchandise and, of course, television broadcast rights. The Tour points out that more than US$40 million has been raised for charity from tournament proceeds over the past 12 editions of the Cup, mainly from the $250,000 fee each player is paid which is forwarded to the charity of their choice, and that is certainly impressive enough, but what I'd be really interested to learn is how much the Tour makes from this event. And on that score, the figures are rather opaque: no-one is really sure.

The PGA Tour has long relied on the Victorian government and its promotional arm, Victorian Major Events, to fund some of its tournaments that have needed an overseas home. Melbourne therefore scored the 1998 Presidents Cup (which was a success on almost every measure), the 2001 WGC Match Play event at Metropolitan GC (which was staged for some unknown reason in the first week of January 2001 and attracted barely a handful of the world's top 20 players), the 2011 Presidents Cup and, most recently, the 2016 World Cup of Golf. So excuse my scepticism and scrooginess, but there are many international sporting events that deserve taxpayer support – just not the Presidents Cup.

A better idea might be resurrecting the World Cup of Golf. Once an annual feature on the global golf calendar, the World Cup has recently spluttered and staggered from host venue to host venue; sometimes played every three years, sometimes every two. It was supposed to be held at Mission Hills in China until 2025, but the tournament's main sponsor, Omega, pulled the pin after 2011. It seems no-one knows quite what do with this event.

But here's a thought that should appeal to all 'stakeholders', and guarantee the tournament's future: leave it in Melbourne, or Australia more generally, for at least the next three editions. The sandbelt courses in Melbourne – or Royal Adelaide or New South Wales GC, for that matter – would ensure a decent field and help give the event a platform from which to build some momentum.

The World Cup was once golf's premier international teams event. With some clever marketing, a semi-permanent home and a bit of willpower from the International Federation of PGA Tours, it could be again.

Meanwhile, the Presidents Cup is a fun tournament that produces some world-class golf, but until there's some deep-seated passion, intensity and theatre – and the occasional win for the Internationals – it's not much more than a glorified exhibition with a scoreboard.

JASON DAY, MARC LEISHMAN, PLEASE CALL HOME

As a boy, **Mike Clayton** was beguiled by the skills of local champions such as Peter Thomson, Kel Nagle, Bruce Devlin and Billy Dunk who kept the Australasian Tour alive. Today, he is dismayed at the modern trend of the country's best players turning their back on the local tour – when it needs them now more than ever.

I grew up in the extraordinary era of Australian golf when IMG boss Mark McCormack arranged an endorsement deal with Dunlop/ Slazenger for his clients, who just happened to be the best three players in the world: Gary Player, Jack Nicklaus and Arnold Palmer.

One, two or even all three would come down to play the big events each summer, promote the clubs with their names on the back and even play the occasional exhibition. Player did one at Yarram, Nicklaus played a match with the club pro at Shepparton and Palmer featured in one at Northern.

New South Welshman Bruce Devlin, too, came home every year, playing Slazenger clubs after using Spalding all year in the United States.

For the time it was a significant endorsement even for the best three players of the era but it was a deal way ahead of its time.

Flying all the way to Australia to play with the small ball and a different set of clubs, let alone an 18-hole exhibition at a not very famous course, would be an unimaginable imposition for today's best players.

As important as 'The Big Three' were to the Australian Tour, the British Open champions, Peter Thomson and Kel Nagle, were the backbone of the local circuit. They would play Australia's major tournaments – The Dunlop International, The Wills Masters, The PGA and The Open – plus many of the state opens and some, or all, of the handful of tournaments at the end of every season in New Zealand. While the prizemoney was pretty small, it was a proper tour going on for three or even four months. David Graham – just starting to make a name for himself in the late 1960s – played every week, as did Billy Dunk.

Billy was a fantastic player. The former New Zealand player, now Golf Channel commentator, Frank Nobilo summed Billy up with this story in a *Golf Digest* interview in 2016: 'You might not have heard of Billy Dunk. He's one of the great Australian players of all time, winner of five Australian PGAs and twenty-nine tournaments on the Australasian Tour. My first pro tournament in Australia was the Victorian Open. I was twenty, unknown, and as such was assigned the first tee time of the day.

'I was on edge about it because I was staying at a cheap motel well outside of town, didn't have a car and would have to depend on a cab picking me up before sunrise. The evening prior, I ran into Billy, whom I idolised. After a little small talk he asked, "What time you going off tomorrow?" I told him and expressed my concern. "No worries; you can ride with me," he said. The next morning at five am, there came the knock at the door from Billy. "Rise and shine," he said. "We leave in thirty minutes." Still squinting, I noticed Billy was still in his pajamas. "Why aren't you dressed?" I asked. "Aren't you playing?" He said, "Of course I'm playing, but I don't go off until this afternoon." I said, "Why are you giving me a ride in?" He said, "Because you needed one." I'll tell you, they don't make them like Billy Dunk anymore.'

Pioneers like Billy made the tour into what it was, which gave Greg Norman and my generation a chance to play and earn enough to compete overseas. They barely played for any money – Thomson made $55.75 for his 23rd place in the 1971 Australian PGA at Surfers Paradise and Dunk pocketed $1710 for winning – but they were promoting the game and giving local fans the feeling they were watching really important golf.

The big money followed the PGA, with the Wills at Victoria and the Open in Hobart ($20,000 both), and the biggest of them all, the $25,000 Dunlop at Manly. One of Australia's leading amateurs, Tony Gresham, caddied for Jack Nicklaus there when he had a chance to break 60 in the second round and eventually took off with the $3800 winner's prize.

What he must think of today's top players getting a million dollars just to turn up is anyone's guess.

Norman, too, was an unstinting supporter of the local tour. Sure he was well paid for his attendance, but he was clearly one of the best two or three players in the world from the mid 1980s to the mid 1990s. In 1986 he came home as The Open Champion and played a long run of tournaments including The Queensland Open (first), NSW Open (first), South Australian Open (first), The Australian PGA (second behind Mike Harwood), Australian Open (seventh) and finally the West Australian Open where he unsurprisingly won again, beating Terry Gale by a shot. The only week off he had was between the PGA and The Open when we all went to the Victorian PGA in Warrnambool. Which neatly segues to the problem with today's local tour.

Marc Leishman grew up in Warrnambool and has become one of the best players in the world. Not only that, he stared into the reality of a life without a wife and mother to his children when the most unlikely of illnesses threatened to take her life in early 2015. I understand it's a long way from his home in Virginia, it's at the end of a long year, there is always a tournament the week of Thanksgiving, and it's time away from the kids. But – and here's the but – it's also important the best Australians play as much at home as they can. It takes an effort and maybe it's a pain at times but if the tour, or what's left of it, is going to carry on, Marc Leishman turning up to play the tournaments would be a huge help. Not only does his presence help, his absence hurts. Is the Australian Open really such a big deal if our best player isn't playing?

Jason Day has been a pro since 2006. Leaving out the World Cup and the Presidents Cup, he has played six tournaments in Australia since then and three were co-sanctioned Web.com events when he was playing that tour and a fast start early in the season was important. If you turned up at school as rarely as that, the teachers would have a hard time even remembering your name. It's fine to come back and say all the right things about how much you care about winning the Australian Open, but those comments don't ring true when you only play it twice in 10 years.

Nor are our two best players coming back for nothing. Their fees, or rather the fees charged by their manager, are enough to buy a nice apartment in Sydney or Melbourne. Well, maybe not Sydney.

When Robert Allenby and Stuart Appleby were our two best-performing players in the 2000s, both came back unstintingly to support the big events, as did Geoff Ogilvy after he won the US Open. And no-one has ever questioned the commitment of Adam Scott. He came back in 2013 after winning the Masters at Augusta, playing the Masters, PGA and the Open here, enduring all the pre-tournament dinners where everyone wanted a picture and a minute of his time, when I'm sure he'd have rather been back at home with his feet up.

Perhaps this is a slap at Leishman and Day, but there will be more Leishmans and Days. In a very old-fashioned way, it is important the best of ours come back and support the local tournaments.

It's too easy for them to think of these tournaments as small beer – which they are compared to the riches on offer each week in the United States. It's even easier for an American manager – both Leishman and Day are represented by Bud Martin – to think of Australian tournaments as irrelevant and an aggravation they don't need. But they would do well to remember the contribution of on the one hand Nicklaus, Palmer and Player and on the other Thomson, Norman and Dunk, because without them, there may not have been a tour at all. And you can bet at some point in the early development of all Australian players, the Australian Open would have seemed like the biggest thing in the world.

Now, more than ever, the local circuit needs them to play, and to play every year. All of them. No excuses.

VIVA MEXICO

A World Golf Championship event was played for the first time in Mexico in 2017, a bold step for golf into alien territory. In spite of some misgivings, the tournament proved a wild success and, as **Charles Happell** argues, it should embolden the game's decision-makers to take elite tournaments to other 'non-core' countries.

The highlight of 2017's World Golf Championship debut in Mexico was not the quality of the golf – which featured eagles, aces and 50 or more hole-outs from off the green – but the simple fact that one of the sport's elite tournaments was being staged outside the United States at a new destination, one not normally associated with the game.

The decision to hold the event in Mexico City, at the Club de Golf Chapultepec, was a bold one, but golf's chiefs only needed to look at the size and enthusiasm of the crowds, and the number of children milling behind the gallery ropes, to realise they had been vindicated in making it.

The layout was perhaps not the greatest championship venue on the roster but other benefits that flowed from the week, and the fact a whole new audience was exposed to the game, more than made up for that minor drawback.

For too long, professional golf has been the province of the US – and the sport as a global proposition has been the poorer for it. For the past 80 years, three of the four majors have been played in the US; and since 1999, three of the four individual WGC events have (usually) been scheduled on the same continent. Homogeneity rules; predictability has been the order of the day. Meanwhile, golf outside the US has often struggled for traction.

That's part of the reason Peter Thomson 50 years ago, and Greg Norman 30 years later, became such strong advocates of a world tour. Both had extensive careers in Europe and while Thomson remained largely a 'world player', Norman settled in the US and played the PGA Tour. Both, however, remained high-profile supporters of their home circuit in Australia.

They basically felt for all its strengths the US PGA Tour was hogging the whole show, including the best players, and the rest of the world was being short-changed. So when the World Golf Championship concept was first mooted in 1999, Thomson, Norman and many others were delighted: at last, the International Federation of PGA Tours (of which the US PGA Tour was clearly the dominant member) had listened to the global golf community, and world-class tournaments were going to be played in the provinces and distant outposts. But their joy was short-lived: two of the three inaugural WGC tournaments that year ended up being staged in the US; the third at Valderrama in Spain. That event, the WGC-American Express Championship, as it was known, soon ended up back in the US – at that well-used, well-trodden venue at Doral in Florida.

Talk about same old, same old. How utterly tedious.

The PGA Tour's major sponsor and television broadcast revenue comes in a steady stream from US companies, and they want exposure at home, not abroad, so it's entirely reasonable that much of the tournament schedule remains within the borders of the US. But there seemed to be no appetite for adventure and to test the waters elsewhere – be they in emerging markets such as Mexico or South America (though, to be fair, the HSBC Champions event has been staged in China for more than a decade), or established golf nations such as Australia and South Africa.

When, in 2001, the WGC Match Play event came down to Melbourne, at Metropolitan GC, the tournament was scheduled (for reasons never properly explained) in the first week of January. As a result, only a handful of the world's top 20 players turned up – the rest were spending New Year's at home with their families. Steve Stricker ended up defeating Pierre Fulke in an underwhelming final – for which tickets had to be given away – and the tournament was widely regarded as a fizzer, and an opportunity wasted. Spooked by the experience, which was entirely the fault of the poor scheduling, the International Federation scampered back the next season to familiar territory, in this case, Carlsbad, California – where the host venue was markedly inferior to the one they left behind in Melbourne.

PGA Tour players themselves must get a little tired of turning up to the same old courses week in, week out, where the fairways are usually lush, greens receptive and wind (outside Hawaii and Texas, anyway) rarely much stronger than a zephyr. And where a certain country-club monoculture rules.

England's Paul Casey, a PGA Tour regular for several years, was one player who revelled in the move south of the border and wondered why tournament scheduling wasn't always this creative and adventurous. 'It's important to the brand of the PGA Tour,' he said. 'There are so many fantastic events in the US, but it's almost to the point of saturation. PGA Tour members get a bad rap that they don't like to travel but plenty of us do. It'd be a shame to miss out on a week like this. Mexico City is damn cool and so is this event. It has a different flavour, just a nice feel to it. And it's still in its infancy. It's going to be fun watching this tournament grow up.'

Of course, for every Casey there are less intrepid types like Billy Horschel, a Florida resident as it happens, who wanted the WGC event to remain at Doral. 'I just wasn't sure if I wanted to go to Mexico City,' Horschel said. 'I just didn't want to go. A lot of guys don't want to go to China; I didn't want to go to Mexico.'

Horschel, who did not end up qualifying for the event, cited security concerns as the basis for his reluctance to travel to Mexico City: 'It's the first year of the event, and I just want to see how it went. I want to see how everything was run, I want to see the feedback from the players, and then I'd go from there.'

One wonders how players such as Jack Nicklaus, Gary Player and the late Arnold Palmer – three of golf's great adventurers and pioneers in the 1960s and 1970s, when long-distance air travel truly was an ordeal – would react when hearing a comment like that. A trip to Mexico would have been a doddle compared to some of the journeys they set out on. Palmer won the Panama and Colombia opens in 1956, for example, while Player took out the Egyptian Match Play in 1955 and, later, the Brazil and Chile opens – while based in South Africa.

Professional tennis is – in this writer's opinion, anyway – a significantly less appealing proposition to watch than tournament golf. Yet the ATP and WTA tours display their sport to the world in a way that golf can only dream of. The tennis circus comes to Australia every year in early January, packs up its big top then proceeds to travel around the world for the next 12 months – from Montpellier to Memphis, and Munich to Marrakech. It hardly needs to be mentioned that tennis's four grand slams are played in four countries – Australia, England, France and the US – on four different surfaces.

It's time golf's grandees got with the program, and understood that for the game to prosper outside the US's established, well-manicured boundaries, more tournaments like the WGC-Mexico event need to be showcased to the world. Otherwise, in an increasingly globalised planet, it risks becoming a staid and conservative curio.

PART 3
COURSES

Some years ago, a representative of the man who would become the president of the United States approached a golf-course architect to build a course. The architect listened to the spiel, politely thanked the man for his time and, to the astonishment of the pitcher, declined the offer. He couldn't comprehend any architect passing on the work.

'Let me put it this way,' said the architect. 'Mr Trump would hate what we like to build and we would hate building what he wants, so it's not going to work for either of us.'

– Mike Clayton

AUGUSTA: TOO MUCH PERFECTION

Augusta National is the most gleaming, pristine championship course in golf, showcased each year at the Masters. **Mike Clayton** argues, however, that its perfection creates unrealistic expectations among club members everywhere. But they shouldn't worry, he says. 'Scruffy is okay.'

I have an old friend who is perhaps the greatest authority on public parks in America, who is frequently expressing his preference for grass that is green. The best golfing grasses vary in colour. They may be red, brown, blue, dark green, light green, yellow, and at times even white and gray. A golf course that is consisted entirely of one shade of green would be merely ugly. There is great charm and beauty in the varying shades of colour on a golf course.

– Alister MacKenzie, 1931

Augusta National is perhaps the most famous course in the world and it's certainly the one best known by people who have never been there. The Masters is the biggest television show in golf, the tournament most want to attend, and Augusta itself is a hugely influential place. But among both architectural purists and superintendents the world over – the latter who are expected to produce Augusta-like perfection but without an Augusta-like budget – praise for it is often tinged with negativism.

Fairways uniformly green and without blemish, and bunkers uniformly consistent, are most golfers' idea of perfection. Augusta provides that, and they are seemingly impeccable to hit from – even though players are heard to complain (but not so loudly as to upset their hosts) about 'mud balls', the annoying phenomenon where a glob of mud attaches itself to the ball, making the flight of an iron at best guesswork and at worst uncontrollable.

Critics of trees imposing themselves on the stage – as opposed to simply being a part of the scenery, as legendary designer Harry Colt preferred – lament the intrusion of additional trees onto the original golfing lines to the right of the 11th and 17th holes and the left of the 15th. It would be hardly unreasonable to suggest that if Alister MacKenzie had wanted trees there when he designed the course, he'd have planted them. And it was Bobby Jones – Augusta's founder and the Masters' co-founder – who once said to his friend British journalist Alistair Cooke, as they looked down Augusta's sweeping downhill 10th, 'I myself don't see any need for a tree on a golf course.'

Architectural purists lament the loss of the character of the original MacKenzie bunkers. Their original irregular and imperfect edges have been rounded off so perfectly they look like someone has taken to them with a Gillette. The sand itself is so improbably white Dulux could call the whitest of their white paints 'Augusta White'.

The greens, too, are famed for their extreme speeds in the second week of April. And with the television commentators seemingly unable to express any opinion other than obsequious praise, there is only fawning about the slickness of the surfaces: fast is good, faster is better.

Of course Augusta can do whatever it wants with its golf course and its tournament. It's theirs, and no-one does championship golf better. The problem comes when committees and golfers all over the world think Augusta is the ideal and the aim. It's a problem because none of them have an unlimited budget. Nor is there anything wrong with 'scruffy'. If you ask Bill Coore, the game's premier course architect, what he appreciates most about Melbourne's sandbelt he might just say, 'I like the scruffiness of it all.' Augusta is anything but scruffy and 'perfection' doesn't always mean perfect for golf.

Despite Augusta's fame and exposure, it has very little influence over the way the average American golf course is set up. How often on the PGA Tour do you see greens surrounded by short grass? Or wide fairways, as opposed to narrow ones lined with the infernal concept of 'graduated rough' – a modern theory attempting to make a game with an inherent element of unfairness attached to it as fair and sanitised as possible? It's amazing more courses haven't adopted the principles of the perfect mowing lines of Augusta, where there is no long grass close to greens and all the bunkers are surrounded by short grass. It's a uniquely American trait to build fairway bunkers in the rough, and many times they simply become refuges from even worse lies in the long grass.

At the 2002 US Open at Bethpage Black, Scottish journalist John Huggan asked Rees Jones, the architect hired to restore AW Tillinghast's wonderful and brutally difficult course, why all the bunkers were in the rough. He didn't really have an answer. Not a good one anyway.

The best courses in Australia are cut almost exactly as at Augusta and even though most Australian courses look quite different, the golf, especially on Melbourne's sandbelt and in Adelaide, is closely related to the game MacKenzie and Jones were trying to encourage at Augusta. Unquestionably it's the most interesting form of golf away from the British and Irish links.

Perhaps there is a place in championship golf for the typical US Open–type set-up, where narrow fairways are bordered by high grass demanding Trevino-like straight driving – but surely the great lesson of Augusta is the original principles championed by MacKenzie and Jones make for a more interesting game.

COURSE WITHIN A COURSE, OF COURSE

The noted American golf-course architect George Thomas devised a concept of a 'course within a course' where some holes would be played from different tees, with different lengths, and even have different pars. **Mike Clayton** thinks it is a great idea – and decries the handicap system that hampers its implementation.

I don't really understand the 'new' handicap system but one of its early proponents told me I would need to, because it was 'going to change the way you design golf courses'. That alone was enough to dissuade me from thinking it was an all-out good idea. Donald Ross seemed to be perfectly capable of designing great courses without understanding the handicap system.

The system, not so new anymore, grades courses by a mathematical formula, taking into account the length of the course, the width of the fairways, the depths of the rough, the contours of the greens and the placement of the hazards. It attempts to standardise handicaps, to make them portable and to give everyone a decent chance of winning the club competition of the day. No harm in that, but sometimes it's worth playing for fun without worrying about what you might score or what a good, or a bad, round might do to your handicap. (No country is as obsessed with competition golf and the notion of 'putting a card in' as Australia.)

What the system also seems to have done is eliminate any real creativity of course set-up, because superintendents stick pretty rigidly to a formula – one element of which is the length of the course doesn't vary more than 90 yards over the 18 holes. Maybe that isn't exactly the theory, but from my experience, that is exactly what happens in practice. Superintendents play it safe with the set-up, which means there will be no criticism from the vast majority of members. Only the most sporting of players will understand how opportunities are being missed.

George Thomas grew up in Philadelphia, privileged and wealthy, and became one of the US's great golf-course architects. He wrote one of the early and finest books on the subject, *Golf Architecture in America*, and he designed two of California's best courses, Riviera Country Club and Los Angeles Country Club.

At Los Angeles, Thomas devised and implemented the concept of a 'course within a course', where holes could be played from varied tees and with different pars. It is a mystery as to why this did not become standard practice among architects everywhere, because it certainly makes for variety and interest without any significant extra cost. Thomas was simply showing how adaptable the game could be.

The Depression and World War II intervened, stopping all of the great architects in their tracks. Few survived much beyond the war and with them died both their ideas and their uncommon skills. MacKenzie himself died earlier, in 1932, bankrupt and pleading with the people at Augusta to pay him money owing. He also agreed with Thomas's concept, arguing in *The Spirit of St. Andrews*: 'The charm of golf is the variety and there is no doubt that greater variety can be attained by changing the holes and tees from day to day. It has been repeated ad nauseam in this book that golf is a game and not a mathematical business, and that it is of vital importance to avoid anything that tends to make the game simple and stereotyped.'

In 2009 and 2010, Gil Hanse and Geoff Shackelford expertly restored Los Angeles after years of tinkering had seen it lose much of the original Thomas character. They regained the original look of Thomas's bunkers and the barrancas (best described as a cross between a bunker, a sandy waste and a drainage swale) as well as restoring the original tees – so important to the concept of a course within a course.

Thomas had made alternate tees at the second hole, a long two-shotter fronted by a barranca. Played off the front tee it was a long two-shot par four, and off the back, a par five where you had the option of attempting the long carry (think 15 at Augusta but with a sandy hazard, not water, at the front) with the long second, or playing safely short and pitching across the hazard.

At the fifth hole, a brutal, long, uphill, 485-yard par four, Thomas added a tiny front-right wing to the green stoutly defended by the bunker and created a pin position seemingly all but inaccessible from far back on the fairway with a wood or a long iron. Both Shackelford and Hanse long pondered why Thomas would have made an almost nonsensical section of green until they found an old plan showing another tee far up in the woods on the right. 'It all made perfect sense then. When they cut the pin in the corner they moved the tee up and it played around 350 yards – the perfect length hole for Thomas's one diabolical pin position,' said Shackelford. In just that one hole you lose all of those precious 80 yards so important to a rigid interpretation of the handicap system.

Then, at two of the long par threes, the seventh and the 11th, Thomas made tees set far enough behind the regular ones to have both holes play as short par fours. Not all par-three greens or holes would work so well, but the two he made were on ground perfectly suited to the concept. Not only are they two of the best long par threes in the US, they are also two of the most interesting short par fours.

Thomas then finished off his 'course within a course' at the par-three 15th. Originally his idea was to do what he so brilliantly did at Riviera's sixth hole: build a bunker in the middle of the green. In the end he didn't, instead shaping a green-dividing knob, which separates the narrow front third of the green from the back.

At the 2016 Walker Cup, the pin was cut in the front corner, the tees moved forward far enough up to shame the players into going for the flag, as opposed to playing safely away. The hole was only 78 yards and it made for fascinating viewing because the landing area was so small.

At the Masters, the 16th hole on the second day often plays with the tee far forward to a pin cut in the front right corner of the green. Like Thomas's fifth at LACC, the landing area is tiny, but no-one is suggesting that if someone shot a 62 on the Friday it wouldn't be a course record because the course 'wasn't playing its full length'.

For many years – certainly in all the Australian Opens I played from the late 1970s to the late 1990s – there was never a tee set more than a pace or two from the back markers. It was boringly predictable, and it missed so many opportunities to vary holes and the questions they were asking.

When the Open went to Royal Melbourne (and for every other tournament we played there), on the final day the pin was always in the far back left corner of the uphill par-three 16th on the Composite Course (4 East). The tees were always left back at 190 yards, and so everyone played 40 feet right and putted across the green because no-one – not even Greg Norman at his flying best – could stop a long iron anywhere near the hole. If the tee had been moved up 40 yards and players got to use a six or seven iron, rather than a four iron, then perhaps they would have been tempted, or shamed, into an unwise gamble. Or a great shot would have given them a chance at a birdie.

The problem with the handicap system is each of Thomas's options of length and par at Los Angeles needs a different course rating. What is the daily rating if the second hole is a par four, the fifth is playing to the front pin and 100 yards shorter than it does from the back, the seventh is a par four but 11 is a par three and the 15th is playing at 80 yards as opposed to 150? What is then needed is an understanding superintendent who isn't just setting up the course one hole at a time but rather as an 18-piece jigsaw where each part is related.

It all gets awfully confusing when it's really a simple concept and a simple game. Finally, it needs a committee and a membership embracing the concept and committing to it. Then the dog (golf) would be wagging the tail (handicap) and not the other way around.

SAWGRASS 17TH: GOLF'S TREASURE ISLAND

The island-green 17th at TPC Sawgrass and stadium-hole 16th at the Phoenix Open have proven hugely popular with fans, who flock there each year in droves. The holes might be gimmicky, but **Charles Happell** argues that tournament promoters elsewhere should sit up and take notice: this unconventional approach could help attract a whole new audience to the game.

It's become the most talked-about hole in golf, more so perhaps than the 12th at Augusta, the 16th at Cypress Point, the Road Hole at St Andrews, the long 18th at Carnoustie or the Postage Stamp at Royal Troon. From the time it was designed in the late 1970s by Pete Dye, the island-green, par-three 17th hole at the Sawgrass stadium course in Florida has attracted controversy.

Not because it's a unique design – island greens have been around a while – but because the punishment for a slightly mishit or misjudged shot is totally out of whack with the 'crime'. Hit a wonky shot at virtually any other par-three on the planet and you might end up on the apron, or in rough, or sand, or heather, or ti-tree. At Sawgrass's shortest hole, there's no doubt about where you'll end up – in water, meaning you'll have to re-load and take a penalty shot.

As Phil Mickelson said of the island green in 2007: 'Most holes, almost every golf hole in all of golf, has one side that's a severe penalty and the other side that's open, that's playable. And this is one of the few holes I can think of that has no bail-out, no margin of error, no area for recovery. It's an all-or-nothing shot.'

That's why the debate rages: should such a boom-or-bust hole feature so late in a round at a tournament as prestigious as the Players Championship?

In one sense, it's a straight-away par three of 137 yards – a sand wedge or wedge for most players – to a generously proportioned green. In another sense, it's a gimmick, a tricked-up made-for-television contrivance that is played in front of an amphitheatre of masochists.

Since its unveiling in 1980, the 17th has had a long and colourful history: some players love it, others would love to see the bulldozers move in and get rid of the damn thing. Bob Tway would be firmly in the latter category: four shots into the water were followed by a three-putt for a total of 12 in 2005's TPC third round.

After early complaints from some of the leading tour pros, Dye redesigned the green. But that didn't help much in 1984 when winds blew up to 65 kilometres an hour during the first round, causing chaos. The stroke average on number 17 that day was 3.853, and 64 balls were hit into the water, a record that still stands.

American Tom Lehman has played the hole just about as well as anyone since Dye first inflicted it on the world. The 1996 British Open champion has managed to avoid the water in 61 of his 62 attempts at number 17, while going 11 under par. His fellow American Jim Colbert, who competed in six Players at Sawgrass, used to try to appease the golf gods by tossing four balls in the lake before the tournament began.

Mark Calcavecchia said the prospect of having to negotiate the island green hung over him like a dark cloud all TPC week: 'It is like having a three o'clock appointment for a root canal. You're thinking about it all morning and you feel bad all day. You kind of know sooner or later you've got to get to it.'

The two greatest players of all time, Jack Nicklaus and Tiger Woods, aren't fans; they think the 17th is too severe to be the penultimate hole on a tournament layout. 'I know it's exciting and adds a lot to the tournament,' Nicklaus has said, 'but maybe almost a little bit too much at times, because it really becomes such a big factor in the golf tournament, where a guy has played great all week and he can make a six or seven pretty quickly there, and all of a sudden he's gone from first place back to about tenth.'

Woods agrees: 'I've always thought that hole is too gimmicky for the seventeenth hole of a championship. I think that would be a fantastic eighth hole, but not as the seventy-first hole of a tournament, or seventeenth hole of your round.'

Despite having among the poorer cumulative records at number 17, Woods played one of the great shots at the hole in the 2001 Players Championship, holing a long, curling 'impossible' putt from the back of the green that clattered into the hole and caused pandemonium among the crowd.

Tiger's long-time caddie, Steve Williams, wrote in his autobiography *Out of the Rough*: 'The island green is like a Roman coliseum. The players live and die by whether they can hit that green. You're happy to be anywhere on there so the crowd doesn't hand you your ego on a plate. If you miss, the ball is in the water and you have to suffer the ignominy of hitting from the drop zone in front of a bellowing crowd.'

As for Australians, for a long time, Robert Allenby held the record for the number of consecutive rounds (36) in which he avoided the water at number 17. And Marc Leishman has hit the green 26 times successively since his first Players' start in 2010. On the other hand, Aaron Baddeley has found the water more than just about any other player. He's played the hole 40 times and splashed down with 13 of those shots – a waterball strike rate of one in three. Ever the contrarian, Greg Norman won't hear about the hole being too hard for the players – he has said he'd like to see it lengthened slightly due to modern equipment.

In response to the criticism, Pete Dye himself has a simple response: 'Golf is not a fair game, so why build a course fair?'

Wherever you sit on this debate, and there are passionate arguments on both sides, one thing is clear: the hole is massively popular with the fans and television execs. It's like the par-three 16th at the Phoenix Open in Arizona, where tournament organisers in 2018 built a three-tier grandstand around the hole to cater for the growing number of fans who wanted to see the action. Music is played by a DJ, alcohol is served, noise is made, a party is enjoyed and the players have nowhere to hide: they are completely surrounded by this wall of sound and spectators.

Yes, both holes are gimmicks and naked attempts at drawing people through the turnstiles – and they would never be allowed at the British Open – but they work. Crowds queue up at the gates before opening time then sprint to find one of the best available spots around the greens at Sawgrass and TPC Scottsdale. At the 2018 Phoenix, 215,000 people attended on Saturday, and a record total of 720,000 rolled up during the week, making it the most popular tournament in golf. How can you argue with numbers like that?

And for that reason alone, perhaps other golf tours around the world could take a leaf out of the Sawgrass and Phoenix books and organise a similarly tantalising, if ghoulish, hole to feature at some of their regular events.

Where would the harm be in golf trying to change its image just a bit: from dowdy to downright fun? Not go the full Happy Gilmore, just make an attempt to enliven proceedings a smidgin.

It's not a popular view, I know, among the purists – which include the co-author of this book. Noted American designer Tom Doak, for example, has called the 17th at Sawgrass 'the germ that started the plague'.

But at a time when the business of marketing and promoting golf has never been more critical, and a new audience is desperately being sought, tour officials can't afford to be squeamish. Radical holes clearly capture the public imagination and get people talking – and attending. As a sometime-fan, would you rather watch Kevin Na or JB Holmes or Jason Day take two minutes to select a club, or line up a putt, or see the same pros squirm under the spotlight, where you are close to the action and can feel the tension – perhaps with a beer in hand?

Young Spaniard Jon Rahm certainly seems to be on board. After the Phoenix tournament in 2018, he predicted a day when all this fun might spread to every event. 'I really feel like every course could have something similar to this, to have an atmosphere like this. It makes it a lot more fun.'

COURSE RANKINGS? OKEY-DOAK

Ranking golf courses, as magazines are wont to do each year, is a fraught business. There is the architecture to take into account, then the aesthetics, ambience, accessibility and affordability, too. **Mike Clayton** tries to bring some order to this inexact science.

The most reliable ranking of golf courses is Tom Doak's book, *The Confidential Guide to Golf Courses*. It started off as a series of humorous, informative and occasionally caustic notes written for friends who travelled widely across both the United States and the rest of the world, who were tired of reading about a flash new course, spending the time and effort to see it – only to come away disappointed, often considerably out of pocket. Or they would travel somewhere and miss the hidden gem because no-one spoke about it, the club was happy to stay out of sight and it didn't appear in any magazine ranking of the 50 or 100 best courses.

Doak originally ranked well over 800 courses from all over the world, marking them on a scale from zero to 10. MacKenzie's masterpiece, Crystal Downs (a 10 on Doak's scale) in northern Michigan, was one example of a hidden star, as was Brora (seven), a James Braid links in Scotland even further north than Dornoch, which few had heard of until Peter Thomson started talking about it. More recently, people are starting to discover Arrowtown in New Zealand, a course sure to become a cult classic among Americans, Britons and Australians.

You can play Mr Trump's courses at Turnberry (eight) or Aberdeen (seven) for about 350 quid a round – or for the same price you can play nine rounds at Brora; you might even be able to join for a whole year for not much more. Maybe those courses are better than Brora, but they are nowhere near nine times better, plus the people in Brora will likely appreciate your custom a little more, and the hotels are sure to be cheaper as well.

The Confidential Guide morphed into a book of 1000 copies, then later came a commercial run of 10,000 with shiny paper and photos. Currently Doak and three co-authors are in the midst of a five-volume upgrade covering Britain, winter and summer American destinations, Continental Europe and, finally, Asia, Australia and New Zealand.

Doak devised his zero–10 scale to measure the worth of travelling to see any particular course. A zero denotes 'A course so contrived and unnatural that it may poison your mind, which I cannot recommend under any circumstances. Reserved for courses which wasted ridiculous sums of money in their construction and probably shouldn't have been built in the first place.' A 10 is 'Nearly perfect; if you skipped even one hole, you would miss something worth seeing. If you haven't seen all the courses in this category, you don't know how good golf architecture can get. Drop this book and call your travel agent immediately.'

Doak's methodology works better than a simple one–100 list because it categorises courses into groups without having to suggest Metropolitan (six) in Melbourne as a better or a lesser course than Adelaide's Kooyonga, Virginia Water's Wentworth or Washington's Congressional, all of which are also sixes ('A very good course, definitely worth a game if you're in town, but not necessarily worth a special trip to see. It shouldn't disappoint you.').

Magazine rankings of 100 courses assume Barnbougle Dunes at, say, number two in Australia, is a better course than Kingston

Heath (let's say number three), when at that level the judgement is purely subjective and both will most likely be nines in the new Doak edition. ('An outstanding course, certainly one of the best in the world, with no weaknesses in regard to condition, length or poor holes.')

One of the inherent problems with the magazine rankings is they try to define what makes a course special by using criteria – memorability, condition, 'resistance to scoring' and 'shot values' (whatever they mean), design variety and ambience – which can only ever be subjective. The ambience, the mood, the character on the dunes of Anderson Bay on Tasmania's north coast at Barnbougle Dunes, for example, is entirely different late in the evening when the sun is going down than it is in the middle of the day. Does that mean it's a better course at eight o'clock on a perfect summer's evening than it is at midday in the middle of winter? Of course not, but it's a better experience late, which is why I always tell players to tee off four hours (three if you play quickly) before the sun goes down. Rankings must be clear on exactly what it is they are ranking.

Trying to come up with a formula to measure worth and position is fraught, because people look at different things and measure the worth of courses so differently. Some put great store in condition. For others it's the views, which no doubt are a huge part of the ambience. Would California's Pebble Beach (nine) and New South Wales (seven) be ranked so highly if not for the stunning ocean views? Some rate NSW a better course than Royal Melbourne, but I think they are rating the quality of the experience. The experience is one thing, but it should be an entirely different ranking from one measuring the quality of the architecture.

Others think difficulty is a primary and worthwhile measure of a course, which is fine, but it would mark down Swinley Forest (eight), Woking (seven), Sunningdale (eight), Cypress Point (10) and Royal Melbourne West (10), none of which are particularly difficult courses if resistance to scoring is the measure. Is Royal

Melbourne a lesser course for Ernie Els' 60, or Sunningdale for Bobby Jones' 66 in 1926, or Cypress Point for Harvie Ward, Ken Venturi, Ben Hogan and Byron Nelson all shooting in the low to mid 60s in 1956? Of course not, because the only ranking criteria should be the architecture – and the architecture is primarily the focus of Doak's scale. How good are the holes? How well does the routing use the land and how easy does it make the course to walk? Does the course 'sing', as famed American developer Mike Keiser is fond of saying?

How interesting are the questions it asks of the golfer? How interesting are the questions it asks relative to The Old Course (10) – because The Old Course asks the most interesting, the most confusing and the most varied questions? Does the condition let you play the course the way it was intended? If the greens are mush and the fairways soft, then the answer is normally pretty clear.

The memberships who best understand the strengths and weaknesses of their courses have tended to do well in the more recent rankings because they have understood what to change and, just as important, what to leave alone.

Kingston Heath was always good, but no-one in the late 1970s thought it one of the best 20 courses in the world. But since then, it changed its fairway grass to couch all year round; the greens were all rebuilt and three of them (6, 13, 18) changed significantly; bunkers were restored and tee carries re-vegetated; and trees were rationalised with many of the imported ones removed, opening up views across the course and lowering the profile. Many lamented the loss of the trees but over time their arguments lost all merit as the course garnered universal praise from all who visited, not just from the golf pros who played the many tournaments over the years.

Tournaments don't hurt rankings either and now there are so few in Australia they are keenly lobbied for by the best clubs. But using fewer golf pros to rank courses seems to have helped the listings. For a long time the assumption was that good players made good judges of a golf course, when often that is not the case.

So focused are they on conditions and fairness that they tend to judge a course on those two criteria, which have very little to do with the merits of the architecture.

The early ranking lists were so poor that magazines were forced to find judges who saw more courses more regularly and had the knowledge to get them in a roughly sensible order. The two Australian magazines in the ranking business, *Golf Australia* (for whom I have written a monthly column since 1992) and *Golf Digest*, have improved in recent years. Perhaps it's just the fashion of the time but, in 1989, *Golf Digest* had The Australian (six on the Doak scale) ranked above Kingston Heath (nine), and Royal Canberra (not seen by Doak) as the fifth best course in the country – yet by 2012, the same course had fallen all the way down to the mid 70s.

Would the game be better off without rankings? Certainly it would be better off without one of the awful world top 100 lists where courses in effect buy their credibility by inviting swathes of rankers and plying them with the best 24-hour experience they can offer. But in Australia, they serve to show how far golf architecture – and the appreciation of it – has come in the past three decades.

In *Golf Australia*'s 2018 ranking, four of the top eight courses in the country are Tasmanian public courses. Given the state barely had a course in the top 70 two decades ago, it's an impressive accomplishment. And rankings have spurred clubs to lift their game. The committee at Bonnie Doon got serious about fixing their course – which sits on a good piece of Sydney's sandy dunes – when it didn't make the top 100 a few years ago. That commitment to get the design company I'm with to rebuild the course has been reflected in its improved 2018 ranking, placing 34th in the list by *Golf Australia*.

The lists are going to be around as long as there are golf magazines, but if they ever do go away there are always Doak's books. They are more accurate and you will learn more from them than skimming down a list of 100 courses just to find your own.

QUESTIONS ONLY SEVE COULD ANSWER

The golf demanded by St Andrews and Alister MacKenzie's Royal Melbourne and Augusta is different from all others – and only one man has won at all three courses. **Mike Clayton** explains.

St Andrews, Augusta and Royal Melbourne are my three favourite courses in the world. Like St Andrews and Augusta you can almost slam it anywhere off the tee at Royal Melbourne and you can still get to the greens but the putting is going to be crazy if you play it that way. It is really so dangerous around the greens and you can make a bogey from anywhere. And when the wind blows it's, Oh my God, how do I manage this course?

– Fred Couples, 2012

The Scottish golf course architect Alister MacKenzie was a fan of the American Walter Hagen, a man of equal significance to the development and popularisation of the game. Hagen opened the doors of clubhouses all over the world to golf pros and put on one of the great shows in golf, a show he took all over the world in a time when the biggest draw in the game didn't pocket the equivalent of a million dollars for showing up.

'Did I make it look hard enough?' he once asked a young caddie just after pulling off what looked like, but wasn't, a difficult shot from the trees.

Hagen understood one sure way to thrill an audience was to make easy shots look difficult and difficult shots look easy. MacKenzie understood that the same principle applied to what he was trying to do with golf courses. 'It is an important thing in golf to make holes look much more difficult than they really are,' he wrote. 'People get more pleasure in doing a hole which looks almost impossible and yet is not so difficult as it appears.'

In *The Spirit of St. Andrews*, his must-read 1932 book on golf course architecture, MacKenzie wrote of his initial encounter with Hagen and his rare talents. Hagen was playing the Road Hole in the 1921 Open at St Andrews, but all MacKenzie knew was the player who had pulled his long second into the famed 17th green was an American.

'I said to the friend who was with me, "Here comes an American. Watch him pitch over the Road bunker and land in the road beyond." Instead of doing so, he played at a little hillock, only three feet across, to the right of the Road bunker, and his ball curved in a complete semicircle and lay dead to the pin. I said to my friend, "That is the best player I have ever seen. Let's follow him to the clubhouse and find out what his name is." We did follow him and we found his name was Walter Hagen.'

Years later at Royal Birkdale, after pulling a long second shot into the final green of the 1976 Open Championship, a teenager stunned a world-wide television audience by playing a similarly breathtaking chip through a gap 3 feet across between two bunkers. The ball trickled down by the hole and the birdie earned Severiano Ballesteros a second-place tie with Jack Nicklaus behind Johnny Miller. Just as MacKenzie had became a Hagen fan after witnessing a single, magical stroke, so the world fell in love with the Spaniard and his astonishing chip.

* * *

MacKenzie had written *Golf Architecture* in 1920 and had already formed his views of how the game is best played. In the tiny book he laid out thirteen principles, the tenth of which was, 'There should be a complete absence of the annoyance and irritation caused by the necessity of looking for lost balls.'

He expanded on that thought in *The Spirit of St. Andrews*, arguing, 'Narrow fairways bordered by long grass make bad golfers. They do so by destroying the harmony and continuity of the game and in causing a stilted and cramped style, destroying all freedom of play.'

This principle is exactly what opponents of regulating the modern golf ball fail to understand when they suggest the answer is instead to narrow the fairway and grow more rough.

No doubt with visions and memories of Hagen's golf in mind, and keen to put his principles into play on the other side of the world, MacKenzie sailed for Australia and his commission to redesign the relatively new golf course that the Royal Melbourne members were playing in Sandringham.

To dictate the strategies at his new holes at Royal Melbourne, he made wide fairways allied with one of the great sets of green complexes in golf. The middle of the fairway was only rarely the ideal place from which to attack the flag; rather the perfect lines were along the edges of the fairways and along those edges he cut the hazards. It's a simple philosophy, one not simply demanding straight hitting but instead asking for thought as to where best to drive and then accurate hitting to the chosen spot.

There is a subtle but significant difference between straight hitting and accurate hitting, and every course MacKenzie made championed the principle of accurate driving over simple straight hitting to narrow slivers of fairway bordered by long grass. It's what distinguishes The Masters from the US Open.

Golf pros want equity of punishment, consistency of condition, fairness and predictability. They want good shots rewarded and poor shots punished. It sounds perfectly logical but MacKenzie argued otherwise. 'Many poor golf courses are made in an endeavour to eliminate the element of luck. You can no more eliminate luck in golf that you can in cricket, and in neither case is it possible to punish every bad shot. If you succeed in doing so you would only make both games uninteresting and no one would want to play them.'

The demand for accurate hitting is the basis of the golf at The Old Course, Royal Melbourne and Augusta. The former was MacKenzie's favourite course and the latter two, along with Cypress Point, his best courses.

MacKenzie himself thought St Andrews a clear level above. 'St Andrews cannot be compared with Cypress Point. St Andrews is first class, there is no second, and Cypress Point comes in a very bad third.' He went on. 'The old stalwarts of St Andrews were perfectly indifferent to these criticisms. They knew that most of the critics had never seen or played a real golf course before so they could not be expected to appreciate its virtues.'

While The Old Course, Royal Melbourne and Augusta look quite different, the golf that they demand, in both its physical and mental aspects, are recognisably related, clearly born of the belief the game is not simply about the execution of good shots.

So here we have the three great characters, Hagen, Ballesteros and MacKenzie – two of the game's greatest-ever players and arguably its greatest-ever architect – connecting through an understanding of what makes the game thrilling to watch and thrilling to play.

* * *

It is no coincidence only one man has won championships at Augusta, St Andrews and Royal Melbourne.

Tom Watson has won at Royal Melbourne and Augusta, but not St Andrews.

Hagen never got to play Royal Melbourne and competed at Augusta only when he was long past his best.

Nick Faldo, Jack Nicklaus and Tiger Woods have won at Augusta and St Andrews – but not Royal Melbourne. Faldo tried a few times, Nicklaus just the once as a 48-year-old. Tiger has played the course in a couple of Presidents Cups, calling it 'the best second-shot golf course I've ever played'. Nicklaus on the other hand called it a 'good member's course', although he later clarified his thoughts in a letter to the club committee, in which he was in accord with Woods' comment about testing second shots.

The only man to win at all three is Severiano Ballesteros.

Ballesteros first played Royal Melbourne in the 1978 Australian PGA and came back until he eventually and inevitably won in 1981. No hole better exemplified his approach to the game than the short par-four 10th hole on the West Course in 1978. It's the eighth on the Composite Course and arguably MacKenzie's greatest short par four. (If it's not, it's in the final with the ninth at Cypress Point.)

The hole doglegs around a massive pit bunker embedded into the hill, and from there five is much more likely than four even though it's only 20 metres short of the green. Over the green is dead and everyone back then, Greg Norman included, was hitting long irons or three woods out to the right and pitching from there.

People thought Seve was a bad driver, and sure, he could hit some crooked drives, but that was how he played. If the 14-year-old Seve had decided to be a straight 260-yard driver, does anyone think he couldn't have managed it? He was a great driver if the standard was the variety of shapes and shots he could hit and how he took advantage of his great power without it costing him too much.

He came to the hole early on the first morning and pondered his choices, running his hand over the two iron and the driver. What to do? Here was MacKenzie tempting with the promise of great reward for the bold drive but offering a simple way around for those happy to play sensibly.

The green was just out of reach but there is a small patch of scrubby heath and sand just to the left of the bunker and short of the green – probably about half the size of a normal green. Off came the headcover, and Ballesteros ripped a perfect drive, high and hard, at the green. His ball finished up in the sandy heath but from there it was none too difficult for a man of his talents to blast a sand wedge out to a few feet and make an easy birdie. He repeated the show every day, making three birdies and a par – only a great driver could have done what he did.

MacKenzie obviously didn't know it, but when he designed Royal Melbourne, he was designing a course for Ballesteros: this was the type of player he wanted to encourage and the type of golf he thought was the most interesting to both play and watch. You had to size up a hole, determine the question it was asking that particular day, and play accordingly. There was always an easy way around the question, but would those who took the easy way around have a chance to win by the end of the week? Perhaps if they did the other things well, but more likely those who won on Royal Melbourne – and Augusta and St Andrews – were able to because they were prepared to lose. Seve could easily have hooked it just left of the patch of heath into the cypress trees, or he could have necked it a bit into the pit bunker, but no, he buttoned four drives, showing off not only a willingness to take the line no-one else thought of but also an uncommon level of skill.

To win on two of the best courses MacKenzie designed and at MacKenzie's favourite course, his model, took the most special of talents. The fact that only the incomparable Ballesteros has done it – and the golf he and Hagen played – is the best proof possible that the golf MacKenzie designed is the best form of the game. It's the most interesting to watch and the most interesting to play. Those charged with arranging the game would do well to understand it. It's all there in his book, *The Spirit of St. Andrews*.

CONQUERING FEAR: PINE VALLEY

Pine Valley, on the outskirts of Philadelphia, is regularly ranked the number one course in the world. Yet few people have seen it, and even fewer have played it. **Richard Allen**, a member, gives some insights into what makes George Crump's gem so special – which is much more than its slope rating of 155, which deems it as difficult as a golf course gets.

Several years ago, a visitor to Pine Valley went searching for his ball in the woods on the right of the fiendish par-four 13th hole and didn't reappear. His playing partners and caddies looked for him, yelling loudly as they stomped through the undergrowth, but to no avail. They decided they should keep playing. Search parties were dispatched.

Over dinner, sometime between entrée and main course, the fellow appeared, dishevelled and thirsty, with twigs sticking to his sweater. He explained that when searching for his ball he had got disorientated and lost. After stumbling about in the woods for two or three hours, he eventually came across a dirt road, which returned him to civilisation. Not only do balls get lost at Pine Valley; sometimes people do too.

The famous American course designer AW Tillinghast liked to tell people that Philadelphia hotelier George Crump spotted the land on which he would build his golfing masterpiece, Pine Valley, from a speeding train on a trip to Atlantic City in 1909. Indeed, a railway line is still there to this day.

Crump had systematically searched the outskirts of Philadelphia for several years, eventually finding what he wanted – rolling hills of sandy soil – in the Pine Barrens area across the Delaware River and across the state line, in south Jersey, 40 kilometres south-east of the city. His aim was simple: to build the US's most spectacular and difficult golf course, one to test the best players in the land and, possibly, to produce a US Amateur champion.

Crump bought the land – 184 acres – for $8750. For the first few months he camped on the site, poring over plans by firelight, before moving into a bungalow he built beside what would become the fifth tee. He strode the grounds, club in hand, playing shots to imaginary greens. Many well-known course architects of the time were consulted as Pine Valley took shape, including Harry Colt, Hugh Wilson, George Thomas, Charles Blair Macdonald, Walter Travis, Tillinghast, Alister MacKenzie and Donald Ross.

The first tree was felled in February 1913 and the first five fairways seeded seven months later. The first 11 holes were completed within 19 months. Those who attended the course opening in November 1913 were aware that they were witnessing something special. Crump's creation attracted huge praise. Donald Ross pronounced Crump's goal achieved: 'This is the finest golf course in America.' English golf writer Henry Longhurst later wrote, 'I look on it as the greatest of all inland courses, the perfect examination of the golfer's physical and psychological powers.' More recently, when asked to name his top three courses in the world, Colin Montgomerie replied, 'Pine Valley, Pine Valley and Pine Valley.'

Today, Pine Valley – with its manicured fairways, vast areas of sand, glorious vistas, intimidating tee shots over barren wastelands, hard and fast greens, and diabolical bunkers (there are no rakes at Pine Valley) – is regularly voted the world's best, and toughest, course. Despite the lofty position Pine Valley consistently occupies in world rankings, many golfers know little about it. It is, for instance, often confused with Pinehurst in North Carolina, more than 600 kilometres to the south. This is largely because the club does not host major championships; there would not be enough room for the crowds.

The most notable tournaments it has hosted have both been amateur events, the Walker Cups of 1936 and 1985, both won by the US. In 1961, it hosted a Shell's Wonderful World of Golf match between reigning US Open champion, 31-year-old Gene Littler, and 49-year-old Byron Nelson. Nelson won the match, which was filmed over two days – the results are on YouTube, which will give you tantalising views of the course. Each September the club hosts another major amateur tournament, the Crump Cup, featuring elite mid-amateur players principally from the US. The redoubtable Jay Sigel won nine of them before he turned professional and joined the Senior Tour.

At Pine Valley, the game is the thing. The club is not for corporate heavyweights, nor those with an eye on the social ladder, although celebrities are not unwelcome: joining the rank-and-file members over the years have been former US presidents, much-loved professionals, the odd television and film star, golf writers and course designers. The membership consists almost entirely of good golfers, or those who simply love the game.

While many American clubs are highly conservative, making visitors feel they are treading on eggshells, the dining room at Pine Valley (where the signature dish is the club's famous snapper soup) is invariably awash with stories, laughter and lively banter between members, visitors and friendly staff. If a storm lashes the course and play is suspended, it is not unusual for members to set up a chipping or putting competition inside the clubhouse.

And everywhere in the clubhouse are nods to the club's great founder. There is a mighty portrait of Crump, and a mural of the course painted in 1929 by Canadian Benjamin Kilvert, which carries words from Sir Christopher Wren's tomb in London's St Paul's Cathedral, *Si monumentum requiris, circumspice*: 'If you seek his monument – look around you.'

The club is happy to remain under the radar, and one senses that even many people who live locally in the Clementon region are unaware of its existence. Visitors heading down East Atlantic Avenue towards the front gate – past an old fun fair and a line of modest bungalows – often wonder if they are on the wrong road. But when you cross the railway line and drive past the sentry box (where hopefully your name is on the list) and along the road between the 18th fairway and a small lake guarding the final green, all doubts are dispelled.

Given the course's penal reputation, conquering fear is a key ingredient to playing Pine Valley. As is resisting the temptation to steer the ball. The golfer stands on the first tee knowing that, over the next four hours, one false stroke could be the ruin of the round.

Notably, the course has a slope rating of 155 from the championship tees, which is the high point at which the scale stops. (By contrast, the toughest slope rating in Australia – held by Bonville in NSW and the Heritage in Victoria – is 148; the lowest possible rating is 55.) There is no real rough, in the generally accepted sense of the word. The golfer's ball either finds the fairway – which are more generous than they appear from the tees – or it is in the trees or sand. Notably, the club recently undertook a program to clear out some trees and undergrowth, particularly around the greens.

The greenkeepers can make the course as hard as they want. At the 1983 Crump Cup, the club kept an eclectic worst score for the 18 holes from the qualifying round – an eye-watering 158. Only three players broke 80, while 17 recorded more than 100. And this from the best golfers in in the land.

To list the great holes at Pine Valley is almost a disservice to the holes that are left out, but those that deserve special mention

Karrie Webb with her then fiancé, Todd Haller. The pair set out from the small Queensland sugar town of Ayr in 1995 to conquer the world. (Glenn Harvey/Alamy)

A 19-year-old Adam Scott tees off in the Victorian Open in January 2000, one of his first big events. Playing alongside him was Mike Clayton, who after seven holes was moved to say, 'Can you believe how good this kid is?' (Robert Cianflone/ALLSPORT/Getty Images)

Greg Norman falls to his knees after his chip for eagle at Augusta's par-five 15th narrowly misses the hole. It was to be his last hurrah at the 1996 Masters; he dunked his ball in the water at the 16th and went on to lose to Nick Faldo by five strokes.

Steve Williams and Tiger Woods high-five each other after Woods' stunning chip shot from the back of Augusta's 16th green for a birdie, one of the greatest shots seen at the course. He went on to win the 2005 Masters in a playoff.

(Harry How/Getty Images)

ABOVE: All smiles now ... Tiger Woods at the Australian Open in 2011, alongside media centre manager Kathie Shearer. The pair had an infamous run-in during a tournament in Thailand in 1998 but, over the years, became good friends. (David Cannon/Getty Images)

BELOW: Peter Alliss, the BBC's much-loved golf commentator, receives an honorary degree from St Andrews University in 2005, alongside Peter Thomson and Nick Faldo. (PA Images/Alamy)

LEFT: Bob Shearer holds aloft the Stonehaven Cup, the Australian Open's trophy, after his win in the 1982 championship – despite calling a two-shot penalty on himself in the opening round while playing alongside Jack Nicklaus. (Golf Australia)

Five-time Open champion Peter Thomson signs autographs during the centenary Open at St Andrews in 1960. In this book, Thomson writes: 'The Old Course is the rock on which the game of golf anchors itself ... it is without doubt the place where the game as we know it now evolved ...' (PA Images/Alamy)

The 17th green at St Andrews' Old Course (looking down the 18th fairway), which is guarded by the infamous pot bunker at the front, and a road and stone fence at the back.
(Newscom/Alamy)

LEFT: The prince of golf-course designers: Scotsman Alister MacKenzie, who created some of the greatest courses in the world, including three in the top 10 – Augusta, Royal Melbourne and Cypress Point – and whose architectural principles are still revered today.

(Alister MacKenzie Foundation)

BELOW: A notable example of the bunkering at Royal Melbourne (designed by MacKenzie and his Australian partner, Alex Russell). This is the 18th green on the east course, with the first hole on the west course running alongside it.

(Gary Lisbon/Royal Melbourne)

TOP: The inimitable swing of Ben Hogan, a feisty perfectionist who played golf in the 1940s and '50s with a machine-like precision that few, if any, have matched since. (PA Images/Alamy)

LEFT: Australia's Geoff Ogilvy, the 2006 US Open champion, driving perfectly down Shady Oaks' 9th fairway with one of Ben Hogan's special, fade-only drivers. 'I tried to hook that and still couldn't make it go left,' Ogilvy said. (Mike Clayton)

Seve Ballesteros told Mike Clayton this was the greatest shot he ever played: a chip from light rough beside the 72nd green at Royal Lytham in 1988 which he nearly holed. The up-and-down par gave him a two-shot win over Nick Price, and his third Open title.

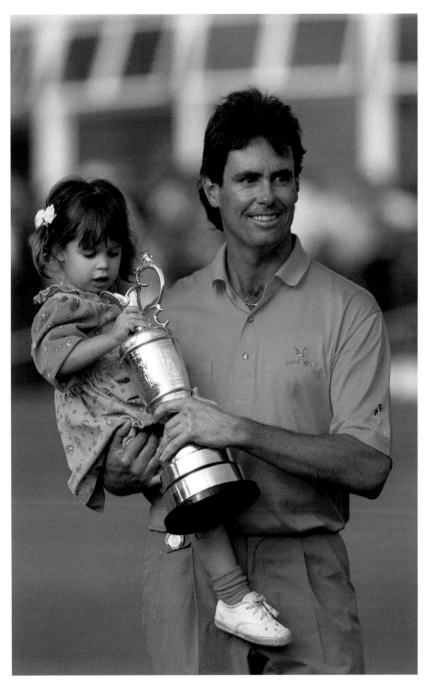

Australia's Ian Baker-Finch lets his daughter, Hayley, hold the Claret Jug after winning the 1991 Open Championship at Royal Birkdale. Seven years later, he was given a memorable reception when he returned to the Merseyside links before the '98 Open.

ABOVE: Jack Nicklaus hits off the 10th tee at Royal Hobart during the 1971 Australian Open. The game's greatest player chose to forsake a lucrative US PGA Tour event to travel to Tasmania (where, naturally, he won), causing local golf officials to beam with pride. (Royal Hobart Golf Club)

BELOW: The unlikeliest trailblazer in Australian golf: Tasmanian cattle farmer Richard Sattler, who chose to build two world-class golf courses, Barnbougle Dunes and Lost Farm, in sand dunes on his farm in the state's north-east. (Scott Gelston/Fairfax)

The par-three 10th hole at Pine Valley. George Crump's Philadelphia gem is consistently rated the number one course in the world. (Mike Clayton)

The 15th hole at the Hague GC in the Netherlands – proof that wonderful golf can be played on the Continent. Mike Clayton writes that it provides for 'an exhilarating' test. (Mike Clayton)

Matt Kuchar hits his tee shot into the notorious island green at the TPC at Sawgrass's 17th hole, a green that has attracted no end of controversy since Sawgrass began hosting The Players Championship in 1982. (ZUMA Press, Inc /Alamy)

Swinley Forest's 14th hole. Harry Colt's layout, near Ascot, is one of the premier inland courses in England. Short but beautiful, the summer swathes of purple heather and firm fairways that wind through mature pine trees make this a must-visit. (Mike Clayton)

The stunning clubhouse at Morfontaine, outside Paris. A Tom Simpson classic, the course is rated the best in France – just remember to play Simpson's short nine-hole 'Valliere' course, as well, to get the full Morfontaine experience. (Mike Clayton)

New Zealand prodigy Lydia Ko poses with her trophy after winning the Women's Australian Open at Royal Melbourne in 2015. The 17-year-old became the youngest winner of the Open, a co-sanctioned LPGA Tour event. (Newscom/Alamy)

Su Oh lobs a water bottle to her lowly paid assistant (read caddie), Mike Clayton, during the 2018 Victorian Open at 13th Beach. (Justin Falconer/Golf Victoria)

Jason Day and his caddie/coach/mentor Col Swatton embrace after Day holed the final putt at Whistling Straits to see off Jordan Spieth and win the 2015 PGA Championship, his first major after several near-misses. (Jamie Squire/Getty Images)

Crowds flock to the 2010 Ryder Cup at Celtic Manor in Wales, illustrating the extraordinary popularity of the event, which has been transformed since Europe's admission in 1979.

(Jeff Morgan 05/Alamy)

International captain Greg Norman and his team at the opening ceremony of the 2011 Presidents Cup at Royal Melbourne – a contest that resulted in yet another US victory.

(Action Plus Sports Images/Alamy)

are the medium-length two-shotter second, the fifth (which Gene Sarazen described as 'an anthology of hazards' after Gene Littler racked up a seven there against Nelson in 1961), the monumental par-four 13th and the 574-yard par-five 15th. The other par five, the seventh, is cut in half by a 110-yard-long area of wilderness. It is well acknowledged that one former club president played at the club for more than 20 years and never once cleared this wilderness with his second shot. Notably, when *Golf Digest* listed the US's 99 greatest golf holes in 1999, Pine Valley provided seven of them – 2, 5, 7, 10, 13, 15 and 18. Visitors are often surprised that there are six par fours of less than 370 yards.

Every hole at Pine Valley, so the saying goes, is a double-bogey waiting to happen. First-time visitors, including many single-digit players, are sometimes offered a bet that they cannot break 90, and many lose. Crump's warning nearly 100 years ago – 'On most of the holes, just a pretty good shot is of no use at all' – is worth remembering.

All members at Pine Valley have horror stories. A five-handicapper once reached the 200-metre fifth green with his tee shot – no small accomplishment – and went aggressively for a birdie. His ball rolled into a bunker. He exploded out, found himself back where he was after his tee shot, and then putted into the bunker again, ending up in the footprint he had left from his previous visit. He finally found the green's fringe, from where he chipped and two-putted. On in one, in in ten.

The accepted rule at Pine Valley is simple – if, or when, you find trouble, the first aim must be to hit out onto the fairway and proceed from there. Most big scores at Pine Valley result from a player following a mistake with another mistake. In match play, of course, anything can happen. Players winning from five or six down are commonplace. Hence the other Pine Valley mantra worth remembering: 'Never pick up, never give up.'

And never brag. In 1983 Bob Barrett, a visitor from Pinehurst, told people in advance of a round at Pine Valley that he was expecting good things after taking a lesson from three-time Open winner Henry Cotton the previous spring. He shot 131. Cotton heard of this and sent him a cable: 'Please don't mention my name.'

To spend time at Pine Valley with a group of friends is as good a golfing experience as there is worldwide, even though you may end the day wondering if you really can play the game. But it's important to leave your pride at the gate; all golfers at Pine Valley learn very quickly to deal with humiliation.

And for those for whom one round is never enough, there is also the 10-hole short course, designed in 1991 by Tom Fazio and former club resident Ernie Ransome, to test the wits. It's not just any old short course; several of the green complexes are replicas of greens on the big course. Nothing is commonplace at Pine Valley.

ENGLAND: SOME CORNERS OF THEIR FOREIGN FIELDS

In his 40-odd years as a playing professional, golf tourist and course designer, **Mike Clayton** has teed up in dozens of countries around the world. His favourite for variety, quality and old-fashioned fun? The inland courses of England.

Australia has better weather and the United States has many more great and varied courses, but there is surely no better country to play golf in than England.

It is somewhat mystifying that people will fly all the way across the world to play all the famous links in Ireland and Scotland yet miss so much of the great English golf, much of it inland and far from the coast (well, as far as you can get from the coast in England). Perhaps the English like to keep their best golf to themselves.

Wayne Grady came back from Europe with less-than-effusive praise for English golf after his singularly unsuccessful first foray on the European Tour in 1979. 'If it wasn't for black and white stakes you couldn't play golf in England,' was Grady's assessment of what he had found, but he would be the first to admit that most of what he found was on Mondays at the pre-qualifiers – none of which were held at Swinley Forest, Rye, Sunningdale or Ganton.

Ten years later, he would lose The Open Championship in a playoff and that brought about a grudging acceptance on his part that golf in Britain wasn't all bad. By then he had come to understand it, appreciate it even.

In Scotland and Ireland the links courses are brilliant fun and while everyone knows the famous ones there are so many second-tier links falling into the 'as good as Barwon Heads' category. Places like Brora, Fraserburgh, Panmure, Gullane and Nairn are all links worth the time and effort to play. They are neither difficult, unless the wind is up, nor expensive, and in the summer you can still tee off at seven in the evening and make it around easily. The King's and Queen's courses at Gleneagles are beautiful places to play golf and provide an experience you won't find anywhere else in the world. (The new Ryder Cup course across the street, the PGA Centenary Course, however, is indistinguishable from anything you might find in parkland United States, and if you were going all that way to play golf I'm not sure why you'd play it over another round on either the King's or Queen's. As my friend John Huggan wrote, it's 'the fourth-best course in Auchterarder'.)

But inland golf just isn't as good in Scotland. The extraordinary scenery that makes it one of the most stunning of countries is hardly conducive to making good golf holes. Unlike Scotland, inland English golf is a joy.

At Swinley Forest, Harry Colt's 6020-yard, par-69 masterpiece just up the A30 from Sunningdale, there are no signs and the only reliable instruction is to turn left at the small red post box on the corner. It is as good a place as any to start discussing the merits of English golf and why you should consider seeking out the famous, and not so famous, English courses.

I played there occasionally in the 1980s and 1990s thanks to the friendship of the late golf writer Tom Ramsey with the club secretary, but I knew no-one there. Sometime around 2010, I was staying close by and thought asking if I could walk the course was a chance worth taking. I knocked on the wooden door of the secretary's small office and a woman, who turned out to be very kindly, opened it. I introduced myself and asked her if walking the course would be a problem. 'Why would that be a problem? I'll let them know you're out there so they don't annoy you,' she said.

Don't try the same at Augusta. Unless you have unimpeachable contacts, so many of the US's great courses have locked gates to the curious traveller.

The heathlands are the London equivalent of Melbourne's sandbelt.

So impressive was Colt's reputation that Royal Melbourne hoped to entice him to Australia to make its new course. Too busy, unwilling to travel, or both, he recommended MacKenzie; unsurprisingly, in London and in Melbourne there are great similarities in the look and design of courses. Both cities have an abundance of beautiful mid-length par threes, making it easy to imagine the eighth at Sunningdale and the fifth at Royal Melbourne being transposed to opposite sides of the world with few noticing much difference.

Wentworth, the famous heathland tournament course, is the home of the British PGA and formerly the World Match Play, but it's far from the best of its ilk and is proof that difficult courses – even ones made famous by the longtime hosting of big events – don't bring certainty of greatness. Worse, the previous owner decided Colt's course could be improved by an Ernie Els redesign replete with a finishing hole low-lighted by a completely out-of-place creek across the front, which turned a historic two-shot par five into, for most, an 80-metre par three with a drive and a dull lay-up to start.

Still, it's better to leave tournament golf there rather than try to make the shorter, smaller and better courses nearby long enough and difficult enough to host professional golf. Not that there is much European tour golf left in England. Indeed Australia, with the PGA and the Perth International being co-sanctioned events in 2018, has as many tournaments on the European Tour as England, while South Africa, with four, has twice as many. It would have been an unimaginable development for those who developed the tour in the mid 1970s, but it's now a proper world tour and the most interesting one to play.

For the travellers, though, the heathlands are the easiest place to camp out for a few weeks and play great golf every day. If you're flying through and don't fancy paying $500 to play Sunningdale, try Woking, Worplesdon, West Hill, West Sussex, New Zealand and, if you don't much like bunkers, Royal Ashdown Forest.

It's in a royal forest where any artificial construction was banned so the club was forced to use the natural features to make the interest. It is proof that bunkers can be overused as hazards and there's an abundance of interest around the greens at Royal Ashdown Forest without the sand.

The heathlands are important, too, because they were the first concentration of great inland design. Architects including Colt, Tom Simpson, Herbert Fowler and JF Abercromby showed how good inland golf could be by using the advantages of sand, ideal low-growing heaths and heather, and undulations to make perfect golf. It's not particularly difficult golf in this modern era, but there is no shortage of difficult shots and it's always both interesting and beautiful.

South of London are the famous links at Royal St Georges, Royal Cinque Ports and Rye. The latter two aren't big enough to hold The Open nor are they hard enough, but they are easily good enough.

Royal Worlington and Newmarket in Suffolk is a nine-hole course and evidence those who think golf needs to be 18 holes to be worthwhile should think harder about what makes for good golf. Crammed into 50 acres, the drive at the third plays across the green of the second hole, a long par-three into a tight corner, and the tee shot at the par-three fifth plays over the fourth green, while off the sixth you drive over the fifth green. It sounds like a shooting gallery but it works because the course isn't overly busy, members are used to it and the architects, Tom Dunn (1892) and Colt (1906), understood the golf would be better if they didn't waste any of the limited land they had to work with. If any architect suggested building it now they would be presented with myriad reasons why it couldn't work, yet it does, and perfectly well.

Driving further north to Leeds are MacKenzie's earliest courses at Alwoodley and Moortown, the home of the 'Gibraltar' hole, which MacKenzie referenced when he was making the 15th at Kingston Heath. He constructed the hole first to show off the possibilities of golf at Moortown – and its singular quality attracted the members and the investment needed to finish the course.

'It is not only a delightful hole to see, which at any rate appeals subconsciously even to the dullest minds, but it is equally delightful to play and is less difficult than it appears,' wrote MacKenzie after he'd built Royal Melbourne and moved to California. 'Now I am a resident in America and my restraining influence so far removed, I should not be surprised if it were altered. Some of the committee, backed by leading professional players, although admitting it is the best hole on the course, suggest that if the unfair tilt of the green was flattened out it would become still better. It wouldn't – it would become as flat as ditch water and just as uninspiring.'

The roughs at Alwoodley highlight one of the advantages of golf in England over Australia, where the roughs struggle to capture the look and texture of the perfect off-fairway grasses, heaths and heather of English inland golf. And courses like Alwoodley do a better job of keeping trees away from the golf, encouraging the roughs and allowing expansive views across the course.

On England's north-east coast near Scarborough is Ganton, a difficult course but one not so easy to define. Even though it is close to the sea, it's not a links but neither does it feel like a heathland or a parkland course. Still, it has abundant good golf and will make the drive off the beaten track worth the effort.

All the way across to the west coast is the collection of links around Liverpool and Southport. Birkdale, Lytham and Hoylake are the most famous, not least for Peter Thomson winning four of his five Opens around them. The big Open courses always have smaller ones close by and to travel so far but to miss Formby, Hillside and Southport and Ainsdale would be disappointing. Tom Doak is a fan of Silloth on Solway, a course 'existing in relative anonymity, due to its unfortunate location in a bit of golfing no-man's land between Scotland and England'.

During my time on the European Tour, neither I nor any of my fellow travellers would take the time out to visit, say, Woodhall Spa or St Enodoc, Brancaster or any other of the old classics. It was a time when no-one was much interested in design and the country itself was in the midst of making a lot of new golf courses, designed either by Americans or with an American influence, with no thought for the legacy left by Colt, MacKenzie, Simpson and Fowler. But the classics are all still there – and it's the classics that offer, as a collection, the best golf in the world.

HIDDEN TREASURES: FRANCE, BELGIUM, HOLLAND

France, Belgium and Holland are not regarded as five-star golf destinations but **Mike Clayton** says each country boasts some wonderful courses, many built by Tom Simpson and Harry Colt between the wars, and are well worth a visit.

One of golf's delights is travelling and discovering far-off golf courses, and some of the best golf to be found is in places you'd least expect.

In Europe the best golf is that from the era when the wealthy wanted clubs and courses to match the best across the English Channel. It was an elitist game on the continent and Tom Simpson and Harry Colt sailed across from England to make some of the game's still largely undiscovered treasures.

One of golf's unlikeliest tourist roads begins in Paris and heads north through Belgium and into Holland. Anyone willing to make the effort will be delighted by a collection of courses as compelling and as beautiful as any in the world.

Simpson designed three world-class courses in Paris: Chantilly, Fontainebleau and Morfontaine. Chantilly, just up the road from the famed racecourse and the extraordinary chateau (think James

Bond, *View to a Kill*, Grace Jones) was for a time in the late 1980s the home of the French Open before it moved sadly (at least to me) to a new, modern course, Le Golf National, with not an ounce of a hint it was even in France. The ground at Chantilly is relatively hard, more clay-based than the sand of Fontainebleau and Morfontaine, which are both reminiscent of the heathlands of Sunningdale and the great courses south-west of London.

Simpson worked on his pick of beautiful sites for wealthy clients making joyous, easily walkable courses, and the 27 holes at Morfontaine display his architecture at its best. I first played the course, an hour's drive north-east of Paris, as part of an Australian amateur team playing the French and British Amateur championships. Tony Gresham had beaten John Kelly in the French Amateur at Chantilly and, the day after, they took us to Morfontaine, the most beautiful course I had ever seen.

The Morfontaine driveway is one of those long winding ones through the forest and the course all the way to the clubhouse. The club is small, private and elegant; the course not quite as good as Sunningdale or Swinley Forest, but no matter, it's one of the game's great experiences. However, be warned: its gates are among the toughest to open – which is made clear on their website, pointing out that golf is <u>strictly reserved</u> to its 450 members and their guests (the underlining is theirs).

Golfers often talk about big greens as though they are a bad trait born of modern design, yet Simpson made a few huge greens fully 50 paces from front to back – and Morfontaine is no exception.

There are an extra nine holes at Morfontaine: the Valliere, a short course with wild greens and fun shots many would think too extreme for a 'normal' course. Maybe, but it's the sort of golf the game needs more of in order to better utilise small pieces of land. I see basic, dull and often poorly conditioned 18-hole public courses in Australia that people defend passionately because, as MacKenzie says, 'Every man has an affection for the mud heap on which he plays.' They don't see any reason to make nine-hole courses, seeing them as somehow diminished, but one round on the Valliere (or Royal Worlington and Newmarket in England) and they'd understand how great nine-hole golf can be.

Fontainebleau offers the same experience as Morfontaine, with its beautiful clubhouse, secluded golf and world-class architecture.

Simpson was a great architect who was independently wealthy; as a consequence, he wasn't one for governance of clubs by committee or being told what to do by men who understood less about the game than he did. Given the free hand he demanded, he made brilliant golf.

Peter Thomson has always wondered how golf in Melbourne would have differed if Harry Colt and not Alister MacKenzie had taken up Royal Melbourne's initial offer to remake its course. All three were visionaries who changed the game: Colt in Britain, MacKenzie in Australia and the US, and Simpson on the Continent. As Thomson wonders what Colt may have done, so do I of Simpson. He was of the philosophy, 'No tee shot can possibly be described as good if the proper place to be is the centre of the fairway.' Golf, he thought, was an adventure as opposed to 'an examination of stroke production'.

Simpson died in 1964 at about the same time professional golf was becoming increasingly popular and influential. The majority of players saw the centre of the fairway as the perfect place to drive and any adventure or quirk as a trick, a potential threat to an orderly procession of threes, fours and the occasional five. It was a pity but for the professionals the elimination of chance and luck was the way they liked their courses.

Over France's northern border and into Belgium: the European tour played a couple of times at Waterloo, the course you'd most like to play if you needed pars on the last three holes to make the cut. All three were par fives, none of them particularly onerous. A decent enough course, but the one really worth visiting is the Colt-designed Royal Zoute in Knokke, located in the sandy dunes in the north of the country. I haven't seen it for 25 years and have read that the conditions can be spotty at times but no matter, the holes are very good – and there is always the local chocolate if the fairways aren't perfect.

Holland is the unlikeliest place to find good golf because it's the flattest country on the planet, making it hardly a surprise they ride bikes everywhere and are good at football and hockey.

In 1980, I played the Dutch Open at Hilversum as an amateur. Like so many of the best courses on the Continent, it's a Colt heathland course through pines and birch. Even back then, when I only had a basic understanding of how trees might adversely affect a golf course, it seemed there were too many of them and it might have been better for a culling, because opening the view across the undulating site would have made for a better experience and better golf, too. (Seve Ballesteros was out in the final round that year with the brilliant Sandy Lyle and duly won, playing controlled golf on a narrow course, the sort many assume would not suit him – but at his best Seve could play any course.)

A few weeks later at the Dutch Amateur we played The Hague, a tumbling dunes course just outside the capital city. The land reminds me of Victoria's Portsea, with the big changes of elevation and the thrilling-looking shots it allows for. As with Portsea, not every shot is perfect because the land offers up a few blind shots and a few steeply uphill shots (the pitch up the hill to the second is a lot like the same shot at Portsea's ninth) but the payoff is some of Europe's most exhilarating golf. The double-storey clubhouse with a thatched roof is more evidence that Europeans understand better than anyone what makes a great clubhouse. It's quite small with one main room, but with interesting corners, nooks and crannies.

A couple of years later I was back, this time as a pro at the Dutch Open at de Pan in Utrecht. Colt again; it's a heathland course neither long nor particularly difficult but first-class in every category except the ludicrous 'resistance to scoring' – one criteria used by magazines to measure the merit of a golf course. Any view that perpetuates the myth that hard is good and easy is somehow deficient is to be abhorred – and de Pan is proof easy can be great. Of course it isn't easy so much as fun, interesting and very playable for a normal club membership.

One highlight is the superb short par-four 10th, a hole where the driver is always too much club from the tee but the pitch is played between a couple of high heath-covered dunes to the green beyond. It is not a difficult hole, but is both beautiful and memorable. It is to the game's eternal discredit the modern ball has made courses like de Pan and Sunningdale too short for professional golf, and it is poorer for having to stage tournaments at lesser courses simply because they are more resistant to the onslaught of titanium, graphite and hot golf balls.

Kennemer and Noordwijk were the other two Open courses we played in Holland in the 1980s and '90s. Both are in the seaside dunes, but neither is as wild as The Hague. Noordwijk has an odd run of holes from the fifth to the seventh through a pine forest, completely out of character with the rest of the holes running through and over the dunes. The seventh in particular is – or perhaps was, because they have worked on it – a shocker, doglegging to the left with a blind tee shot over a forest of pine trees.

Kennemer has 27 holes, 18 of Colt and a new nine, which we disappointingly had to play in a couple of Dutch Opens after 1983 when we played the original course.

On a side note, the 1983 Dutch Open was held two weeks after Jack Newton had walked into the spinning propeller of a plane at Sydney airport and I well remember Irishman John O'Leary, one of Jack's best mates, telling us he'd just heard Jack had died. Fortunately, like Mark Twain, news of Jack's death was exaggerated. The week before in Germany, I'd played with Seve Ballesteros on the last day of the German Open in Koln and he was particularly upset about the accident. When Seve won at Augusta 1980 he'd played the last day with Jack, who finished up tied for second. Jack, in his typically blunt fashion, had told the American press after the tournament he was tired of hearing all the talk of Seve being a lucky, wild hitter, suggesting the sooner they realised 'this guy is a great player the better'. Seve remembered and always appreciated it.

It was Seve, of course, who brought the professional game to life on the European continent, whose best old courses, primarily gifted to us by Colt and Simpson, are some of the game's great treasures. If you ever get the chance to play any of them it's well worth the effort of writing a nice letter to the club secretary. But it probably won't help you at Morfontaine.

THE OLD COURSE: ORIGINAL AND BEST

Peter Thomson first played The Old Course at St Andrews in 1954 and immediately fell in love with its quirks and unspoiled beauty. The following year, he won the second of his five British Opens around the fabled links. Here, he describes what makes it so special.

The Old Course at St Andrews is the rock on which the game of golf anchors itself. It was not the first ground on which the game was played, but it is without doubt the place where the game as we know it now evolved and revived itself.

In the beginning, four or more centuries ago, it was a wild place on which to hit a small wooden ball across country, and it did not enjoy a sunny, warm climate except for the short summer months. Yet the game of golf from its infancy not only survived – it flourished. Today, St Andrews links is called the 'Home of Golf' although, in truth, golf has no home. It is worldwide.

St Andrews, though, is the true home of the Royal and Ancient Golf Club, in whose hands the game is entrusted by all the world of play, outside the United States and its sphere of influence. The 'R&A' made The Old Course what it is and, in its turn, the course made the R&A. Had the club not nurtured and enhanced its dignity, the custody of the game would probably have drifted somewhere else.

The Old Course emerged on a strip of territory that started on the old town steps, taking from there a crooked path along the coastal route until it ran out of westward land at the estuary of the Eden River. The golfers then reversed their progress and returned whence they came, ending their matches at the town limit.

As history tells us, originally there were 22 stages along the golfing journey there and back, but in the mid–19th century the golfers of the Club decided that as the balls they struck increased their trajectory, some of the stages were too short. There was merit in joining a few together, they decided, thereby settling on 18 stages as adequate. Eighteen holes consequently became universally accepted as the standard number of holes to comprise a full-size course.

The Old Course at St Andrews is the model and prototype for golf courses everywhere. Not only have they accepted and followed the number of holes set, but all courses everywhere across the world will have sand bunkers strewn in emulation of links features, and a fair ratio of fairground to rough areas to complete what has come to be accepted as a full-featured playing arena.

The lakes and swamps of Florida courses featuring water hazards are imitations of the Swilcan Burn, which crosses the first hole of the Old, albeit usually with a considerable distortion of dimension. Even so, the innumerable illogicalities of the St Andrews course have been largely ignored in other places. Who indeed in their home state tolerates a golf hole with a green sliced in half like the Road Hole, or put up with a hole without a visible fairway like the seventh? These things undoubtedly troubled the minds of the early Greens Committees of the R&A, and their astute judgement to leave the course as nature provided was certainly cursed by the many who suffered the punishment of inadequate shots.

Even so, pressure must have built up until the Club appointed 'Old Tom' Morris as Keeper of the Greens, then charged him with widening the course to make more space for the increasing numbers of golfers, which was a momentous step. We can only surmise that the ordering of this exercise was a bold demand for more fairway and less hazard to make the game of golf a more enjoyable experience. Certainly it made a huge difference. More freedom to divert from the rigid straight and narrow must have brought joy to many hearts.

As a result of this work, The Old Course took up approximately 92 acres, which is its scope today. More than 80 per cent of its territory is now given over to fairground, and the broken sward (112) bunkers add up to just one acre of total catchment area – surprising given its fearsome reputation.

I first played The Old Course in 1954, in the British Match Play (*Ed: which he won*), and I was awed. I loved it instantly.

But The Old Course is on trial in this modern era and I fear for it. Unfortunately, there is currently a demand for courses to be green and lush, which runs counter to what links golf should be about. If the course is firm and bare, as it should be, and the wind blows, and the greens are given just a little hand-watering, then I would say you need more discipline here than on any other course, because you have to play approach shots away from the flag ... in those conditions, you can't play stone-dead golf.

I would say the simplest piece of golf course architecture is the first hole at The Old Course. There is no bunker, the fairway is about 150 yards wide and it is a beautiful piece of turf. When you play the Championship there, it is a frightening hole. The wind is blowing and the flag indicates that the cup is perhaps three yards from the burn in front of it. You are a professional so, of course, you attempt to get close to the flag and you sometimes get caught. The simplicity of the whole thing intrigued me when I played all those years.

The ninth hole doesn't have a greenside bunker, aside from one tucked away in the gorse bushes on the left edge of the green. The hole is dead flat. I remember Greg Norman one year elected to drive to avoid the bunkers that divide the ninth and the 10th holes. He ended up no more than 80 yards from the flag, so he got out his wedge and launched his second shot, which came up about 12 feet short and then screwed back a bit as well. So he was now quite a few yards from the pin and a bit cranky because the hole is so simple you should get a three every time.

Norman gave the putt a good whack, missed and sent the ball about 6 feet past the hole. Then he missed that one coming back. I was standing there and I had to laugh. After that beautiful drive he had this simple approach, yet contrived to take five.

That is what I think is marvellous about golf: an intriguing hole you think should be easy and expect to walk off with a birdie, yet you walk off disappointed. It is wonderful.

Players would also be wise to pay attention to the 17th, the Road Hole. It is a very odd hole and one where players can make a very high score. When I won tournaments at St Andrews, I dodged that road to the right like the plague. Quite often you are better off to not try to hit your second shot stone dead, but to play short of the green. You have to be able to swallow your pride, approach with caution and be happy walking off with a par four.

The course is a beautiful bit of nature at work, although it is not entirely virgin territory. The hand of man has added or subtracted from the original micro-landform at every juncture. And nature itself is a dynamic force that has its own way of changing things.

What we have in The Old Course is an environmental partnership that arranged a playing arena and gave the game a suitable shape. Yet the major issue facing the keepers of the course has been the ever-developing technology that threatens to render the course irrelevant. At various dates, the governing body set specifications for the balls used that were intended to control its performance. A weight limit of 1.62 ounces was set and a minimum size of 1.62 inches was added to attempt to limit the balls' flying performance. Later still, in modern times, a speed restriction was imposed. This particular imposition was thought to be the ultimate stopper to the balls' increasing length of flight. Alas, what was overlooked was the aerodynamic factor of dimpled-cover balls. Balls today are carrying greater distances than ever and so the battle goes on, overshadowed by commercial legalities.

All courses are, to varying degrees, copies of The Old, but no-one anywhere in the world has been foolish enough to try to copy The Old Course as an entity. It wouldn't work. On another piece of ground in a different climate, it might look ridiculous. It is just as well. The Old Course is unique, and long may it be so.

CAN'T SEE THE COURSE FOR THE TREES

Trees have their place on the golf course, argues
Mike Clayton, but not as part of the play, only as part
of the scenery.

The last time I saw him, I told him about a rather morose
Scottish caddie I'd recently had who took a dim view of most
things American, but especially the golf course, which, he'd
been told, had lots of trees. We were sitting on the porch of his
Augusta cottage and Jones looked down at the towering pines,
the great cathedral nave, of the plunging 10th fairway. 'I don't
see,' he said deadpan, 'any need for a tree on a golf course.

– Alistair Cooke on Bobby Jones

People think I hate trees. I don't. Who doesn't love a beautiful tree?

Well, George Thomas, the architect at Riviera and Los Angeles
Country Club, certainly didn't. 'Trees and shrubbery beautify
the course, and natural growth should never be cut down if it is
possible to save it; but he who insists on preserving a tree where
it spoils a shot should have nothing to say about golf course
construction,' he said.

Trees inevitably became a part of golf once the game grew and
moved to inland sites much different in look and character to the
original courses by the sea. Golf on the links was based around

the wind and the features of the ground, including the bunkers, undulations (some wild and some not so much), wispy roughs, heather, the boundaries of the course (few courses use the out-of-bounds hazard as well as the links) and greens both wildly rolling and close to flat, very often orientated to favour an approach from one particular side of the fairway. What the ball did on the ground was as important as what it did in the air, and understanding the ground and what it was doing was a critical part of a golfer's examination.

At two of Australia's best courses, Kingston Heath and Royal Melbourne, the interest is primarily created around the things on the ground. Likewise for other great courses: Sunningdale, Woking, Ganton, Notts, Morfontaine, Oakmont, Shinnecock, Paraparaumu Beach. Any trees on those courses add to their beauty, but they are mostly peripheral to the golf and the playing strategies. 'Trees should serve perhaps as the scenery, but never part of the stage,' was how golf architect Harry Colt put it.

Three of the best par fours in Australia are the medium-length sixth and the drivable 10th at Royal Melbourne, and Royal Adelaide's long and difficult 14th. They are lined by trees, but all of their strategy and all of their brilliance is made by the hazards on the ground cut into the inside corners of the dogleg.

Colt's contemporary, AW Tillinghast, expressed a similar view of the place of trees in golf when he said, 'I sometimes take my very life in my hands when I suggest that a certain tree happens to be spoiling a pretty good golf hole.' Then there's Alister MacKenzie: 'Playing down fairways bordered by straight lines of trees is not only unartistic but makes tedious and uninteresting golf. Many green committees ruin one's handiwork by planting trees like rows of soldiers along the borders of the fairways.'

But as time moved on, members and committees couldn't contain themselves and the great architects of the Golden Age were not as revered in the 1950s and 1960s as they are today. Trees got on to the stage, blocking off views across the course, getting in the road of the shots, especially when the incursion was too close to the inside corner of a dogleg, and just generally cluttered up the course. 'Nothing,' argues American architect Bruce Hepner, 'has negated the strategic value of classic course design more than loss of fairway acreage due to tree planting and overgrowth.'

Of course, one man's trash may be another's treasure, but clutter in the end is clutter, and none of the very best courses are cluttered. Clutter is never elegant, it can never be made elegant, and all the best courses have elegance at their heart. They are also largely faithful to the vegetation as it was before the course was built.

In Australia we didn't do the faithful part well at all – either with the flora or the fauna. (Some even thought rabbits, carp, cane toads and kikuyu would be a good idea.) It was unsurprising the early English settlers and the founders of Australia's original clubs and courses wanted to capture some of the essence of home. They couldn't resist the lure of trees reminding them of home, especially conifers – pines, spruce and cypress mostly. Variety was also seen as a virtue. Why not import eucalyptus from all over the country, or plants from all over the world?

Why not? 'Because they don't belong' would seem to me to be the answer. Ask any golfer if they think a course should feel natural and all, without exception, will answer in the affirmative. If nature had wanted tall mahogany gums by the sea, it would have grown them by the sea, but nature worked out tall trees with fragile limbs worked well in forests but weren't such a good idea in heavy coastal winds.

There was barely any reverence for the locally indigenous plants, the plants best suited to their environment, when it came to golf course planting schemes in suburban Australia. Who really cared, aside from Claude Crockford, the long-time green-keeper at Royal Melbourne, and his few acolytes, about all those beautiful little indigenous heathland plants? It is an easy argument to trash them because they 'only affect the highest handicappers' and 'slow up play'. Maybe, but they add beauty, texture and character to a hole.

The next 50 years are going to be important, as committees, architects and members will inevitably have to re-vegetate their golf courses. Old and dangerous trees will need to be removed. If they are to be replaced they should be relegated to their proper place as a part of scenery. The clubs that do it best will de-clutter, ridding their courses of their inappropriate odds and ends and resisting those who think them somehow treasured parts of the vegetation. It will be a time of argument and passion on both sides, and the clubs making the hard but necessary decisions will finish up with better golf and better golf courses for it.

Every single architect, writer or commentator over the course of time argued the role of trees was limited. Jack Nicklaus said it as well as anyone when he spoke of Pinehurst No. 2, the Donald Ross masterpiece in North Carolina: 'It is the best course I know of from a tree-usage standpoint. It's a totally tree-lined golf course without one tree in the playing strategy of that golf course.'

Scenery, not stage. Indigenous. Simple, really.

A DOZEN OF THE BEST

As a touring pro, course designer and golf tragic, **Mike Clayton** has been lucky enough to play all over the world, from New Zealand to Nebraska. Here, he selects 12 courses he wishes everybody could see.

The experience of playing a golf course is a subjective thing: most of us love a beautiful view, but a beautiful view can mask the architectural flaws of a golf course. Some will be bothered by those flaws; some will not.

A perfectly conditioned course inevitably earns more praise than one in poor shape, but would you rather play a well-designed course in average condition or an average course in perfect condition? Many in my experience would opt for the latter. It just shows that everyone has their own tastes, and likewise everyone has his or her favourite courses. Likely they are courses where they have enjoyed a pleasing experience, played well, perhaps they won something or savoured spectacular views over the ocean or the mountains.

The first course I played with any regularity was the nine-hole public course at Bulleen, in what was then outer-suburban Melbourne. The green fee was 30 cents, or 40 if you went around twice. We used to sneak from the seventh hole back to the fourth to get in a few extra holes, something the guy in the caravan who collected the money probably knew but kindly never said anything about. It was rudimentary golf at its most basic, but we loved it because all we cared about was hitting the ball and learning to play.

Eventually, I ventured far from Bulleen and saw a decent amount of golf all over the world in all its forms, some great, some good, some average and some just plain bad. Professional golf can find any number of very logical commercial reasons to go to lousy golf courses.

Favourite courses are not necessarily the best courses, but here are a dozen courses I wish everybody could see. All in their own distinct way show off just how great, and how varied, golf at its best can be. The first six are really hard to access, maybe not worth selling your first-born for a game, but if you ever get the chance don't pass it up. The rest shouldn't be too hard to get onto. Just write a nice letter to the club secretary or even turn up and pay the green fee.

Cypress Point – California

Beauty is unquestionably an important part of golf and there is no more beautiful place than Cypress Point. Designed by Alister MacKenzie in 1928, its 6536 yards wind through the Del Monte Forest, which is dominated by Monterey pines, before heading back to the sand dunes of the Californian coast, where players not only get cliff-top views of the Pacific Ocean, but play over it on the long par-three 16th. If every golfer in the world could play Cypress Point, it would be the favourite course of all of those who didn't pick St Andrews. Not that many will get the chance; it's probably the world's most exclusive club, and only an invite from a member will get you through the gate.

Swinley Forest – south-west of London

This reclusive club just off the A30 is a kilometre or two past the road up the hill to Sunningdale. You turn left at the little red post box because, unsurprisingly for a club doing absolutely nothing to advertise itself or its magnificent course, there are no signs.

Designer Harry Colt called it his 'least bad course', proving he was hardly a brilliant self-publicist. The par is 68 and there is 6200 yards of proper golf. In other words, it's the perfect-length course for about 80 per cent of people who play.

National Golf Links of America – Southampton, New York

The National was the first great American course. Its construction in 1913 began the Golden Age of golf architecture, which ended with the opening of Augusta in 1933. CB Macdonald spent time studying the great links of Scotland then came home to build his ideal course, one made up of holes replicating the principles of the best he had seen on the other side of the Atlantic. The third hole at National is his Alps, based on the principle of the blind 17th at Prestwick, a hole no sane architect would dare build today for the inevitable torrent of criticism that would come their way. It is followed by a long par three, a Redan asking for the same right-to-left draw as the 15th at North Berwick. Macdonald's description of such a hole is duly famous: 'Take a narrow tableland, tilt it a little from right to left, dig a deep bunker on the front side, approach it diagonally and you have a Redan.' The National is right next to Shinnecock Hills and if you can swing that double, it is likely to be your best 36-hole day in golf.

Sand Hills – Mullen, Nebraska

Bill Coore and Ben Crenshaw made Sand Hills for developer Dick Youngscap and it is probably the best course built in the US since Augusta. So brutal is the climate in Nebraska, it's open only from May to the end of October, but as there is nothing else to do out there, you may as well play golf all day to make up for it. The sandhills are 60 square miles of tumbling dunes in Nebraska, not unlike the dune country of Melbourne's Mornington Peninsula – there's just a lot more of it, although being snow-covered five months a year is disappointing to say the least. The only visible man-made structure is the halfway house above the ninth green and it goes without saying for a Coore and Crenshaw course that all the holes are first-class. If you missed any one of them, you would have missed something worth seeing. The only rule for the members is you cannot be rude to the staff; the one member who broke this rule is no longer a member. Every club should have a similar rule.

Merion – Philadelphia

David Graham became the first Australian to win the US Open when he piloted his way around the short and treacherous Merion on the final day in 1981, doing nothing much aside from hitting every fairway and every green and making a couple of decisive putts along the way, one on the first green, the other on the 15th. The holes here are all terrific but I love it for being another course thumbing its nose at convention. There are only two par fives, the second and the fourth. The run of holes from seven through 13 is very short but demands precise shots – David Graham–type shots. Then at the end comes a run of three uncommonly difficult holes, the last one made famous by the black-and-white Ben Hogan photo from the 1950 US Open.

Morfontaine – north-east of Paris

Morfontaine's small stone clubhouse is one of the most beautiful in golf – what else would you expect from the French? My other two favourite clubhouse – Fontainebleau (south-east of Paris) and Saint-Nom la Brèteche (near Versailles) – are also French. There is no pro shop at Morfontaine, but you can buy a hat and some golf balls from a closet-like room by the manager's office. Tom Simpson's course, as beautiful as the clubhouse, is made on sand and plays through a mix of pine and heather, making it reminiscent of the golf at Sunningdale and the rest of the best of the London heathlands. If you ever get there, do not finish the day without playing Simpson's wild little nine-holer complementing the big course.

Royal Hague – Netherlands

Holland may well be flat, but just out of Amsterdam is a Harry Colt course made in big coastal dunes by the sea, which are anything but flat. I've always enjoyed playing at Portsea on the Mornington Peninsula, and The Hague is a lot like Portsea but with even better holes. Scotland's North Berwick is what golf was before someone decided it needed to be 'fair' and golfers developed rules and conventions as to what was good and what wasn't – and Royal Hague is one of the best two examples (Prestwick being the other) of wild golf that many would describe as 'unfair'. Yet Royal Hague provides one of the most fun days you can have hitting a ball across interesting ground; if you don't like hitting at fairways and greens that you can't see, look for something more conventional.

The Old Course – St Andrews, Scotland

No other course shows off such day-to-day variety and variation in the playing options and choices. Alister MacKenzie called it the 'only first-rate course'. And St Andrews is one of the world's great towns. The greatest thing about golf on The Old Course is that, aside from making you pitch over the burn at the opening hole, nothing is dictated to the player. You can drive down opposite fairways, hit shots along the ground or in the air. Each time you play, the course will be subtly (or sometimes in a gale not so subtly) different and ask you endlessly fascinating questions. People often go there, play the course once and wonder what the fuss is all about. There is almost no point playing it once without having at least walked the course first just to see what the holes are doing and how best to play each of them. Frank Nobilo, one of New Zealand's finest-ever players, played the old Dunhill Cup there for years and always said he learned something new each time he played it – and that makes it the most extraordinary of courses.

Woking – south-west of London, near Sunningdale

Woking is one of the best examples of elegant, understated English heathland golf. No green in the world is as close to the clubhouse as the 14th, a par five with a pitch sure to scare those liable under pressure to hit the 'sickening knee-high fizzer', as John Huggan (himself one of the great practitioners of the shot) calls a bladed wedge. No committee or insurance company would let you build that hole today but it's like those little laneway roads bordered by hedges all over England: they are safe because they are so unsafe, and everyone is as a consequence so much more careful.

Notts – near Nottingham, England

In the middle of England, Notts has one of the best entrance drives in golf and a testing course with holes worth going out of your way to see. Most people who travel to England to play would sail past it unknowingly on the motorway on their way north from London, but they would be missing one of England's finest inland courses. Being near Nottingham and Sherwood Forest may incline some to think it a forested course, especially as it sits within Kirkby Forest, yet it's anything but, with the early holes having a heathland feel and the holes at the far end of the course playing over some wild hills. The middle is more wooded but never is there the feeling of playing a course disjointed by the different sections. It is a brilliant design, one showing off the diversity of English golf and why it's the best country in the world to play.

Arrowtown – Queenstown, New Zealand

'Unique' is an overused word, but Arrowtown has some truly unique holes. The course travels through rocks and valleys on a site only a group of intrepid designers would dare build. It's still largely undiscovered despite Queenstown becoming a hugely popular tourist destination. The better-known and much more expensive courses in the area attract most of the attention, but Arrowtown offers up golf like you have never seen anywhere in the world. There are a few ordinary holes, but the rest more than make up for them; many will blow your socks off. With architects Tom Doak and Greg Turner singing its praises, it won't stay undiscovered for long, and you can play almost 20 rounds here for the price of one on the more famous courses nearby.

Paraparaumu Beach – North Island, New Zealand

An hour out of Wellington, Paraparaumu is a proper links, with the beautiful seaside turf and tumbling, hard ground making what the ball does when it hits the ground as important as what it does flying through the air. Alex Russell built some good par threes at Yarra Yarra and Royal Melbourne East, but his second, fifth and 16th here may be his best set. The latter two don't have a bunker and the second does but none of them are in play. For the longest time it was the best course in New Zealand, but the new courses at Tara Iti and Cape Kidnappers have slipped ahead of it on the rankings. No matter, it is still more than worth playing as many times as you can and, like Arrowtown, you won't need a second mortgage to pay for it.

PART 4
CADDIES

'Do you know the rules?' Peter Thomson would ask when looking for a caddie. 'Good, you'll do me.'

The coming of Tiger Woods brought much increased incomes, and not only for the players. Ten per cent of a million-dollar winner's prize is a caddie windfall unimaginable to the bagmen of eras past.

Despite their increased incomes, the demands of the job haven't changed. Arguably they are lessened. Long past are the days of making your own yardage books, 'foxing' balls after the practice round and driving from tournament to tournament in a beaten-up old car filled with men and luggage.

Ultimately it's still a job of calculating the right yardage and offering sensible advice to the question, 'What do you think?' The best caddies answer with assurance and confidence even if they are neither sure nor confident.

Raymond Floyd, the 1976 Masters Champion, paid his man, Steve Williams, the ultimate compliment when he said, 'He's the only caddie I ever had who never choked.'

– Mike Clayton

MASTERS COURSE IN CADDYING

A veteran of 40 years on the circuit, **Steve Williams** has carried the bag for Greg Norman, Tiger Woods and Adam Scott, among others. The most successful caddie in history, with 14 majors to his name, he explains the role of the bagman – which is far more complex than it looks.

I first started caddying in 1976 when my father asked Peter Thomson if I could carry his bag in the New Zealand Open that year. I was 12. Peter paid me $150 for the week, an amount beyond my wildest dreams, and also gave me a bag of balata balls. I was hooked; from that moment on, I wanted to be a caddie.

As soon as I was old enough to leave school – 15 – in late 1978, I decided to work over summer on the Australian and New Zealand golf tours. And that's really how my career started … and didn't stop until the end of 2017, when I told Adam Scott that enough was enough and I felt it was time to do something else.

I've been lucky to caddie for some of the game's greatest players and have a ringside seat at some of the most memorable moments in golf's biggest tournaments. But I've had to work damn hard, stay fit and be diligent about my job, so I feel like I've earned some of that luck.

At the start, caddying was an existence for most of us; it was a great way to be involved in a game we loved, and see the world, while earning some money. We never really thought about making a decent living from the game. That was a luxury reserved for a handful of caddies working for the top players.

Not much was expected of us in those days. As the old cliché goes, we just had to show up, keep up and shut up. We carried the bag, occasionally gave some input – when we were asked for it – and worked out the yardages. A lot of people looked down on us; some called us glorified porters.

The yardage books in the early days were very rudimentary. Sometimes, players would have made a few notes on the back of a scorecard: 'The big tree on the right is 150 yards to the front of the green, and the green's 35 yards long', and that'd be all the information he'd have on that hole.

When I caddied for Peter Thomson, there were a lot of variables when trying to calculate how far each shot would travel. The golf balls weren't all identical, being made to contrasting specifications; some brands would fly different distances to others. Every clubhead was different; shafts had variations in weight and flex. Now, everything has become far more predictable; depending on the conditions, I will know how far my player is hitting each club to within a metre or two. The equipment used these days is so precise, so advanced.

Then there is the professionalism. In my early days, I didn't know how some of those caddies made it around the course given the amount of alcohol they'd consumed the night before. I distinctly remember some of the older players keeping their distance from their caddies because of how badly they stunk of alcohol. That hardly happens these days. Caddies know they have got to do a good job because they're replaceable; there's always someone waiting to take their place if they slip up.

The role of every person on tour has evolved in these past 40 years: players, coaches, managers, trainers – and it's no different with caddies. Now, he or she is an amateur psychologist, an on-course coach, a confidant, and that's just the start of it. The whole dynamic has changed.

If you look at the guys caddying on the PGA Tour now, a lot of them have a very good understanding of the golf swing and ball flight; they can video a player's swing on the range and have the skills to identify things that might be slightly out of kilter. The modern guys really understand the game.

They also have a lot more information at their disposal to help a player. The detail that goes into yardage and green books now is incredible. They're all done by lasers. That level of detail was unthinkable when I was starting, with a bagful of non-matching balls.

* * *

When a player's playing well and everything is going to plan, you basically just try to stay out of their way and keep them on that roll. The very best caddies make a difference when their player's not playing well. That's when you've got to think clearly and find a way to get your player out of the funk he's in. It can be difficult pulling out of that tailspin.

When the player has had a bad stretch of holes, you might say: 'Okay, let's set some small goals – we hit every fairway and every green for the next three holes.' Or: 'Let's see if we can make a couple of birdies over the next six holes.' Just mini goals. That's a good way to distract your man from his triple-bogey and get him to focus his concentration on a target.

At the 2005 Masters, Tiger bogeyed the 17th and 18th holes to finish in a playoff with Chris DiMarco. We were riding down to the 18th tee for the playoff on a golf cart and I could sense Tiger was feeling a bit deflated, so I said to him: 'You're Tiger Woods, you've won eight majors; he's Chris DiMarco and he's won none. He'll be trembling; he'll be nervous. So just show him who's number one.'

That wasn't meant to be disrespectful; Chris is a wonderful player. I just wanted to give Tiger some positive reinforcement and get his head in the right space. As everyone knows, Tiger sank a 15-footer for birdie and victory.

The best caddies are also the ones who aren't afraid to speak their mind. They have the courage of their convictions, even in the tensest moments in the final rounds of tournaments, and are prepared to back their judgement.

I remember caddying for Greg Norman at the Daikyo Palm Meadows Cup in Queensland in 1988. He came to that last hole at Palm Meadows needing just a par five to win the tournament. There was a lot of water well down the right-hand side of the hole, and a huge clump of bamboo as well, so there was danger lurking everywhere.

Greg pulled the driver out. The adrenalin was flowing and all he would have been able to see then was a driver flying down the middle of the fairway. Greg's a pretty strong-willed guy and sometimes hard to convince, but the driver was clearly not the percentage play at that moment. If he'd pushed his shot right, he could have easily taken a bogey or double bogey. He had to go with an iron to take that trouble out of play.

I was standing next to him with the bag, between the tee markers, and I wouldn't move – until he took an iron out of the bag. I stood strong and convinced him there was no way he's going to hit a driver. He took two iron, seven iron, wedge, made his five, and won the tournament by a shot.

That was a big moment for me. That was my first time of being forceful with a player and really asserting myself. It really improved our relationship, because Greg knew he could trust me to make the right call in a pressure situation.

I must give credit here to Greg for teaching me so much about the professional game. He was instrumental in my career. He took the time to really explain everything to me; it was extraordinary. I was a very good player as a junior but I didn't really understand the nuances of the game. I'd just hit the ball without knowing, for example, how to adjust the ball flight, even how to hit a fade.

Greg taught me how to think, how to approach a hole, and the little things about the tour. He treated me like a son. We probably became too close in the end, but I feel an incredible amount of gratitude to him because I'd never have got to where I did without his guidance.

Later, a similar incident happened with Tiger when we won our first major together, his second, the PGA Championship at Medinah in 1999. It was getting tight going down the stretch and Sergio Garcia was making a pretty good run at it, so Tiger had to hole this seven-footer on the 17th to keep his lead. It was a really big moment. He read the putt outside the hole; I read the putt inside the hole. 'Trust me,' I said. 'I remember you had this putt in practice; we put the tee peg down there. It's definitely inside the hole.'

Obviously if I was wrong, it could have cost Tiger the tournament. But he hit it on that line, made the par – and we won our first major together. Again that was the defining moment in our relationship till that point. Tiger knew I wasn't afraid to speak my mind at a big moment.

Again, with Adam Scott when he won the Masters in 2013: at the second playoff hole against Angel Cabrera, the 10th, I knew the putt broke more right-to-left than it looked. I'd had a similar putt with Greg 25 years earlier, and the reason I remembered it is that it's so difficult to get the ball to the back of the 10th green – almost everyone comes up short. So I'd stored away that information. Adam saw it as one cup outside the right; I said, no way, it's at least two cups. 'Trust me, I know this putt.' And so it proved, and Adam was rewarded for 74 holes of magnificent golf with his first major.

I won't pretend, however, that all my decisions have been brilliant; some haven't been. I've had two major regrets in my career – one occurred with Ray Floyd in 1990, the other with Greg in 1989, both at the Masters.

Ray played unbelievably well all that week at Augusta; he just needed to par 17 and 18 and he would have won; he was in complete control of what he was doing.

He drove down the middle of 17, and had 135 yards to the pin – a regulation nine iron. A simple shot given the way he was playing. The last thing he said to me before hitting the shot was, 'Stevie, I'm just going to hit this fifteen feet left of the hole' – because there was a shelf there and the ball would have rolled down quite close to the flag.

I thought, 'That's fine, Ray, if you hit it there; but what if you pull it left? Then you're left with the hardest putt on the course. You'll be very lucky to two-putt.'

If he had have aimed at that flag and missed the green to the right, he's left with one of the easiest chips on the golf course – and Ray was one of the best chippers in the world. But I didn't say anything. It's the only time in a crucial situation that I haven't said what's come into my mind. Of course, Ray tugged his second shot left, hit his first putt 6 feet past, missed the return and made a bogey on 17, then parred the last but ended up in a playoff with Nick Faldo – which he lost.

Ray was absolutely devastated afterwards – as was I – but time heals most things. He and I have laughed about it many times since: 'We'd have two green jackets, Stevie, if you'd spoken up on seventeen,' he says.

The year before, I was at Augusta with Greg. We came to the last hole needing a par to make the playoff with Nick Faldo and Scott Hoch. Greg was playing brilliantly and was six under for the day after 17 holes. On the 18th tee it was cold, dark and raining and Greg asked me what club I thought he should hit. 'Absolutely driver,' I said. 'There's no way you can reach those fairway bunkers on a day like today. You've been hitting the driver well all day.' He disagreed and insisted on hitting a one iron. He hit the shot well but it left him way back in the fairway. He wanted to hit a five iron for his second shot into the green, but I said, 'Greg, there's no way you can get there with a five iron. It's clearly a four iron.'

The flag was front left, as it always is, and I said, 'You can hit your best four iron and you will never carry that slope up to the second tier of the green. It's clearly the right club.'

He kept saying, I can get a five iron there. It's one of the hardest situations in golf when, as caddie, you can't convince your player to hit a certain club, even though you know – you're certain – that you are right. Greg was never going to get there with a five.

Anyway, he hit a five iron about as well as he could, and it landed on the front of the green. Back then he used that Tour Edition ball, which spun an awful lot compared to most balls; the green was soft and the ball just spun back off the front of the green and ran 30 yards down the hill. Greg didn't get it up and down, so we missed the playoff by a shot.

Occasionally, I've watched incidents during tournaments and felt like jumping up and saying, No, stop, this is going to end in disaster.

Like at Carnoustie in 1999, which really stands out as a major caddie malfunction. Jean van de Velde was obviously a really solid European Tour pro; he hadn't won a major, but he now had a chance to win the British Open. In the final round, he got through those really tough holes from 14 through 17 with pars, which was an incredible achievement in itself given how hard they were playing that week. So even a double-bogey six up the last would win.

The walk from the 17th green to the 18th tee at Carnoustie is quite long. He would have been thinking as he walked along that he'd won the tournament. So much would be going through his head.

What the caddie should be saying at that moment is: 'All we've got to do is make a five here and we've won this tournament.' What is the best way to do that – and take out all the trouble? It's pretty simple: five iron, five iron, wedge. But his caddie let Jean hit the driver. A strong caddie would never, ever have let a player take a driver out of the bag in that situation. He hit it way right and ended up on the 17th fairway.

Even then, Jean had a chance to make amends; he could have laid up short of Barry Burn with his second shot, but he chose the wrong option again, trying for the green. He hit some railings on the grandstand, bounced off the burn's stone wall and ending up in knee-deep rough. An experienced caddie would never have allowed Jean to play either of those two shots. It's almost too painful to relate that Jean went from the rough into the water, took a drop, then into the greenside bunker. Triple bogey, playoff – and no major championship to his name.

Then rewind back to Greg losing the Masters in 1996. I was caddying for Ray that week and, funnily enough, in one of our practice rounds, we played with Greg and Tiger – so the group contained my boss, previous boss and future boss.

I'm not saying I could have definitely helped Greg win that tournament, but I would have fancied my chances. I do believe that with a different approach, I may have been able to make a difference that day.

Greg knew if he shot 70 he was going to win the tournament. That would mean Nick Faldo had to shoot 63: a very tall order. But playing conservatively, he came up short on many holes, like the fourth, ninth and 12th, and got himself into trouble. People say he choked but I don't believe in that word. He lost because after three days of playing aggressively he started to go into his shell, trying to protect his lead. It's an easy mistake to make when you're that far in front.

Greg probably won't like the comparison, but I know if Tiger had a six-shot lead, he wanted to make it 10. He never slipped into the trap of playing negative golf.

* * *

Arriving at a tournament on a Monday or Tuesday, every caddie wants to get the best knowledge of the course he can for his player.

One of the first things you want to do is find out where the prevailing wind is. So when you're walking around on your own, measuring the course, you've got to imagine how it's going to look and feel on Thursday when the grandstands are full and there are people milling around the fairways and greens; it really does look different then. You also need to know exactly where your markings are – so even when there are thousands of people around, you know where to take your distances from.

If it's your first time at a venue, it might not be a bad idea to go into the pro shop and ask one of the assistants there about the course and any quirks: do all the putts run towards the water, for example? Same with the greens staff: ask them if there's anything you're missing.

I've always taken notes about courses, and players, and how they've reacted in certain situations, so you get that familiarity. I've got filing cabinets at home full of notes. You're always looking for trends: when players get to certain holes in pressure situations, say it's a dogleg right, what's their tendency then? If you keep writing down trends and tendencies, you'll get a very good feel for what your player's going to do.

Often I could tell before we hit off what sort of day my player was going to have. When you see them practising their putting or full shots, sometimes you get a feeling that this is going to be a good day, or it's going to be a tough day.

They go through their routine on the putting green and will make 99 out of 100 putts inside 4 feet; other days, that number will be right down. Or they're on the range and you can see what target they're firing at but they're not getting anywhere near that target. So a lot of times, when you stepped onto the first tee, you had a pretty good idea of how the next four or five hours was going to pan out.

After you've caddied on tour for a few years, you end up playing many of the same courses over and over again. That's when experience, and all that precious information you've filed away, comes into its own.

* * *

Nowhere is local knowledge and experience more important than at Augusta. It's the caddie's greatest test, because the line between success and failure is so narrow. You hit the wrong club at the wrong time there and it can be very costly, more so than just about anywhere else.

In the caddying world, it's a standing joke that there are more caddies fired after the Masters than any other week (perhaps along with the British Open). It's just a fact.

The three holes that will define your Masters week

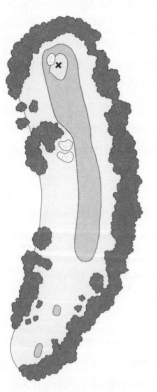

Fifth hole, 455 yards, par four

A sleeper hole that doesn't get the attention it deserves. Invariably, it rates among the hardest five or six holes on the course. A dogleg left, with massively deep bunkers on the corner of the dogleg, you need a drive of 315 yards to carry the trouble. I think the second shot into this green – anything from a five to a nine iron – is one of the most underrated shots on the course, in terms of difficulty and judging the distance. There's a dead elephant buried in the middle of the green; it's one of the most severe surfaces on the course. Basically, you're trying to hit the ball in the middle of the green – regardless of where the flag is. It's such a small landing area (as marked by the cross). The crux of the course to me is at numbers four, five and six. Everyone knows Amen Corner – 11, 12, 13 – is tough, but this is equally as hard; it just doesn't get as much attention. If you can play those three holes in even par for the week, you're likely to have a good score and make up shots on the field because they're three sleepers; they can really undo your round.

12th hole, 155 yards, par three

There's no better short hole, and no greater challenge to get the club right than when you're standing on the tee at 12. You'll see players back off their shots here more than at any other hole. The wind swirls around; that's what makes it so difficult. If this hole was on a normal course it would play under an average of three. When gauging the wind, you've got to remember to look at the flags on top of the big scoreboard behind the ninth green. If they're flying very strongly in one direction, that's a big hint. Also, look at the water in Rae's Creek; the ripples will tell you the way the wind is blowing in that corner of the course. That's always been my guide. Another is the pollen; sometimes early in spring when they haven't had a lot of warm days, there's a lot of pollen coming out of the trees, so you can see which way that is blowing. Sunday's flag is always back right. But unless you really have to make birdie, don't take it on; aim over the middle of the front bunker (as marked by the cross) to give yourself some extra room if you're just short or just long. I pride myself on this hole; I've never really had a disaster here … and generally walked away unscathed.

15th hole, 530 yards, par five

With the second shot into this green, there are only three things that can happen to you: you're either on the green and sitting perfectly; you're short and in the water; or you're over the green and all but dead. That's it. In normal conditions, the drive will travel about 300–330 yards (as marked by the cross on page 192), leaving a player with slightly more than 200 yards to the green. But it's a very shallow target: maybe 20 yards deep on the right, and just 15 on the left. A ball that lands on the green with some height will stay there; anything short rolls back into the creek. Over the green and

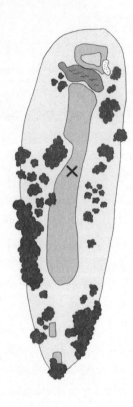

you're chipping off a tight lie to a green that is lightning quick, and runs away from you. So when you're standing in the middle of the 15th fairway and trying to decide what club to hit for that second shot, you really earn your keep as a caddie. It's a very difficult and demanding shot to judge. You're way above the green, the wind can be a factor, and there is simply no bailout area. You have to be so precise: you're either on the green or you're dead. Good luck.

THE CADDIE'S DILEMMA

So Yeon Ryu, one of the leading players on the LPGA Tour, captured her second major title in 2017 after her caddie employed some clever and impromptu amateur psychology over the closing holes, as **Mike Clayton** reveals.

Golfers often wonder what a good caddie does, aside from 'turning up, keeping up and shutting up', as the saying has it.

Tom Watson, an Australian caddie who happens to share a name with the American multiple-major winner, fell into caddying years ago after finishing an apprenticeship to become a pro. He caddied for Brendan Jones in Japan for many years and, since the 2012 Australian Women's Open at Royal Melbourne, for the Korean So Yeon Ryu.

To sum up his job description, he is in effect personal assistant to the one-woman head of a multimillion-dollar-a-year company. The reigning US Open champion when she and Watson first teamed up, Ryu three-putted Royal Melbourne's 72nd green to fall into the six-way tie – and a playoff won eventually on the 74th hole by Jessica Korda. In the ensuing years, Tommy has learned his boss's game, her strengths (hitting greens), her weaknesses (three putting) and her other tendencies ('over-thinking under pressure').

'Many times I knew what sort of round she would play before we started. I could tell by her demeanour when she walked onto the practice fairway and if she was in a funny mood it was hard to snap her out of it,' he told me. 'On those days, I knew I would have to have to do my "psychology best" to get her around in a decent score.'

So Yeon has finished in the top 10 in just over half of their 150-odd LPGA events together, suggesting they have been an uncommonly successful partnership. But it hasn't always been smooth sailing. And it was at the first major of the 2017 season when Watson demonstrated the importance of a clever, switched-on caddie, who totally his understood his boss's idiosyncrasies, during a dramatic final round.

The tournament leader, American Lexi Thompson, walked off the 12th green at the ANA Championship to be told by rules officials she had been docked with a four-shot penalty: two for failing to play her ball from where it originally lay on the 17th green the previous evening, and two more for the subsequent signing of an incorrect scorecard. It was an extraordinary intervention that rocked Thompson, her caddie and legion of fans.

Unsurprisingly the American crowd had their favourite and the nuance of the rule was unimportant to the most partisan of them. As far as they were concerned, some rules geek in his basement poring over videotapes had rung in to dob in their girl and it just wasn't right. Except it was. 'Play the ball as it lies' – it's the most basic of all the rules in a game that can't work any other way.

While this drama was unfolding, So Yeon was playing the 15th hole (the 69th of the week) and after hitting her second shot onto the green, a television cameraman told Tom of Thompson's penalty. So Yeon didn't hear exactly what he said and Tom told her only that Lexi had been given a slow-play warning. 'I knew she would instantly panic if she knew she was tied for the lead,' he explained.

One hole later, a rules official confirmed the penalty but Tom again fudged the truth. 'It's not certain yet,' he told So Yeon. 'They are going to review it after the round so assume you are still behind. You still have to play.'

Not until So Yeon reached the 18th hole did she see a leaderboard, which showed her tied for the lead. By then she only needed to birdie the par-five finisher – a typical, made-for-television, water-infested American resort-course hole made for sports fans looking for the same thing they see at one of those circular car racing tracks where all the drivers do is turn left: a wreck.

With the tee moved well forward, the green was easily within reach, and four was really a par. (At least with the tee forward, the hole is more interesting than when it's back and essentially plays as a 100-yard par three with two boring, almost pointless, shots to begin.)

So Yeon easily carried the pond with a long second, pitched to 6 feet, almost the exact distance she had missed from all those years ago in Melbourne, holed it and waited for Thompson to finish. The American followed her in for a birdie and off they headed to the 73rd hole to decide the winner.

So Yeon ended up making another nasty, sliding, left-to-right six-footer for a birdie on the first extra hole to win her second major championship. It was evidence – writ large – of a quick-thinking, understanding caddie knowing his boss and reading the play three or four holes ahead.

Ironically on the same hole the previous year, the 54th of the tournament, Tommy had taken a measurement from the wrong sprinkler head and So Yeon's perfect lay-up with a six iron splashed into the middle of the pond. Annoying, and not a mistake you'd want to make too often, but he did at least make up for it – and how – 12 months later.

MEMORY LANE

Caddies at the professional level require the golfing brain of Tiger Woods, a PhD in psychology, the hide of a rhinoceros, the motivational powers of Winston Churchill – and a robust constitution. **Charles Happell** spoke with Australian broadcaster Tim Lane who gave it a shot one year ... with mixed results.

Tim Lane, the respected Australian sportscaster, found himself immersed in the bizarre, byzantine world of golf caddying when he took four months' leave from the ABC in the winter of 1988. The corporation had just lost the right to broadcast Australian Rules football, so Lane found himself at a loose end.

While working for the national broadcaster over previous summers, Lane had got to know Vaughan Somers, a charismatic if somewhat combustible Queensland pro whose name was occasionally seen on leaderboards at Australian tournaments. A chance meeting with Somers at the Formula One grand prix in Adelaide late in 1987, a couple of follow-up phone calls, and Lane found himself recruited as Somers' caddie on the European Tour. It was to prove an instructive lesson in human behaviour, relationships, pressure and patience. It also taught Lane there are a thousand easier ways to earn a buck.

One of the first things that struck Lane about his new profession was the disdain in which it was held by so many people in the golf industry. It's true that caddies were, on the whole, a fairly motley, hard-drinking, hard-living crew. There was a time on the European Tour when they would sleep under hedgerows, shuffling on to the first tee the following morning looking, and smelling, like something out of *Steptoe and Son*. Occasionally, they would sleep in their cars and shower in the clubhouse. These days, though, they are more likely to be found in three- or four-star hotels and driving fancy cars, such is the prizemoney sloshing around on the professional tours, of which they can expect around 10 per cent in wages.

Lane recalls in the weeks leading up to his departure for Europe how Australia's leading golf writer at the time, the late Don Lawrence, ticked him off for bringing journalism into disrepute – such was the reputation of the humble bagman at that time. Not long afterwards, that hardline view was reinforced when David Begg, the media liaison officer at the British PGA at Wentworth, barred Lane from entering the media centre to phone through a radio report. Although papers were produced to show Lane's credentials, Begg simply refused to allow a caddie access to the media area.

So this is the world Lane entered. For four months, the Tasmanian lived the peripatetic life of the caddie: one week in England, the next in southern France, the third in the Swiss Alps. Some of his colleagues were experienced and skilled, others were simply looking for work in an environment they enjoyed. Some were career caddies or budding professional players, others were just passing through. Some wanted to make money, others simply wanted to see the world – or run away from it.

All, though, experienced intense one-on-one relationships with bosses who were operating under considerable pressure. As Lane noted, it's a job in which you feel as though every word you utter, every move you make, might affect the performance of the person you're there to help.

Lane's experience was due to begin at Mougins, above Cannes on the French Riviera, in mid April. Somers was late arriving in Europe, though, so employment was arranged with an English player, Neal Briggs, who missed the cut.

There were quite a few caddies and players from the Antipodes, and Lane quickly got to know them. After three tournaments, there was a week's break. Lane and two other new friends drove along Portugal's Algarve, then up the west coast to Lisbon, before taking a train to Santander in northern Spain to meet Somers for the next event.

Never a big hitter, Somers was battling to keep up with the rising generation of the time and the stress was getting to him. This, coupled with a personality that was both excitable and loveable, but given to self-punishing lows, made for a roller-coaster ride. A cycle of emotional boom and bust would repeat, often a couple of times an hour.

Lane kept a diary of the time and recently went back to his account of the second round of the Spanish Open, played at Pedreña (home course of the late Seve Ballesteros). Having shot 71 on the opening day, Vaughan was solidly placed to make the cut. But, as Lane drily noted, Fridays were inevitably stressful.

Here's an excerpt:

Drops his third shot at five when he three putts from 12 feet. Totally lost concentration with second putt and missed from 18 inches. Typically, he birdies seven and eight to get back to plus-2 overall but then he hooks his drive at par-five ninth: into a tree and it stays up there. Lost ball – double bogey! It happened after long delay [on the tee] and joke-telling session. He's got steam coming out his ears by the 12th – has virtually given it away – and hits a hole-in-one! Four iron at 153-metre El Corto ... crowd roars while ball disappears into hole!

What Lane didn't record was that Vaughan was so angry even his ace failed to bring a smile. Subsequently, and in keeping with his fortunes, he birdied the 14th but bogeyed the par-five 16th to miss the cut by one. There, writ large, is the caddie's turbulent existence.

A month or two later, with Lane still toting his bag, Somers tried to qualify for the British Open at St Anne's Old Links, via a 36-hole strokeplay tournament. After a good opening round, Somers smacked his opening drive on day two straight down the middle, while his playing partner, a club pro, hacked his drive into the heather. (The third member of their group had withdrawn with a bad back after the first round.) Full of the joy of life, Somers bounded down the fairway, all but whistling and clicking his heels.

Lane did not want to dampen his man's spirits but – after much thought and knowing his job description involved the role of amateur psychologist – decided to counsel caution, quoting Kipling's famous poem 'If' to his boss: 'If you can keep your head, when all about you are losing theirs ...'

Lane quickly realised that he should have let well enough alone. The advice seemed to deflate Somers. Soon enough, of course, the twin impostors of triumph and disaster were to collide spectacularly. Somers three-putted for his second straight bogey early in the round and, hellfire in his eyes, stormed off the green, hurling his putter at the broadcaster's feet. 'Got any more fucking advice, Rudyard?' Somers spat. Tim never did get to caddie in a British Open.

These days, Lane still looks out during golf telecasts for familiar faces on the players' bags – and was delighted a few years ago to see New Zealander Mike Waite, with whom he had forged a good friendship in 1988, wearing the caddie's bib for Michael Campbell when the fellow Kiwi won the US Open.

As for Somers, he is now general manager at the Melbourne Golf Academy and head professional of Capital Golf Club, jobs that provide him with a steady income while playing golf – something he could only have dreamed of 30 years ago.

And Lane himself? While delighted to have had that experience of being in the cauldron, at the coalface, of professional sport, the veteran broadcaster is even happier now to be plying his trade from the air-conditioned comfort of the commentary box where he knows what he's doing.

SU OH GOES TO RIO

Mike Clayton charts his on-course relationship with child prodigy Su Oh, tracking her winding path – with two important lessons – to the 2016 Rio Olympics when golf made its return to the summer Games.

Su Oh was something out of the ordinary at the 2008 Australian Women's Open. Born in Korea, the 12-year-old had only been playing for four years and the local newspapers that week made something of the curiosity of a child playing among women at Metropolitan Golf Club in Melbourne. Along with many others, I determined to watch a few holes to see how she played. Hardly surprisingly for someone in her first big tournament, she began with 79 and from there making the cut would have been some achievement.

Our design company had recently redesigned the par-three 13th at Metropolitan and Su came to the largely unloved hole needing to play her final six holes around par to make the cut. A pretty decent shot flew long but taking three chips to scramble her way back up the steep bank behind the green finished off any hope of playing the weekend. Our relationship wasn't off to a particularly good start and we didn't even know each other. Strike one.

I'd occasionally see Su's name in the golf magazines as she seemed to win all the local girls' tournaments, and a few years later she was in Hobart playing for Victoria and in the final of interstate matches, up against Western Australia's number one player, Minjee Lee.

I was in Hobart looking at some land for a golf course when a friend asked me if I could caddie for Su in the final. She asked Su, who replied, 'He's way too scary.' Instead, I carried the clubs for Julienne Soo, Victoria's number two player. Strike two.

Eventually we met at the golf club and started playing together, her after school and me after work or on the weekend. Then one night she called, explaining there was a problem with her caddie for the upcoming Australian Open at Victoria. 'What should I do?'

'Why don't I do it?' I suggested.

'Can I call you back?'

Presumably she asked her dad and a few minutes later she called back. 'Do you mind?'

'If I minded I wouldn't have offered.' I'd started golf as a caddie, always enjoyed it and it was a way back into top-line competition without having to play.

Su made the cut with some very solid play on Friday's back nine, and on Saturday she shot the easiest 17-year-old 66 imaginable. One good shot followed another; she made a few putts and eagled the 18th.

I remember a seven or eight iron up the hill to the sixth green. The television tower right behind the green (golf pros spend their lives aiming shots at television towers behind greens) had a 'MELBOURNE' sign on it, and I thought the U was a sensibly safe aiming point.

'I think I can go for the O,' she said.

'Okay, fine – let's not argue about it.'

Sunday was windy, difficult and not the sort of day you hope for if you are nervous and inexperienced. Su birdied the short par four to begin and was tied with Karrie Webb playing in the group behind. Karrie, too, birdied it and eventually signed for a beautiful 68 to win easily as the others all fell away. Su had 78, despite another eagle at the last. Years earlier, in the 1981 Australian Open at Victoria, I'd been in a similar position on Sunday and shot 76 – it isn't much fun. Still, she was clearly a player.

We did a few more tournaments together: her first major a couple of months later in Palm Springs, California; her first tournament as a pro, the 2015 Victorian Open; and then at Turnberry for her first British Open.

In January 2016, Su played again with Karrie Webb, this time in the opening two rounds of the Victorian Open. The eighth hole, our 17th of the day, is a difficult hole into the wind. Karrie hit a short, high hook off the tee and a weak block with a hybrid way short and right of the green. Su, in contrast, hit a great drive far down the right side by the water and flew a beautiful iron in close to the flag.

I said to her after that shot, 'You can make that team in Rio this year. Karrie isn't the player she was and you're getting better.'

Su spent a couple of weeks in early January 2016 beating balls at St Andrews Beach in Victoria and working on her swing, in preparation for the Australian Open at The Grange in Adelaide. A couple of months earlier she'd seen a teacher who had suggested she wasn't good enough to play the LPGA Tour and she'd need to employ the latest and greatest theory. On the practice fairway at St Andrews Beach we looked at a few pictures of her new backswing and she asked me what I thought. Su's swing did need a lot of work but the mentality of players thinking they won't play good golf until the swing is flawless has ruined many. I'm no golf teacher, but I told her: 'What you are trying to do isn't any good and it's never going to work.'

Potentially strike three, but she listened a bit and we worked on a couple of little things. A 14th placing, and $25,000, followed at the Australian Open.

Yet the only way into tournaments was to play the two-spot qualifiers on Monday. We tried one in Phoenix, Arizona, and missed by a shot.

On the way to the airport we dropped in at Geoff Ogilvy's place for dinner. Su had two sets of clubs with her in Phoenix: the set she had used in Adelaide and an old set I thought were better suited to her game. The Adelaide set were game improvers: big heads offset with strong lofts and with no consistency of distance. She asked Geoff what he thought of them. He gave a couple of clubs the knowing golfer's waggle, looked her dead in the eye and said: 'These are really good clubs ... if you're a bad player.' Su's sister uses them now.

From Phoenix we flew to Dallas to see Cameron McCormick, the Australian teacher who'd grown up, as I had, playing at Eastern Golf Club in Melbourne but was better known as Jordan Spieth's long-time teacher. Ogilvy had described Spieth as 'the best-coached player on tour', and that was a good enough recommendation for me.

Cameron watched Su hit for 15 minutes, suggested she turn her shoulders a bit more and then headed to the chipping green where he set up a simple chipping drill. The task was to land six shots in different spots and have them run out and finish within 5 feet of the flag. 'How many shots do you think it will take you?' asked McCormick.

'Thirteen or fourteen.'

'That'd be world class.'

Twenty-three shots later, she finished.

'Jordan can do that in ten or eleven every single time. Get close to that and you will easily compete on the LPGA. Do it every day until you can.'

It was a brilliant lesson, exactly the one she needed, just as Ogilvy's comment about the clubs was something thing she needed to hear. Coming from me, or her father, is one thing. Coming from a US Open champion and a US Open champion's teacher was another.

We went back to San Diego, where Su failed to qualify. Then Hawaii, where she finished 40th. Su went on to San Francisco, finishing 19th in a strong field. She was away. A few weeks later, after second placing in the Kingsmill Championship, care of a 30-foot putt on the final green, a spot on Australia's Olympic team had become a real possibility.

The LPGA Championship was at Sahalee in Washington, a few weeks after Kingsmill, and Su finished eighth, the first decent finish she'd had in a major championship. Amazingly, she had jumped past Karrie in the world rankings; she was now the second-ranked Australian behind Lee.

And that is where she stayed until the Olympic team was finalised at the US Open. As devastating as it must have been for Karrie to miss out, she handled it with more class and grace than anyone could reasonably expect. Su, meanwhile, felt terrible for knocking her idol out of the team. Karrie had helped her for years, playing practice rounds together and hosting her at the 2014 US Open as a winner of one of her scholarships. They played together in a team event in Chicago a month before the Olympics and Karrie couldn't have been more encouraging, especially during the opening fourball when Su played some bad golf, when she'd have been well justified in thinking, 'How is she going to Rio and I'm not?'

And so to Rio, something Su's family could never in their wildest dreams have imagined possible when they arrived in Melbourne in 2004 with eight-year-old Su – who'd never hit a golf ball.

* * *

The golf in Rio 2016 was the first time golf featured in the Olympics since St Louis 1904, and it worked. The crowds were much bigger than I expected, given the fact almost no-one plays golf in Brazil – people watch Olympic sport no matter what it is – and the course was terrific.

American Gil Hanse won the commission to build the course based on his vision of replicating both the look and the play of golf in Melbourne. The golf Gil was trying to encourage was very familiar to Su and I, and he walked our first practice round, something I'm sure drove Su to distraction as we discussed the nuances of the course.

The fairways were wide but you had to play to the advantageous sides to earn the better angles and the shots around the greens – the chips, pitches and bunker shots – replicated those from home. Gil and his partner Jim Wagner, who built the brutal par-three fourth hole himself, had never seen the old 15th at Huntingdale, but Rio's fourth was almost an exact replica, except it was even more severe. The green was orientated from left to right, making the fade a perfect shot. The right bunkers were cut diagonally up into the green so any shot to the right had to be properly struck or it wouldn't carry the sand. With the short edge on the left the overplayed draw, or just a rank pull, was going to hit the left edge and career off the steep back, leaving a brutal shot back up to the green.

One of the architect's tasks is to ask uncomfortable questions and to expose a player's weaknesses as well as displaying their strengths – and Su has always struggled to fade the ball. In that first practice round, and without having to say anything to each other, we knew it had the potential to be a problem.

The first competition round started well. The fairway bunker at the par-five opener was 246 yards to reach, but it was into the wind.

'Can I reach the bunker with a driver?' she asked.

'No.'

She did push it a bit, but it was never going anywhere else but the bunker.

The first shot ever hit by an Australian woman in the Olympic Games, I give her the wrong club and she makes a bogey. You might call that strike three.

A birdie at the third helped, and then Gil and Jim did their job at the fourth. The pin was four paces from the left edge, and the correct shot was to ignore it and play safely right.

The six iron started left of the middle, drew a little too much, hit the back corner of the green and viciously kicked down the slope into the sandy wasteland at the bottom of the hill. Double bogey.

In the end, an even-par 71 was a good score. A 72 the next day was decent enough and six birdies on the front nine on Saturday led to a 66.

Sunday was windy and when we got to the 13th, Su had made three birdies and there was an outside chance of a bronze medal, but it meant parring the three difficult holes and then making birdies at the final three holes, which Gil had deliberately designed to make the three-birdie finish possible.

The unforgivable caddie crime is letting a player hit the wrong shot and the wrong club; one or the other is excusable, but the combination of the two is deadly. From the middle of the par-four 13th fairway, we had 159 yards to the front of the green and 184 to the flag, the wind blowing and long was dead. A running, chipped hybrid was going to be fine as was a hammered five iron landing short and bouncing up 25 feet short. Either way, don't go long.

We went with the hybrid but she flushed it with a draw into the back bunker and, as is often the case in a tournament, you get asked the most uncomfortable question at the worst time. The ball was on the downslope at the back of the bunker in an awful spot, and she made six. In the end, Su's 70 was a decent score, as was 13th place, but, as with most weeks, everyone but the winner has a story of what might have been.

By the end of the season, one she began terribly and with little hope, she was in the top 50 on the moneylist and had at least proved her game was good enough to compete at the highest level.

She continues to refine the swing with Cameron; surprisingly for one good enough to play the Australian Open at 12, Su is a slow, methodical learner, comfortable going at her own pace. There is always some uncertainty in predicting golfers' futures, but there are three things I can guarantee: Su won't beat herself, she won't ever give up, and she won't fail for want of hard work.

PART 5
AND ANOTHER THING

There is a close relationship between the strategies of golf and tennis. In tennis, to win against a proper player you have to hit the ball close to the extremities of both the service box and the court. On the best strategic courses you have to hit the ball close to the edges of the fairways to open up the best lines into the greens. You're rewarded for the skill of hitting the exact shot – but one inch or one foot too long and it's either a point lost or a near automatic bogey. There is no shame in chickening out, but you are less likely to win the point or to make a birdie. On average courses, devoid of much interest or strategy, you just hit the ball down the middle and avoid the trouble down the sides. The equivalent would be a tennis court 3 metres wide, one simply testing who hit the ball straighter.

– Mike Clayton

THE EVOLUTION OF THE BALL

Mike Clayton charts the advances in golf equipment, which he says have had a devastating impact on the classic courses of the world, making many of them obsolete.

There is no limit to science.

– Alister MacKenzie, 1933

In the beginning, golfers used the most rudimentary pieces of equipment, and it was a properly difficult game as they experimented with grips and swings to see what worked and what didn't. It wasn't as though the first players adopted the Vardon grip and went from there. Nor have players lost any enthusiasm for experimenting with swings as they try to find the elusive secret to improve their game.

Shafts were made of wood and so difficult was it to attach the heads to the shafts that the necks of the clubs were thick and heavy, moving the sweet spot closer to the neck of the irons – and a sweet spot close to the neck isn't good.

The early balls were hand-stitched leather with feathers inside and you can imagine how well they flew. Players soon noticed that the balls improved as they got older and scuffed a little. Aerodynamics 101.

The courses weren't as long as they are now, but the balance between course and equipment was clearly in favour of the course. Shooting in the high 70s was a worthwhile achievement for the best players, and it took 40 years for someone to do better than even 75s in winning an Open Championship. Perhaps the R&A took umbrage at Jack White's 1904 routing of Sandwich in 296 strokes because, a year later, James Braid won with a score only two shots under even 80s.

Not until the 1920s – the years of Jones, Sarazen and Hagen – did the Open scores come in under 300 and by the early 1930s the new stars – Byron Nelson, Sam Snead, Ralph Guldahl, Ben Hogan – were enjoying the benefits of much improved golf balls, Gene Sarazen's sand iron and steel shafts. The balance of power moved toward the equipment, but not so far that it wasn't a fair fight. Bobby Jones was the first to break 290, in 1927, and it took 23 more years for someone, Bobby Locke, to break 280.

Jack Nicklaus was a huge man, an athlete with a great and powerful swing who dominated his era. It was Bobby Jones who watched as Nicklaus took Augusta apart in 1965, saying famously, 'Nicklaus played a game with which I am not familiar.' One could argue even back then the balance was tipping slightly in favour of players over courses. Nicklaus regularly reached par fives in two and wedged onto par fours, but it was still a reasonable contest. No-one was suggesting limiting the flight of the ball (although MacKenzie had warned of it in the very early 1930s) to bring the middle irons back into the game or to have the classic courses play somewhat closer to the way their original designers envisaged them.

The change really started in 1979 when Gary Adams set up a factory making metal woods. Within a couple of years TaylorMade was an increasing presence on the tour and, as a result, in amateurs' bags. They weren't any easier to hit, or any better, than persimmon drivers, and they suited some players more than others, but the balance was tilting further towards the equipment.

Ely Callaway began his company and made a driver with a bigger head than TaylorMade's. Then came another model with a bigger head still, which was followed by the biggest of them all, The Greatest Big Bertha. When it came out, it looked so utterly ridiculous no-one could believe it. Now it looks utterly ridiculous because it's so much smaller than the frying-pan heads that pass for drivers now.

But the biggest change was in the smallest object – the ball.

In the 1970s there were two sorts of balls: the balata balls, which good players used, and 'rocks', principally Acushnet's Pinnacle and the Spalding Top Flite. The problem was that balata balls cut easily. If you weren't paying for them, that wasn't a problem. But one bladed wedge or bunker shot and they were done because the edge of the wedge went straight through the cover.

The rocks were great balls for average players because they could withstand a huge amount of leading-edge wedge abuse and they travelled further, especially into the wind. You just didn't want to be going downwind with one into holes such as the 15th at Kingston Heath, because it wasn't going to stop.

The Top Flite came out about the same time Neil Armstrong walked on the moon – and if man could calculate how to get a man to the moon and back, it surely wasn't too hard to make a golf ball that would spin but wouldn't cut. Spalding produced one in the mid 1980s, the Tour Edition, and Greg Norman won the British Open with it, but it was a high-spinning ball and, in comparison to the best balls of today, very rudimentary.

A month later, at the US PGA Championship, Norman viciously spun a wedge off the 72nd green at Inverness and five minutes later Bob Tway holed a bunker shot to beat him. Perhaps a Titleist would have stayed on the green? We will never know, but the Tour Edition was like the original TaylorMade drivers: it was a window into the future. There was no way you would use it unless Spalding were paying, and almost a decade elapsed before the game would have a great ball that would spin but not be easily cut.

Titleist's Pro V1 in the early 2000s was that ball. Combined with massive drivers with long and ultra-light graphite shafts, it transformed the game at the top level and utterly distorted the balance between the equipment and the course.

In 2016, Henrik Stenson lowered The Open record when he shot 264 at Troon, an unthinkable 20 under par on a difficult golf course.

You can argue that modern players are better athletes, and that they have better swings, and that fairways are cut shorter, and anything else you can think of, to make sense of how far the ball goes, but give Dustin Johnson a persimmon driver and a 384 Titleist (circa 1984 and a great ball) and he isn't driving it 315 yards. Maybe he would be longer than Nicklaus or Norman or Ballesteros, but not 30 to 40 yards longer.

Few more important issues face the modern game than the insidious creep of distance and the subsequent ruination of the original intent of the great old architects who left us the game's great treasures.

In 2017, the first time Dustin Johnson hit a six iron into a par-four green was in Boston in October. Consider that for one moment: for almost ten months, Johnson needed no more than a seven iron into any par four he played. By way of contrast, Arnold Palmer, a pretty good athlete himself, played the opening round of the 1969 US Open at Champions GC (7200 yards) in Houston and hit nine shots with clubs between a two iron and a five iron into the dozen par fours. (For that matter, Deane Beman, who ended second that week, went with fairway woods into the par fours eight times.)

To have Johnson play the sort of golf Palmer was playing, the course would need to be something beyond 9000 yards, a number clearly both insane and unsustainable.

Ultimately the best players were nearly always the most powerful but there was always room for the clever shorter hitter who showed off uncommon skills elsewhere. Hale Irwin and

Corey Pavin were masters of the fairway woods. Gary Player was the genius in the sand. Bob Charles almost never missed from 6 feet. Graham Marsh drove it like an arrow, Lanny Wadkins did the same with the irons, and Peter Thomson possessed one of the great minds to play the game.

Setting the rules is the province of the United States Golf Association and the Royal & Ancient. While they have occasionally talked a good game, they have yet to initiate anything worthwhile with regards to modern equipment. The game got away from them with the combination of the Pro V1, the frying-pan head driver and the lightweight graphite shaft.

They can perhaps be forgiven for allowing the Pro V1, but how they failed to regulate the maximum size of a driver head is unfathomable. Instead they wasted their effort arguing with Karsten Solheim over an infinitesimal amount of space between grooves on his Ping irons.

Larry Summers, an advisor to Barack Obama, once gave some advice to Senator Elizabeth Warren. Ms Warren wrote that after they had dinner together, 'Larry leaned back in his chair and offered me some advice. I had a choice. I could be an insider or I could be an outsider. Outsiders can say whatever they want. But people on the inside don't listen to them. Insiders, however, get lots of access and a chance to push their ideas. People – powerful people – listen to what they have to say. But insiders also understand one unbreakable rule: They don't criticise other insiders.'

Here is the problem with the ball debate. The insiders are the current players – and they won't criticise other insiders, such as ball or club manufacturers, because they are 'owned' by them. The outsiders are former players, such as Jack Nicklaus and Peter Thomson – but no-one is listening to them.

And we end up with the nonsense spouted by 2014 Fed-Ex Cup champion Billy Horschel, whose argument against bifurcation – one ball for pros and another for club players – is that it would reduce 'manufacturers' revenue and mean less money for sponsorship of players'. If ever you thought the players' opinions should be considered, Horschel's reasoning might dissuade you of that notion.

Some argue it doesn't matter how the best courses play for the small percentage of players who drive architecture-distorting distances, but not so. Australia's best courses were not only designed for member play, they were also designed to test first-class play in state and national championships. One of Australia's problems is the best courses are landlocked suburban layouts already stretched to within an inch of their lives in an attempt to remain relevant for championship play. Already almost all of the best long par fours in the country have become drives and short irons (unless defended by a big wind).

But Australia doesn't get a say – the R&A and the USGA make the rules. We just sit here at the bottom of the world watching as Jon Rahm, in the 2016 World Cup, drives to the top of the hill on Kingston Heath's 'blind' 17th hole, rendering it no longer blind because he's driven so far he can see the green 60 yards away – on a hole designed as a par five.

The game has always evolved, but in this era of unimagined scientific advancement it's time we thought about the courses – the most important things in the game – and defended them against the ravages of advancement in ball and club. The pendulum has swung too far. It is time for the authorities to do their job and defend both the skill it takes to play the game and the integrity of the courses.

DO NOT THINK. EVER.

For amateur player **Rob Sitch**, on a mission to get some respectability into his golf, the secret one day hit him like a bolt of lightning: it wasn't about the titanium drivers or 'turbulator' technology he was using, it was all about the 6 inches between his ears.

Nearly every really smart thing I've ever heard about golf has been a piece of psychology. We're all afraid to admit it, but in a game that has undergone more technical innovation than any sport I can think of, psychology is still more important than equipment.

Years ago, driven by the realisation that 25 is not a handicap, it's a participation ribbon, I resolved to improve. I'd be methodical. Every part of my game needed attention, so I'd start with putting. I bought a book. That made sense at the time. It was so thick it should have been broken into A-K and L-Z.

I then asked my pro for a putting lesson. 'Absolutely,' he said and strode to the practice green. I could sense he had a lot to teach. This was great. I could work my way through that putting encyclopaedia in between lessons.

He started at the very beginning, the grip. He made a small but deliberate adjustment. I really should have a pen, I chided myself. I took my stance. He suggested that I position my eyes directly over the ball. Hmmm, I thought, he's clearly jumped to chapter two. Ease up buddy.

Then, after choosing a target line, he suggested I look at the target one last time and hit the putt. It was feeling very chapter 11, or even later.

This 'grip, stance, target' combo, he suggested, was the way to approach every putt. Then he said what I've come to believe is the single smartest thing I've ever heard on a golf course: 'Now, I don't want you to have another mechanical thought while putting ... [*deliberate pause*] ... for the rest of your life.' He allowed that to sink in and turned towards the practice fairway. 'Let's go work on the hard stuff.'

I still have the putting book. In fact I have two after a family member mistimed their birthday gift. Both are in pristine condition. I'm happy to send you one.

The pro and I did work on some hard stuff. There's a lot of hard stuff in golf. Really, really, really hard stuff. Most golf holes begin with what must be the single most difficult-to-master athletic movement in sport: the drive. Oh my lord, it's hard to get right. Swinging back a club head at the end of a metre-long graphite shaft on a precise plane and delivering the clubface to within a millimetre at 200 kilometres per hour at an exact angle of attack in order to launch a small white ball nearly 400 yards with a one-degree tolerance ... on a repeating basis ... on live television ... with a million dollars on the line ... while wearing pink check pants? That's the hardest action in sport.

Sadly for a professional golfer, that's usually followed a couple of shots later by a 4-foot putt, the simplest action in sport. Kids can putt, complete novices can putt, 60-year-old blokes that look like they've come from a darts competition can putt. Trust me, if you've never played golf in your life, you can putt. So for a touring pro there is simply no excuse to miss. They stand on the 18th green knowing that not a single person in the gallery could have matched their drive, but even the lady on the mobility scooter could make this three-footer. So why would every pro in history admit that at times they can barely keep the 'flat stick' from shaking?

The reason is simple. It's our thinking. It's why golf has been investigating the role of psychology and using its insights for decades. It's arguably why the most sought-after coach in the game is not a swing guru but a psychologist.

As players walk out for the Wimbledon final they pass under an inscribed arch. It bears a quote from Kipling: 'If you can meet with triumph and disaster and treat those two impostors just the same ...' Every golf locker room should have something similar with a quote from Dr Bob Rotella, the famous sports shrink: 'You cannot hit a golf ball consistently well if you think about the mechanics of your swing as you play.'

It's true. We all know it's true. Happy Gilmore knew it was true. In order to get good at golf you have to think about swing mechanics nearly every second of your practice time and in order to play golf well you need to forget you've ever heard the word 'pivot' or 'plane' or 'transition' or 'lag' or, more recently, 'TrackMan'.

In a previous life, I was required (forced) to study neuroanatomy and neurophysiology. This placed me in the rare position where, when I played like crap, I could often explain the neuroscience behind playing like crap. It was an enormous comfort. I would often reflect as I searched for a wayward drive how much neuroscience backed up the doctor's quote. According to the great Dr Rotella, a single swing thought is allowed, but only one. Frequently, as my tee shot would veer towards what aviation maps call a 'designated remote area', I would remind myself that 'Check stance, alignment and grip ... now, one piece takeaway, full shoulder turn, flatten the plane, left hip first, allow the arms to fall, keep your spine angle and turn through the ball, then finish balanced on your left side' is not a single thought. It's a monologue. In neuroscience terms, it has an inhibiting effect on cerebellar coordination.

My tip is, don't study neuroscience, just trust the quote. The golf course is not the place for mechanical thoughts.

I've likened a swing change to puppy training: You tell it to sit; it doesn't. You say it again, then you force it to sit. After which it stands. Repeat 100 times a day and permanent progress will emerge in a year or so. The good news is your brain does learn to sit. Even shake hands and fetch. Eventually, though, you have to go back to playing the game. That means feel and trust and target and scoring and competing. And not yelling at yourself!

The first week I got to single figures coincided with the club championship. I went from being in the B group, under the semi-official title 'Bandit', to the A group, where I had a similar status to the Test cricket title 'Substitute fielder'.

I knew a few blokes in this division. I'd congratulated one of them on breaking the course record a couple of weeks prior. Eight under off the black tees felt like a shot across my bow. 'Challenge accepted, my good man!'

Intimidated, I headed to the first early. I didn't know where the black tee was and asked the starter for directions. I confessed my nerves. He then passed on one of the cleverest pieces of psychology I've ever heard. 'Really?' he said with encouraging dismissiveness. 'I always thought club championships were the easiest comp of the year. Nerves take out half the field.' Half the field! He's right. He's bloody well right.

If you've never played competitive golf you may not realise how clever that is, but it's genius. I've since heard Jack Nicklaus say something similar about the majors.

Armed with that knowledge, my whole psyche changed. Not my swing, my psyche. I was only playing half the field.

I couldn't wait to tee off. I would play conservatively, back off with the driver, bail out when necessary and putt from just off the green – even from another fairway if I could get away with it. It worked a treat. Nobody noticed me. I didn't notice me.

I wasn't even thinking about my score as I took the honour again on the seventh and teed up my ball. As I stepped back to pick a target, the delightful low handicapper who was marking my card exclaimed, 'Bloody hell, I reckon you'd be leading the tournament right now.' I never saw that ball again. Or the one that followed it.

Within two hours I'd had nearly the smartest and the dumbest thing ever said to me in the same round. One was designed to relax and the other to resurrect every swing thought I'd ever had.

Being a 36-hole stroke event, played on two courses, I reluctantly fronted up the next day if only to experience more back tees I never knew existed. My playing partner, a future club champion, was off scratch. He didn't start well and for some reason that relaxed me. Hearing the word 'provisional' coming out of a partner's mouth rather than your own has a calming effect.

On this occasion the vibe never left. I didn't even think about golf. I was only vaguely aware well into the round that I'd hardly dropped a shot. A fact noted by my marker on the 15th tee: 'I tell you what, not many break 80 off the blacks on this course.'

I was ready for it this time. 'Do not think about swing thoughts ... Do not think about swing thoughts ...' That ball was never seen again. Nor its twin brother. (Spoiler alert: I didn't break 80.)

It wasn't his fault. I'd been in the 'zone', but my 'zone' wasn't really *the* zone', more a large, ill-defined postcode, open to all sorts of unproductive thoughts such as 'I better not hit it onto the front lawn of that house over there'. Again, that's not golf, that's psychology. (Spoiler alert: it didn't go onto his front lawn, it went into his pool.)

If you've never read a Bob Rotella book, I highly recommend them. They're full of great stories. My favourite concerns a dinner he had on the eve of the final round of the Masters in 1992. Fred Couples, not one of his clients, was intrigued. He asked Rotella what he thought of his mental game.

'It looks pretty solid to me,' the psychologist responded. 'What do you do?'

'Well, you know, when I come up to a shot, I just pull up my sleeves and shrug my shoulders to try and get them relaxed ... And then I try to remember the best shot I ever hit in my life with the club I have in my hand. Is that okay?'

'I think that will do just fine, Freddy,' the psychologist responded, 'just fine.'

(Final spoiler alert: Couples won.)

If you think like Freddy, then forget you ever read this piece. However, if you don't, the next time you're standing in a golf store with an $800 driver in your hand weighing up whether 'turbulator' technology is the difference you've been looking for, put it back and head over to the tiny section reserved for books. If you see a copy of *Golf Is Not a Game of Perfect* by Dr Bob Rotella, buy it. You'll save $750 and it'll be the best bit of 'technology' you ever purchase.

FARMER WANTS A GOLF COURSE

Richard Sattler, a Tasmanian farmer, is a name unknown to all but the most ardent golf fan but, as **Mike Clayton** writes, he deserves recognition as a trailblazer in Australian golf because of the extraordinary contribution he has made to the game in his home state.

There are many who have contributed much to the formation and development of golf in Australia. Some would think of the pre-war players such as Norman Von Nida, who unfailingly passed his knowledge down to the next generation, a practice followed by Peter Thomson and one continued to this day by older Australian players who advise those coming behind.

Thomson and Kel Nagle were the backbone of the local tour in the 1950s and 1960s, leaving behind a series of strong events for Jack Newton, Bob Shearer, Stewart Ginn and, a little later, Greg Norman, Ian Baker-Finch, Wayne Grady and Peter Senior to build their banks and hone their skills before heading overseas.

Alister MacKenzie transformed golf in Australia when he sailed here late in 1926 to rebuild Royal Melbourne. His influence pervaded golf in Melbourne, Sydney and Adelaide and even as far north as Royal Queensland, where he visited the site and offered his suggestions, and his influence far outstretched the three months he spent here. One beneficiary was his local design partner, Alex

Russell, who headed west to Perth and made Lake Karrinyup, the best course in the world's most remote city.

Businessman Duncan Andrews funded the rebuilding of The Dunes on the Mornington Peninsula in 1996. Originally built by Colin Campbell, an old pro and one deserving of much more credit than he ever gets, Andrews bought the struggling course at auction for a little over $1 million and made Australia's first public golf course deserving of a rank in the top 20 courses in the country.

If you kept heading across the water from the Mornington Peninsula, eventually you would get to the north coast of the island state, Tasmania, where Richard Sattler lives. Sattler, a burly Tasmanian farmer – potatoes and cattle – is as unlikely a contributor to Australian golf as one could imagine. To begin with he did not even play golf and probably wouldn't have recognised Greg Norman if he fell over him. (Sattler does play these days, and is probably the only bloke in the world to have played more courses in the world's top 100 than out of it.) But Sattler, you see, chose to build a golf course – and then another one – on the dune land between his farm, near Bridport in north-east Tasmania, and the stretch of ocean that is Bass Strait, separating the island from the mainland. The wildly ambitious experiment has been an unqualified success.

The idea for a course at Barnbougle was Greg Ramsay's, a 23-year-old whose family owned a nearby farm. Ramsay understood the potential of the dune land linking the beach to the farmland beyond.

Ramsay, with Sattler's permission, had Bruce Hepner, John Sloan (my partner in our design business) and I visit the site sometime in 2001. Hepner was working for Tom Doak and at the time building Cape Kidnappers in New Zealand.

Ramsay gave us the 'I'll make you guys famous' speech, and while we really were entranced by the land as we drove out the gate, Hepner said, 'I've met those same kids a hundred times and they all make the same spiel. It'll never happen.'

A sceptical Doak came down next, and then Mike Keiser, the visionary behind the extraordinary golf at Bandon Dunes in Oregon. Everyone had told Keiser he was mad to make public golf in the middle-of-nowhere Oregon, but he'd made it work – and without employing a famous tour pro to design his first course. Instead he'd headed down the opposite route and hired David Kidd, a young Scottish architect no-one had heard of. It worked because the golf was great and Keiser marketed it brilliantly.

Between us, we convinced Sattler that the course was worth a shot, but it was really Keiser who showed him how to do it and gave him the confidence it would all work out. Keiser at that point had two courses at Bandon and since then he has added two more plus a 13-hole par three. His wife once told me, 'I thought I'd let him do one just to get it out of his system but the problem is the more he does, the more money he makes.'

Keiser's model is to find great land no matter where it is and build great golf courses. Now there are two more (one by Bill Coore and Ben Crenshaw and the other by Kidd) at Sand Valley in Wisconsin, two in Nova Scotia and plans for a new course up by Royal Dornoch, which is about as far north as you can go in Scotland. And how much market research does he do before he builds a course?

'None at all – we just find good, remote, sandy land and build golf. People seem to like it and come.'

Sattler eventually committed to the course that would 'never happen'. I well remember meeting him in his kitchen with a pretty standard design contract. He took a quick look at the first page and asked me if I trusted him.

'Yes.'

'Well there won't be any need for this.'

It screwed up nicely into the shape of a golf ball and went in the bin.

So Barnbougle Dunes got built, and Keiser came to the opening in December of 2004 and predicted there would be a second course before long.

Sattler, I'm sure, didn't believe him, but people came to the first course, enjoyed it, spread the word, and not only did the course survive, it thrived. Golfers seemed to enjoy the effort it took to get there, with many arriving by plane and landing at an airfield nearby, staying the night in the rudimentary cabins, eating in the clubhouse and then doing it all again the next day. In 2017, overseas visitors outnumbered Tasmanian players.

Sattler is now the biggest employer in north-east Tasmania and thousands of golfers each year make the pilgrimage to experience what they could previously only find in Ireland.

Keiser proved prescient regarding the second course. Bill Coore, the greatest of the modern designers, came out in 2010 and built Lost Farm, named after the part of the farm where lost cows liked to hide away.

It's a different course from the original because the land is a much different shape. The Dunes necessarily goes up and down the narrow strip of land between the beach and the farm, while Coore's land is more of a square, meaning he could change direction with the holes more frequently. One never gets the feeling of playing long runs of holes with, or against, the wind. It's neither better nor worse, it's just different – but it doesn't stop golfers endlessly debating the merits of the two.

The Dunes had set a standard but Sattler's two courses at Barnbougle, for the first time, allowed anyone in the country to play courses good enough to be ranked in the top 50 in the world. Britain has great public courses including St Andrews and Carnoustie, and the US has Pebble Beach, Pinehurst, and later the great modern resort at Bandon in Oregon. Sattler will forever be remembered as one who did something of great significance.

And he did one more, largely overlooked thing, which in time will spread north and in a small way help change the image of the game.

It happened like this. We were in the clubhouse on the opening weekend of The Dunes when the phone rang. Richard answered and looked at me. 'This bloke wants to know if he can wear jeans in the clubhouse. What should I say?'

Remember, this is a bloke who knew barely more than nothing about golf and had no clue that anyone daring to venture into a flash mainland club in jeans would be quickly herded toward the door.

'Tell him jeans will be fine – he just can't play in them.'

And the world didn't fall in. The best clubhouses are like the two clubhouses at Barnbougle: relaxed, classy, open to all and with no pretense.

Sattler's contribution to golf in Australia will be recognised more as time goes on and, long after the feats of famous players have faded from our memories, his monument, I believe, will thrill generation after generation of golfers.

BIG IN JAPAN

A resident of Japan for 30 years and a fluent Japanese
speaker, **Andrew Thomson** describes the idiosyncratic
experience of playing golf in his adopted country – where
the bunkers are shallow but communal clubhouse baths
are warm.

The Japanese language is like a sponge in collecting foreign words –
there's 52,000 listed in one Japanese dictionary of foreign words.
This borrowing applies on the golf course as much as anywhere else,
where Japanese golfers speak a sort of pidgin English as they play.

'*Naisu paa!*' Nice par.

'*Naisu patto!*' Nice putt.

'*Naisu shotto!*' Nice shot.

'*Naisu doraibu!*' Nice drive.

There are plenty of native Japanese words and expressions
available to praise another player's skills, but because golf is
regarded as a foreign sport it's become the accepted etiquette to use
a form of English to do so. More than any other people on Earth,
the Japanese are sticklers for etiquette – in eating, conversing,
bathing, exchanging business cards, even riding the train – which
is probably why golf took such a hold of them when it began to
be played by expatriate Englishmen and Scotsmen in the very first
years of the 20th century.

During the first three decades of the last century, a wave of
Anglophilia swept through Japan. Japanese aristocrats and

wealthy industrialists took to wearing Victorian Era costume, and recreations such as equestrianship and golf were very visible parts of the trend. The obsession with etiquette has its disadvantages. On the green a Japanese golfer will often mark his ball after every putt, leading to interminable minutes while everyone takes his turn to putt out.

Yet golf in Japan is neither British nor American in style; it is uniquely Japanese. Almost no clubs have regular teaching professionals. Almost all clubs insist that players have a meal between each nine holes. Very few clubs allow for someone to turn up in mid or late afternoon and play just nine holes. Every club has a huge bath for golfers to soak in after their exertions out on the course.

The basic philosophy of golf in Japan differs from that in the West. For the average Japanese golfer the game is not seen as a rigorous personal contest against a course strewn with challenging bunkers, dangerous rough or confounding undulations in the greens. Instead it's played on wide fairways fringed with only the shortest rough, shallow ankle-deep bunkers, and generally flat greens.

The thinking seems to be that life at work from Monday to Friday – not to mention exhaustingly long commutes to the office from a tiny home – is enough suffering without the misery of deep bunkers, terrifying rough, and three-putt greens being added to it. We golfers come here to relax, they say, not to do samurai service.

This experience of untroubled golf courses can cause problems for Japanese golfers who venture overseas. Recently I hosted a Japanese friend at Royal Melbourne Golf Club. Before we teed off I warned Tanaka-*san* in general terms to avoid the bunkers. After nine holes he'd had probably 15 sand shots and was looking badly damaged and wishing he were back in Japan. I explained that on a difficult, classic course one had to think of each hole ahead not in terms of belting the ball down the fairway toward the green, but rather where the ball should finish *so as to avoid disaster*. Tanaka nodded, but wandered away bewildered.

Another peculiar aspect of the Japanese way is the lack of informal matches between players. Whereas we Western golfers will usually figure out a match play game using the handicap index and often stableford scoring to encourage faster play, many Japanese golfers seem reluctant to compete vigorously against each other. The usual format is for each player to enjoy themselves by trying to record a decent stroke score rather than lose face by being defeated at match play. The Japanese almost never gamble on golf, a practice regarded as vulgar in the extreme.

Golf courses in Japan come in all sorts. The very earliest were designed by British architects, notably Charles Alison, whose bunkers at Hirono Golf Club in Kobe were so shockingly deep that thereafter a deep bunker became known as an 'Alison bunker'. Since the 1970s a good few foreign designers such as Robert Trent Jones, my father Peter Thomson, Pete Dye, Jack Nicklaus and various others have designed dozens of courses in Japan – but not all of these courses ended up as designed. I recall my father returning to one of his creations near Nagoya to find the originally deep bunkers filled to the brim with sand. When he protested to the club president that the intent of the bunkers had been ruined by rendering them so shallow, the president sheepishly explained that some of the club members had trouble climbing out of them, so it was a matter of physical necessity to fill them up. Hirono is an honourable exception – its bunkers are the same depth that Alison built them, and the club is immensely proud of them.

Another peculiarity my father discovered was the insistence from Japanese clients that shots played close to the green ought to be chip shots only. My father liked to see the aprons of his greens cut very short so that putting is an option from even 30 yards out, much as you'd do in Scotland. Woe to he who suggests this in Japan! Putting is for greens only; thus, after my father left the site the club would grow back its aprons to a length that made putting impossible.

It's a common observation of foreigners visiting Japan that the number of huge golf practice ranges dotting the suburban landscape is astounding. Myth has it that many Japanese golfers never venture beyond such places to play. It's true that practice ranges are common, but most golfers do get out on a course now and then, due to the reduction in green fees that followed the recession of the 1990s and 2000s. But practice range golf is not to be derided. I myself enjoy at least four hours a week hitting balls at my local range near Fukuoka. It costs me $20 for two hours, terrific value for the mental therapy, exercise, and positive effect on your game.

Three decades of growth came to an end in 1937, when the military government began confiscating and closing down golf clubs. After the war ended in 1945, Japanese designers were often given land in the mountains on which to build courses, the result being escalators and funicular cars between some holes, such is the steepness of the slopes.

It was in 1957 that the country's golf boom really began. It all happened when Kasumigaseki Country Club outside Tokyo hosted the Canada Cup, a great honour for Japan at the time. The US sent Sam Snead and Jimmy Demaret over, and the field was a strong one, including my father, then three-times Open champion. To the astonishment of the world, the Japanese team of Torakichi 'Pete' Nakamura and Koichi Ono (known as 'The Helicopter' for his habit of hurling clubs through the air after a poor shot) won the tournament in fine style, delivering Japan a volcanic surge of national pride. Golf was thus established as the recreation of highest status, and the boom began.

By the 1980s, some golf courses were installing lights along the fairways, allowing for play to continue all night. Having once teed off on one of these courses around 11 pm it is not an experience I plan to repeat. Finishing a round at 3 am seemed like a form of lunacy. Yet such was the demand for golf in those days that it made sense.

The boom reached its zenith during the speculative bubble at the end of the 1980s. With a wave of easy money sloshing through the economy, golf club memberships – being transferable securities – became objects of furious punting, along with stocks and real estate. Ludicrous sums were paid for them, and in the end they crashed along with other asset prices. Many golf clubs went bankrupt during the long recession that followed, and the number of golfers relentlessly declined along with the ageing of the population.

Over the years, Japanese professional golf has had some noteworthy characters and a few very good players, especially women professionals such as Hisako 'Chako' Higuchi – who was taught by the aforementioned Torakichi Nakamura – and her great rival, Ayako Okamoto, and of course Hideki Matsuyama on the men's side. Beyond doubt the 1980s were Japanese golf's golden years, when Isao Aoki, 'Jumbo' Ozaki and 'Tommy' Nakajima were in their prime. Jumbo, a burly former baseball player, was the rough-tough man of Japanese golf, very much the common man's hero. Aoki was a clever, strategic player and mentally very tough. Nakajima was a great player too, and a delightful gentleman, though the world will likely best remember him for his disaster in the third round at the Road Hole in the 1978 British Open Championship, first putting into the world's most famous bunker and then taking four shots to get out. Peter Alliss christened the incident 'The Sands of Nakajima'. Nakajima was equal leader when he teed up on the Road Hole – and out of contention when his final putt dropped. 'Sorry, Neil,' he said softly to his teenage caddie.

These days professional golf in Japan is a puzzle. On the Japanese ladies circuit, Korean professionals are dominant; they attract admiration from fans for their relentless perseverance, and prizemoney is still good enough to attract dozens of new players every year at qualifying school. But prizemoney for the men's circuit has dwindled, along with the number of tournaments. The best players head for the US PGA Tour, depriving the home galleries of local heroes. The flag is flown by Matsuyama, who went to number two in world rankings after placing second in the US Open in 2017.

While golf in Japan is not as popular as it once was, it isn't going to die off anytime soon. Sure, the population is falling and younger people are not so keen, but there are millions of golfers who flock to the practice ranges and courses every day of the week to enjoy their game. Golf comics and magazines sell vigorously, and hickory golf is played with the old-fashioned clubs by a small group of dedicated traditionalists. Even sumo wrestlers are occasionally seen trying their hand at the game. That, I can tell you, is a sight to behold.

Slow play is a serious issue on all the tours with the exception of both the men's and women's tour in Japan. Playing slowly and losing your place in the field isn't tolerated and if they fall behind on one hole, they run on the next to catch up. In comparison, on the PGA Tour, the LPGA Tour and in Europe, they are closer to crawling than running. If they introduced a shotgun finish – that is you have, say, four hours to play and every five minutes over that attracts a one-shot penalty – they would all finish in four hours, just as they do in Japan.

– Mike Clayton

WHAT WOULD BOB SHEARER DO?

The 2017 season witnessed a spate of players breaking rules – unwittingly or otherwise – which prompted **Mike Clayton** to recall an incident from decades ago that typifies golf's integrity and sportsmanship.

Every professional season has its share of rules oddities and controversies, but 2017 was a particularly wild one. (Or perhaps with Twitter we just notice them a little more.) We had Lexi Thompson's ball marking – or rather mismarking – at a major championship; the controversy of putter anchoring on the Champions Tour; Charley Hoffman and Branden Grace in separate incidents squeezing their feet far enough into bunker sand to find the new asphalt linings; and Jon Rahm replacing his ball in a different place on the green at the Irish Open – then officials, for the first time ever (Bobby Locke in the 1957 Open Championship aside), deeming near enough was good enough.

Perhaps, on reflection, it wasn't so unusual. Players have always broken rules, mostly unwittingly but not always. John Huggan, the Scottish golf writer, conducted an anonymous player survey on the European Tour a few years ago and of the 40 players he asked, 37 admitted to witnessing a fellow competitor cheating. 'It's golf's dirty little secret,' says Huggan.

The rules can be complicated and confusing. Late in 2017, Englishman Matthew Southgate's 8-foot putt for a par in a Web.com tournament in the US was knocked off track by a leaf blowing across his line and hitting the ball. He did what probably every single pro in the world would have done: cursed his luck and tapped it in for a bogey.

It all seemed perfectly sensible. The game isn't supposed to be fair. The problem was he should have replaced his ball and putted again. So he was docked two shots for not proceeding correctly and two more for signing the wrong scorecard – a pretty harsh penalty, but at least everybody now knows the rule.

Southgate, and Lexi, can count their luck, though. For the longest time, signing an incorrect card was a disqualifiable offence.

Bob Shearer was a brilliant Australian player in the 1970s and early 1980s and rated one of the possible winners of the 1982 Australian Open, even if he didn't think so. When his wife, Kathie, dropped him off at Melbourne airport for the flight to Sydney at the start of the week, he said, 'I'll see you at home on Friday night.'

The Australian Golf Club's old clubhouse had only just burned down, leaving everyone housed and entertained in a big tent, which worked just fine. The course was deemed to be the most difficult in the country by some way, and Shearer was out with Jack Nicklaus in the opening two rounds. 'You don't want to make a fool of yourself when you're playing with him,' said the Australian.

Shearer was playing well in the opening round when he came to the long, difficult par-three 15th. His long iron found the bunker just to the right of the green and he hit a poor bunker shot. The ball got out onto the edge of the green and Shearer whacked the sand with his club in annoyance. Then, to his horror, the ball turned and rolled back into the bunker. He got the next one up and down and told Nicklaus to assess him a two-shot penalty.

Nicklaus suggested Bob wait until the round was finished and they could get a ruling. The rules officials and Nicklaus all agreed after watching the tape there had been no infringement and therefore no penalty was due, because the ball was out of the bunker when Bob's club hit the sand.

Shearer was having none of it: 'Jack, thanks for your help but please add the two shots to my score. I'm not having anyone questioning my integrity.'

His 73 became 75, not a mortal blow but hardly one that improved his chances of beating Nicklaus and Payne Stewart. As fate or karma or providence would have it, three days later Shearer holed a crazy putt up the slope at the 13th, pitched a wedge in from 70 yards on the 14th and then hit what must be the best three iron in the history of Australian tournament golf – given the pressure and circumstances – across the water and onto the green on the par-five 18th. In the end, he beat Nicklaus and Stewart by four shots.

Not many players would have taken that two-shot penalty but Bob was not having anyone even hinting he'd taken an unfair advantage.

The hinting of taking advantage is the dark spectre of the anchored putter controversy. The rules lawyers should have drowned the long putter at birth but they presumably reasoned few players used it and, besides, no-one was winning any of golf's majors with the broomstick, so why worry? Of course that argument is a real trap, because what do you do when, within a couple of years, Adam Scott, Webb Simpson, Keegan Bradley and Ernie Els all win major championships with anchored putters?

Eventually a ban, of sorts, came into place on 1 January 2016.

Almost everyone abandoned the long putter then except for a few on the Senior Tour including Bernhard Langer and Scott McCarron. Both deny disrespecting the rule or intending to anchor the putter, but using the Bob Shearer 'no-one is going to accuse me of cheating' rule, long putters would have been consigned to the cupboard ages ago.

The real problem, and why Langer and McCarron are put in a difficult position, is it's almost impossible to tell if the putter is anchored and many times on television it looks awfully like it is. The administrators could have avoided it all by simply decreeing the putter had to be the shortest club in every professional's bag. Raymond Floyd was the only player I ever saw who had a putter (38 or 39 inches from memory) longer than a standard wedge (37 usually), but he'd have managed. In trying to avoid the lawsuits from manufacturers that would result from an outright ban, officials legislated instead to change the way the putter was used – and it's messy. (At least they killed off the 'belly putter' because it was likely to be the widespread method of choice in 20 years, rendering extinct the traditional 35-inch putter.)

More recently, the phenomenon of 'backstopping' has become another thorny issue as players leave balls around the hole when others are chipping. It's clearly done to aid the other player by offering a backstop to an incoming chip shot or bunker shot and stop it nearer the hole than might otherwise have been the case. The players are all claiming it's done to speed up play. If that's true, it's the only single instance of modern professionals doing anything to speed up play in this era of five hour-plus crawls around the golf course.

The collusion rule is ambiguous: 'In stroke play, if the committee determines that competitors have agreed not to lift a ball that might assist any competitor, they are disqualified.'

In the era I played, it hardly ever happened, in part because players respected the spirit of the rule and the game. One player giving an advantage to another at the expense of the field is clearly the wrong thing to do – but it now seems par for the course even in important situations.

In the final round of the 2017 US Open, Brian Harman was playing in the final group and, on the second green, chipped to within a couple of feet of the hole and left his ball there as Justin Thomas chipped from over the back. That Thomas's ball didn't collide with Harman's isn't the point. There is a fine line between 'agreeing not to lift the ball' and silent collusion in aid of another.

Players defending the new practice argue about where the line is drawn. It used to be obvious. You marked when your ball might have assisted another player.

Then there is the concept of what is a reasonable amount of time. Waiting 15 or 30 seconds while a ball is marked is reasonable; a minute is not. Walking 20 yards to mark a ball is reasonable, but 50 is probably too far. Every previous generation seemed to manage it just fine.

One of Australia's most experienced rules officials saw what he considered a breach of the rule at a major tournament only to be told 'the PGA Tour aren't enforcing Rule 22'. I wonder who thinks that's a good precedent?

The Lexi Thompson mismarking controversy at the 2017 ANA Inspiration in Palm Springs was a case brought to light by an eagle-eyed television viewer who pointed out Lexi didn't play the ball 'from where it lay'. At the 17th hole during the third round, Thompson putted from 20 feet to a couple of feet, went to tap it in then changed her mind and marked the ball. With the tape slowed down, she clearly failed to replace the ball in the same place – leaving it a centimetre or two closer to the hole. Some think it's a difficult thing to do; others argued the small distance was unimportant – but an inch may as well be a mile when it comes to playing the ball as it lies.

The respected British commentator Peter Alliss had a typically black-and-white view of it all: 'I've watched it a few times. I'm a purist in many ways, but as far as I can see she came up to her ball and moved it to the side. She cheated for goodness' sake. Or had a mental aberration. Whatever. But she didn't put the ball back in the right place.'

Thompson should have been thankful her mistake was pointed out when it was, because had it been revealed on Monday morning, her 'win' would forever have been tainted by her 'carelessness'.

Whether she believed she had erred or not, the American should have come out and said she was eternally grateful for the mistake being pointed out before the end of the championship.

Whether she moved the ball intentionally or not only she knows, but those who expressed the 'poor Lexi' sentiment would do well to ask themselves what Bob Shearer would have done.

IF YOU PLEASE, PETER ALLISS

He's been BBC's voice of golf for as long as anyone can remember, and a unique voice it is. The commentary of Peter Alliss is a delightful mix of knowledge, whimsy, impish sense of the ridiculous and disdain for political correctness. **John Huggan** profiles the inimitable one of a kind.

Right from day one, Peter Alliss was exceptional. Born in Berlin, where his father, Ryder Cup player Percy Alliss, was head professional at the Wannsee Golf Club, the future 'voice of golf' weighed in at a hefty 14 pounds, 12 ounces and was, in 1931, the heaviest-ever baby in Europe.

That was just the beginning of a fascinating life that has taken in multiple aspects of the game Alliss has played so well and talked about so eloquently. If nothing else, his qualifications are impeccable. The phrase 'steeped in the game' is often overused, but this 21-time European Tour winner certainly qualifies.

As a child, Alliss recalls coming back from school in 1940 to find four Open Champions seated around his small kitchen table – Alf Perry (1935), Alf Padgham (1936), Reggie Whitcombe (1938) and Dick Burton (1939), as well as Ernest Whitcombe (runner-up in the 1924 Open) and Alliss senior.

'Players of that era were very ordinary people, in the best sense of that word,' he says. 'I was in my father's shop when he came back from winning the *News of the World* match-play championship, which was a big deal. I would be maybe ten years old. A member came in: "Well done Alliss. You won £250 I see. Now then, what about those shoes you were repairing for me?" So there was no thought of grandeur.'

A few years later, Alliss caddied for golf's greatest-ever amateur, Bobby Jones, in what was the champion's final round in the United Kingdom. Wearing his army uniform, his tie tucked into his shirt, Jones played at Parkstone with the elder Alliss.

'I have either played with or met all but seven Open champions since 1900,' says Alliss. 'People look at me funny when I say that. But it's true. I have seen Walter Hagen. I have seen Bobby Jones. I met JH Taylor. I didn't meet Arnaud Massy, the 1907 champion. And I didn't meet Densmore Shute, who won in 1933. But I have seen or played with every one since the Second World War.'

As a player, Alliss's career was distinguished but not without disappointment. Eight times a Ryder Cup player and 10 times a member of the English World Cup side, his game was characterised by a mixture of majestic ball-striking and, at times, woeful putting. (Not for nothing does the number plate on his car read 'PUT 3'.)

'I have a very good Ryder Cup record, mostly because of my fear of losing,' he contends. 'I always had the attitude that "you weren't going to beat me". I believe you play the man, not the course. I played Arnold Palmer three times when he was at his peak in the early 1960s and the only one I lost was a foursome. I beat him once and halved with him in singles. I also beat Billy Casper, Gay Brewer and Ken Venturi at various times, and halved with Tony Lema.'

Still, despite being good enough to win three national Opens – Portugal, Spain and Italy – over consecutive weeks in 1958, Alliss never really contended in The Open Championship. 'I was very good from tee to green in my time,' he says. 'And, despite my reputation, I could putt too. You don't win twenty-odd times if you can't putt. I would, over the course of a round, hole four or five putts of at least twenty feet. But I'd occasionally miss from no more than fifteen inches. And I never knew why. I've seen film of myself in the mid 1960s and I had hardly any backswing at all.'

The putting yips that would eventually lead to his career ending somewhat prematurely came to a head at Augusta National during the 1967 Masters. Playing with one-time US Open champion Gene Littler, Alliss putted up to about a yard on the 11th green in the second round.

'I remember standing over the ball and the next thing I knew I was fifteen feet past,' he says with a shudder. 'I left the next one about two feet short. Then I was eight feet by again. Gene asked, "What the hell are you doing?" To which I replied, "I don't know."'

'Eventually I got the ball in and Gene asked how many I'd taken. I had no idea. I told him to put down ten or eleven – I forget which. But that bothered me for a long time. I wasn't exactly sure what I had taken. Years later, I noticed that I don't have the record high score for that hole. Which is probably a good thing.' Alliss does himself a disservice – five players share the 'honour' of highest for the hole, and their score was nine.

Alliss played in his last Ryder Cup in 1969 and bowed out of competitive golf five years later. By then, however, the BBC commentary he had dabbled in as far back as 1961 was taking up more and more of his time. Mentored by the legendary Henry Longhurst, Alliss soon brought his own sense of style to his work, simultaneously displaying a deep knowledge of the game, an impish sense of the ridiculous, some delightful departures into amusing whimsy and, more than occasionally, a controversial disdain for modern-day political correctness.

'Several of my fellow players – who will remain nameless – were huge womanisers,' he reveals. 'They would have twenty-five to thirty liaisons per year. And they would book into hotels under their own names. Tiger Woods is a child in comparison to some of my mates. But those were different times. There wasn't the same journalism. Society wasn't nearly so litigious. Girls you went out with didn't rush off to the newspapers. This was before the pill. The big fears were getting a girl pregnant or catching VD. They were the two great contraceptives of the day.'

Alliss is equally contemptuous of the establishment, once turning down an OBE (Order of the British Empire), which he instead labelled 'Other Buggers' Efforts'.

'I was asked if I would accept it for "services to golf", which I thought odd. Why should I get an OBE for doing my job? Now, if it were for work I have done with the wheelchair charity I have been involved with – we have raised about seven million pounds over the years – I could have seen the point. But not for bloody golf. So I said no.'

That sense of right and wrong often manifested itself in Alliss's commentary, whether for the BBC or the ABC network in the United States. Compromise was not a word he recognised.

'I refused to do anything different when commentating in America,' he says. 'I certainly refused to say "back side" or "hole location".'

'I remember one commentator saying, "And here is Faldo at fourteen, with wind gusting from his rear." I thought, "No, I'm not saying that." For me, it was always a bunker rather than a sand trap. I always tried to do what Longhurst told me: "Imagine you are sitting talking to a friend." If there is nothing to say, it is better to do just that. The one thing I rarely do is take my eyes off the screen, which I liken to someone turning to look at you as he drives the car. I am observant. I look at all corners of the screen when I am commentating. I'm always looking for something to talk about. Funny faces. Kids having ice-cream. Dogs urinating. Whatever.'

Towards the end of a career that has naturally wound down with age and the BBC's almost complete withdrawal from golf, Alliss embarked on yet another adventure. With 40 dates all over the United Kingdom, his one-man show – consisting of reminiscences and question-and-answer sessions with the audiences – drew more than 18,000 people and underlined his enduring popularity among those of a certain age. Alliss is a man of his time, with little patience for what he sees as an inexorable deterioration in 'standards'.

'I hate unfairness,' he says. 'And rudeness. And graffiti. The deterioration of manners has been the most shocking thing in my lifetime. I think I have aged well. I don't have any rheumatism. I wish I was a bit lighter. I'm not vain, but I like a decent haircut and a crease in my trousers. I like to have a shave. I like to have my fingernails and shoes clean. Designer stubble makes me think people don't care.

'I've watched Tiger since he was fifteen and marvelled at what he can do on the course. He has been amazing. There was a time when he smiled and was more gracious. But gradually that changed. Even when he is asked reasonably sensible golfing questions, he looks grumpy. He looks like he has terminal piles. He gives nothing back and looks like he hates every minute of it. He has never learned the art of communication.'

Which is not an accusation that could ever be attached to Alliss. Player, broadcaster, raconteur, World Golf Hall of Famer. One of a kind.

'I'M TALKING TO THE BUTCHER NOT THE BLOCK'

Growing up in east London, **Kathie Shearer** knew nothing about golf and no-one who played the game. Yet she has spent the past 40 years as a prominent figure in the sport, married to a golfer, Bob Shearer, and running media centres at tournaments around the world. She looks back on her time in golf, from the raucous early days on the European Tour to her run-in with Tiger Woods.

One of my first jobs was working for a company in London called Carreras cigarettes. And back in the day, the mid 1970s, they were very big sponsors of sport events – the Dunhill Cup, which was a sailing regatta, the Piccadilly golf championship at Wentworth, and so on. That was how I came into contact with the sporting world, and golf in particular.

I met Bob while I was working at a tennis tournament in Bournemouth in 1973. There was a golf tournament, the Sumrie Better-Ball*, being played nearby and Bob's partner was Ian Stanley. The Australian golfers used to watch the Australian tennis players, such as Bob Carmichael and Ray Ruffels, and the tennis players came to watch the golfers; there was a great camaraderie between them.

My friend Jackie Butterworth was having a birthday party and she had been dating Jack Newton for a while before that. So Jackie said to about six of us girls who she worked with: Come to my birthday party; I'm going to be there with my boyfriend and there will be some other golfers there. It wasn't a set-up; it was just lots of young people together. And what fun we had.

At one point, Jack asked me to dance with his mate, Bob Shearer. But I said to Jack, 'I like who I'm dancing with now, thank you very much' – he was a fellow called Harry Bannerman. But Bob and I did end up having a dance later. He'd imbibed quite a lot by then, I think, yet he did make quite a few good moves on the dance floor. You know how Gene Wilder said white men can't dance, and they always bite their bottom lip and give it a bit of a shuffle. Well, he had a good Gene Wilder going, Bob. He gave it the best he had.

Our paths only crossed occasionally after that because he was away playing golf and I was working. He was very easy to talk to and mix with; I didn't realise till later he was so mellow because he'd often had a drink or two. But those were the days.

I made the mistake of telling him and Ian Stanley that I lived in an apartment in north London with my mother. And somehow when my back was turned – it happened quite suddenly – they moved into that apartment because they needed somewhere to stay and to save some money.

No sooner the word than the deed. I don't remember actually inviting them, they just turned up one day. Pretty soon, they were laying around the place on their days off and making themselves at home. My mum was a generous person and didn't mind too much. And I said to her: They're just going to stay for a few days, that's all.

In no time, they had managed to convince the local off-licence down the road to stock Foster's Lager, so there wasn't much incentive for them to move out. Soon my aunts and uncles were asking questions about these two loud Australians who had taken over my mother's home and were making complicated plastic model aeroplanes which, probably after too many Fosters, they were launching out of her upstairs windows – to the astonishment of the neighbours. My grandmother who lived around the corner was particularly concerned. 'I don't know what's going on up there,' she'd say repeatedly to anyone who would listen.

What attracted me to these Australian guys on tour in the early 1970s was they were so different – so uninhibited. They were a fascination to me. You'd see them out and think: they can't do that, but they did. They were such rogues. There wasn't a nightclub, pub or hotel that was safe from the Aussie contingent. They would often be joined by Irish and Scottish players, and a few South Africans, and they would just take over pubs, ending the night as barmen, serving drinks and almost running the place.

It was a time in England when you went on a date and the fellow would turn up in a suit. My first date with Bob, he wore check trousers, a pink shirt and a blue-and-orange striped sweater – and a pair of shoes he'd bought in St Kilda that were like pimp's shoes, with high heels and a spat up the front. I remember he came to pick me up from work, and one of the other girls there said, 'Nice fella, but you're going to have to do something about the way he dresses.' I later found out that whoever among the boys had the date, got the clean clothes – whether they matched or not.

I'm a Londoner from Whitechapel; there's no golf course anywhere in sight in east London. I had no exposure to golf at all; none whatsoever. No-one I knew played golf. I thought Jack Nicklaus was a pair of shoes, and Arnold Palmer sold colourful umbrellas.

When my grandmother said to Bob, 'What do you do for a living, son?' and he replied, 'Golf,' she said, 'No, what do you do *for a living*?' So we had to make up a story that Bob was in the army because it disturbed her so much that somebody might earn their living from sport.

Bob and I got married in Melbourne in 1975. The reception was at Bob's golf club, Southern. I realised what I'd got myself in for when Bob was chaired out of the clubhouse on his mates' shoulders after the reception, like some kind of rock star. My mum and I looked at each other and just shrugged our shoulders as we trailed behind with the rest of the guests.

We were going to spend six months in Europe and six months in Australia, with a little bit of Asia in between; that was the plan when we got married. But Bob decided to try out for the US Tour early in 1976 to see if he could win his card. I must have been the only person who didn't want him to make it. But he topped the qualifying school with Woody Blackburn. So that's where we spent the next nine years, until 1984, living in a condominium in Myrtle Beach, South Carolina.

At that time, Bob played a lot of money games at the local club. He called himself Bob Slazenger from New Zealand, because he had Slazenger on his bag and he flew Air New Zealand. So that was the name he went by when he played all these hustlers. They played every day when he wasn't at tournaments. He's always said that playing for his own money kept his game really sharp.

People came from all over for these big money games. I can remember one guy had a putter in the shape of a woman's foot, with painted toenails. Another one had started up a chain of Wendy's hamburger stores in Kentucky. They had plenty of time and money on their hands, and they would come to Myrtle Beach from all over the country from June to September, then move to California from October to January, then head to Florida for the next four months; these guys were serious gamblers.

Bob would go up to the golf club about lunchtime, have something to eat and then they'd decide who was playing against who. It could take a long time to organise that, and for the gamblers to get set.

About 25 of the local hustlers from South Carolina would be invited to play and they in turn would bring along a player, and that's where Bob came in. Their bets were a quarter, which was $1000, a nickel ($500) and a dime ($100) – which in the late 1970s was quite a bit of money. Bob was often sponsored by the local gamblers when the big boys arrived. He always had his own bets going, but those boys bet really, really big money and Bob played as hard and as long as he could. It was almost like a tournament every day.

I knew if he didn't make it home till after dark, it was because someone had pressed and they'd be playing another nine holes. But the money he made from those games kept us afloat, no doubt.

In 1976 Bob was invited to play the Masters for the first time. Jack Nicklaus, who won the tournament the previous year, was kind enough to ask Bob to play a practice round with him at Augusta. They had played together in 1969 before Bob turned pro, and then were regularly put in the same group in Australian tournaments through the 1970s, so had got to know each other quite well. The relationship with Jack was very special because he was Bob's idol and proved to be such a terrific bloke. Anyway, Bob arrived at Augusta for his first look at the place but didn't realise he had to bring his own practice balls, so Jack went to the pro shop and gave Bob six dozen new balls in a 'shag bag'. He was such a gentleman.

Jack started up his Memorial Tournament in Ohio for the first time that year; it was an invitational event played in late May. Bob received an invitation from Jack, which he was delighted about, so we both trooped off to Akron.

During the tournament, which is obviously held in Jack's home state, we had dinner with him and his wife, Barbara, and one night went to Baskin-Robbins ice-cream shop and just sat outside eating our ice-creams on a park bench. People driving past couldn't believe it; there was one of the most famous sportsmen in the country having an ice-cream. We still swap Christmas cards with the Nicklauses today.

Two weeks after the Memorial (*Ed: Shearer finished in 38th place, earning US$780*), Bob went to the US qualifying school in Myrtle Beach and the rest is history. We were offered a condo to use there, which we ended up buying, and Bob represented Myrtle Beach when out playing tour events.

Bob was just gobsmacked at how kind Jack was towards him. David Graham was also very kind when we first moved over there, as was Bruce Devlin. Bob Stanton showed us the ropes, as well. We owe them all a great deal.

We moved from hotel to hotel in those years, as the circuit went around the country. I became very friendly with the wives – there was Margie Caldwell, Rex's former wife, Charlotte Quigley, Dana's former wife, Gina Shea, Mike's wife, and Tom Watson's first wife, Linda. We also saw a lot of Judy Levi, a New Yorker married to Wayne, who was hilarious, and Irene Burns, who was married to George, and Jerry Pate's wife, Susie. All of the girls got on well. I never felt isolated at all. Later at night, once we'd put the kids to bed, sometimes we'd meet in the lobby of the hotel, pull up some seats together and hoot with laughter for an hour or two about things that had happened that day. I am still in close contact with Margie and Charlotte and consider them some of my closest friends.

One time we were staying in Atlanta, and I rang the tournament office to see how Bob had got on that day. They said he had a 63. No, I said, it's Shearer – S-H-E-A-R-E-R. I didn't believe them. I thought they'd got Bob mixed up with someone else.

He had his best year in the US in 1982, Bob. That's when he won the Tallahassee Open, and lost in a playoff for the Houston Open. I think in six straight events, from March to May, he had finishes of 4, 48, 1, 2, 6, 2, so that was his best period on tour.

At the end of that year, Bob played with Jack again over three days at the Australian Open back in Sydney and ended up winning the tournament by four shots. During the first round, though, Bob called a two-shot penalty on himself after hitting a poor bunker shot then hitting the sand in disgust – but the ball had rolled back into the bunker. Even though Jack was marking Bob's card and said there was no penalty, Bob insisted he'd broken a rule. Luckily, the golfing gods paid him back later in the week.

Bob finished up in the US in 1984; that's when we bought a family home in Melbourne and began to live there full-time.

A few years later, Bob came home after playing in Japan and said, 'I've got you a job.'

'I don't want a job,' I told him.

But he said that Graham Marsh was running the Coca-Cola Classic at Royal Melbourne later in the year, with Isao Aoki as the marquee player, and Graham needed someone to help Jim Webster run the media centre; someone who knew Melbourne and could be the front of house.

So I did that, while Jim helped run the interviews. It was my first taste of working in a media centre. I then went on to help out at the Australian Masters at Huntingdale. The first time I ran one by myself was at the end of 1990 when someone asked me if I could look after the whole show at Huntingdale. I said, Yes, I think I can do that.

And I've loved it ever since. Even though I've never played the game, I love golf and everything about it. I have a passion for it. I love the people, the way they speak to one another, generally so polite. From my first tournament, I thought, Oh, this is nice. People are just so welcoming and nice: 'Yes please, no thank you'.

Managers now come in to the press tent to watch over their players, and when they feel the interview's gone on for too long, they run their finger across their neck as if to say: Cut. I take no notice of that at all, none whatsoever. I won't have managers telling me how to run the interviews. I finish the session when everyone's finished asking questions. That's it.

When we've got a packed interview room, I ask everyone to stay seated so the player and I can walk out without journalists stopping them with extra questions. Some journos don't like it; they say, This doesn't happen anywhere else in the world.

But Bud Martin, who manages Jason Day and several others, came up to me once and said, That's a Hall of Fame move, that, keeping everyone sitting down. He couldn't stop laughing when

I announced to the room, 'My colleague and I are now going to leave, and you lot are going to sit still.' Or sometimes I'd say, 'Elvis and I are now leaving the building.' Bud said a 23-year-old could never get away with that.

The players I've most enjoyed working with? There are so many. I cut my teeth on working with Greg Norman when he was young – we started out about the same time. The truth is he's probably kept me in business for most of the last 30 years. He probably kept the Australian tour in business, too, because he always came in for an interview and he always had something to say.

I have a fondness for all the players in their own special way. And I tried to treat every player the same, no matter what their profile or their ego. From George Serhan and his tie-dye shirts to Greg Norman – the great, the grand and the also-rans, they were equally important in my eyes.

Wayne Riley, who some people thought was a bit wacko, was always fun. Nick Faldo will still call out now when I see him: 'Hi there! What are you up to? What are you doing?' Peter Senior, could you get anyone nicer than him? The same with Jordan Spieth, a gentleman. And Adam Scott, who calls Bob 'Uncle Bob'. Lovely, lovely men. (Though I'm not sure I can say the same about all their travelling managers.)

Then there were also players who were somewhat tricky: Lee Trevino, for example. Those players that everyone loved were often quite tricky. John Daly, Sergio Garcia, Ray Floyd would look at you with those piercing eyes and not say anything. Silent but deadly. If they refused to come in, I'd say, 'Look, it's best to get it over and done with now, even if it's just ten minutes, or they'll start chasing you for an interview.'

I had an incident with Tiger at the Johnnie Walker Classic in Phuket in 1998, and it was all over his manager from IMG, Clarke Jones or Clark Kent or whatever his name was.

Tiger started with rounds of 72, 71 and was well off the pace and he didn't want to come in for an interview. I didn't realise that the European Tour media person had spoken to Tiger's manager earlier in the week and told him that Tiger didn't have to come in if he wasn't in the leading three players. So I walked into the men's locker room to find him after that second round and said, 'Look, you really need to come in.'

Tiger said, 'I don't fucking have to.'

Jones butted in when I was having this conversation and kept repeating the same thing, that Tiger didn't have to come in. That tipped me over the edge.

I said, 'Listen, I'm talking to the butcher not the block. You can fuck off, too.'

I'm not sure he'd been spoken to like that before. It was a colourful confrontation. I'm certainly not proud of what I said, it wasn't my finest moment, but it was a thousand degrees in the shade, people were dropping like flies, the walk up to the clubhouse from the 18th green was so steep. Everyone was a bit frazzled.

With that, Tiger followed me into a golf cart and we drove to the media centre. The atmosphere was a bit frosty, I'll admit, in spite of the heat. But from that day onwards, he's been as good as gold. Fantastic. He hasn't carried a grudge at all.

He was introduced to Bob a little while later, at the Presidents Cup at Royal Melbourne, and catching his surname, Tiger asked, 'Are you related to Kathie Shearer?'

Bob said, 'Yes, I'm married to her.'

Tiger then said, 'Well, you're a hell of a man.' I think it was meant as a compliment.

Ten years later, after Tiger won the Australian Masters at Kingston Heath in 2009, he gave me a hug and thanked me for all my support over the week, which was very nice, but a bit of a surprise. And the following year, he presented me with a lovely Tag Heuer watch to mark my 25 years at the Masters. I still wear it now. I'd like him to come back here again; I think he's with Rolex now!

Golfers have undoubtedly changed over the years. They're more serious now and less fun, but that's hardly surprising given how much money they're playing for. It's a serious business. They're also a lot more protected now; they don't go anywhere near the punters. They leave the 18th green and sign their scorecards upstairs; they have little contact with the public. Instead, they employ people to keep them connected to their fans via social media. I can see the security reasons, but I also think golf might be the poorer for it.

As for the journos, well, not much has changed. I always run a 'wet' media centre, never a dry one. And that means we have a drink at 5 pm every day, for those who are interested anyway. I stock the fridge with two cases of beer and two boxes of wine each day, and we seem to get through it. Some things never change.

* Ed: Jack Newton and Ireland's John O'Leary teamed up to win that same event, the Sumrie Better-Ball, two years later in 1975. After romping home with a final-round 63 to smash the 72-hole tournament record, O'Leary confided to the media afterwards that he and Newton had, in the manner of the time, found inspiration for their win not on the practice fairway but somewhere more convivial: 'We played so badly in our third round on Friday, we decided to abandon our routine. Instead of going out to practice in the evening as we had done all week, we decided to go out and have a drink and forget about our poor play.'

WRITE A WRONG?

Covering the Johnnie Walker Classic in Taiwan in 1999,
Charles Happell found himself impaled on the horns of
a journalistic dilemma: should he dob in two misbehaving
golfers, or leave well enough alone?

As the one-time golf writer for *The Age* in Melbourne, I was sent
some years back to cover the Johnnie Walker Classic in, of all
places, Taiwan. Normally, it was hard to convince the powers-that-
be that it was worthwhile covering a tournament in Traralgon, let
alone Taipei, but because Tiger Woods was playing, along with all
the leading Australians, the request was surprisingly given the
all clear.

On the Sunday night after the tournament, having written up
and filed a report about New Zealand's Michael Campbell beating
Tiger and Australia's Geoff Ogilvy over the closing holes, I got on
the bus that ferried journalists and players back to the airport for
the flight back to Australia.

On to the bus staggered two leading golfers and their caddies,
clearly the worse for wear. One player was from Victoria and
ranked among the top players in the world. The other was a
less well-credentialled player from New South Wales who,
unsurprisingly, given his lack of professionalism, soon dropped off
the face of the earth.

The four of them were friends of Campbell's and, having finished
their final rounds much earlier in the day, had been watching the

New Zealander's duel with Woods and Ogilvy on the television in the clubhouse bar. And naturally they'd been drinking while cheering their man home. For about four hours solid. By the time they got on the bus, each carrying a half-full stubby of local lager, they were totally inebriated and deeply obnoxious. They sat at the back, gurgling to each other.

Five minutes into the journey, the Victorian player shouted out to the Taiwanese driver: 'Hey, mate, where's the dunny in this bloody thing?' It was explained to him that while it was a luxury bus, there wasn't a lavatory on board. 'Oh, f---,' came the reply.

So, amid much giggling and with bladders full to bursting, they each urinated into their by-now-empty stubbies and sat them on the floor of the bus. Which was fine until the bus rounded a corner and, you guessed it, the contents of the bottles spilled everywhere and ran in a torrent down the walkway. The smell was foul.

So, the dilemma: do I write about this episode – as I'm sure one or two colleagues would have – and expose these high-profile players as boorish buffoons? Or do I tell myself that it was adolescent behaviour committed away from the course, away from the general public's gaze (there were only about eight other people on board: the driver, one or two golfers, the rest officials and caddies) and, as a result, hardly in the public interest? I mean, if they carried on like that at a barbecue in their own backyard, who'd have known and who'd have cared? The conundrum is one faced by political correspondents, sportswriters, police reporters and business journalists all the time.

I knew I'd run into these players again and again over the coming years (well, one of them at least) but the prospect of exposing them didn't really bother me, it was more a question of how self-righteous I wanted to be, or should be. I mean, I'd been intoxicated in public once or twice myself.

The situation is like AFL reporters posed with the dilemma of exposing, say, the drug-taking of Ben Cousins, which eventually landed him in prison. Similarly, which American golf writer wants to be shunned by their meal tickets, Tiger Woods or Jordan Spieth? Which British F1 correspondent wants to be frozen out by Lewis Hamilton, or football writer fresh-aired by Harry Kane? We're only talking about two misbehaving golfers here who'd gone out a bit hard on the Taipei special brew, so hardly crime of the century, but the dilemma is the same: should journalists always call out this kind of conduct or not?

In the UK, *The Sunday Times* chief sportswriter David Walsh illustrated this conundrum beautifully in his book, *Seven Deadly Sins*, which must rank among the greatest books ever written on the ethical dilemmas journalism regularly throws up, and the high personal cost that sometimes comes with writing the truth.

Walsh had been a critic of Lance Armstrong ever since the American won his first Tour de France in 1999. As he watched the race, and Armstrong's performance, something just didn't sit right with him. Here was an athlete who had recently undergone chemotherapy for testicular cancer, whose best placing in the Tour till that point had been 36th in four attempts and who was racing in what was expected to be a slow race. The previous year the Festina team had been busted for drug use; the 1999 Tour was therefore supposed to be ridden clean – the 'Tour of Renewal', as it was called.

Yet Armstrong bettered his time-trial performance by eight seconds per kilometre between his first Tour appearance in 1993 and that victory in 1999 – smashing all sorts of records along the way – when, three years earlier, he was having a testicle, lung cysts and brain lesions removed.

In filing his report on that race for *The Sunday Times*, Walsh wrote: 'There are times when it is right to celebrate, but there are other occasions when it is equally correct to keep your hands by your sides and wonder.'

Which is what he resolutely did for the next 13 years, refusing to join in the applause for an athlete he was convinced was cheating, even though it cost his paper hundreds of outraged readers who cancelled their subscriptions – and caused him much personal angst as well.

Armstrong's henchmen, for example, put pressure on the three journalist friends who used to travel in a car with Walsh from stage to stage on the Tour. It was made clear to them that if they continued to fraternise with Walsh, they would be frozen out by Armstrong and given nothing to help them do their jobs. Shamefully, the three journalists caved in to the pressure and Walsh was effectively booted out of the communal car.

Walsh has often said that he refused to fall into the trap of so many sports journalists – being 'a fan with a typewriter' – and said he never worried about being unpopular with his peers: 'A good story is always worth pursuing, no matter how difficult pursuing it might be.'

So where were the American cycling writers when this was all happening? And when, in winning his seventh straight Tour in 2005, Armstrong was recording the fastest pace in race history: an average speed over the whole tour of 41.7 kilometres per hour? Why did it fall to an Irishman writing for a British newspaper to expose the extraordinary scam that the Texan had perpetrated on the sporting world? Clearly, eyes were averted and difficult questions avoided by many in the press pack back home.

Which brings us back to all the sportsfolk who have managed to keep their double lives secret, thanks in part to a less-than-rigorous media.

They give rise to suspicions out there in readerland about the true nature of journalism: is it a 'nudge, nudge, wink, wink' closed shop? Is bad news sometimes contained in-house, to the detriment of any sort of accountability, because that cover-up might later work to a journalist's advantage? Has 'publish and be damned' become a hopelessly quaint and outmoded concept?

Reporters are faced with this problem all the time: in order to protect a valuable source or a friend, do they only tell three-quarters of a story and leave out the bit that upsets their contact?

Of course some do. Only the most courageous and resilient of them, such as Walsh, write without any fear or favour.

This issue for sport journalists, especially young impressionable ones, has long been a vexed one. They've grown up having Tiger Woods or Harry Kane or Lewis Hamilton posters on their bedroom walls then one day they find themselves, pen and notepad in hand, actually interviewing their idols. Or drooling all over them in between questions. It's very difficult to retain objectivity in situations like this. I know, I've been there.

It's only after these young reporters have been in the caper for a few years that they realise sportspeople are often not the demi-gods they're painted as. Or even one-third of one-fifth of a demi-god. They might be good at roosting an inflated pigskin around a football field or hitting a small, dimpled white ball in a straight line, but their talents in life sometimes don't extend much beyond that.

Having worked in Perth, where Ben Cousins played and played up, I can attest to the large number of professional journalists there trying to uphold the trade's noblest ideals. But then there are some who'd prefer to be mates with the big-name footballers and cricketers, drink with them in bars and – joy of joys – be called over by their nickname, and taken into the sportsman's confidence. They are not journalists so much as unpaid PR consultants, groupies in a grubby shirt, or, as Walsh would say, 'fans with typewriters'.

Still, who am I to be throwing stones? That noise I hear is probably my own glass house tinkling around me. Regarding my own personal Taiwanese bus dilemma ... Yep, after much thought, I chose discretion as the better part of valour, and opted not to write the story. I think it's the same decision I'd make today.

THE SHOTS YOU REMEMBER

There are the great shots played to a global audience that everyone remembers. Then there are the great shots that only you, and a handful of others, have seen. **Mike Clayton** recalls the best he has witnessed.

Everyone knows the famous shots: Tom Watson's chip-in on Pebble Beach's 17th hole at the 1982 US Open; Jack Nicklaus's one iron on the same penultimate hole in the same championship 10 years earlier; Ben Hogan's long iron on the 18th at Merion in the 1950 US Open; Seve Ballesteros's three wood out of the fairway bunker at the 1983 Ryder Cup, or his shot through the tree and over the wall in Switzerland in 1993; Larry Mize's chip-in to win the 1987 Masters playoff.

There are, however, lots of shots hardly anyone sees, but which stick in the memory of those who did. So pure was the flight, so unusually sweet the strike, years later you can still see it.

David Jones was the tallest man on the European Tour in the 1980s and one of the nicest. Northern Irish, he was a club pro who came out on tour and played some pretty decent golf. He had a set of old Pings, the model before the Eye Two, with massive grips matching his huge hands. One of the best short holes in Ireland is the 15th at Portmarnock. It plays along the beach on the right, the green is long and narrow and a huge hollow sweeps anything remotely left far from the green. Think the 15th at Kingston Heath but 30 yards longer, no bunkers on the left and the 14th fairway is the Irish Sea. It's a properly hard hole.

The wind could blow at Portmarnock and this day it was really howling off the right. If you started your shot right of the green with a hook it might hit the green, but by the time it had the ball would have moved so far in the air it would likely run all the way across the green and down into the hollow. Jonesy took out his three iron and hit a piercing hard cut back into the wind. The ball never deviated an inch, flew straight at the middle of the green and finished 15 feet from the hole.

Years later, I'd see Jonesy and just say, 'three iron, 15, Portmarnock', and he'd laugh. He's building golf courses in Africa now, but I guarantee if you ever met him and said the same, he'd still laugh. What a shot it was.

English pro DJ Russell, is also now building courses. We played at Birkdale in 1986 and nothing at all memorable happened – except for one three wood he hit at the eighth hole. He'd skied his drive a bit (it was back in the day when people sometimes skied wooden-headed drivers) and had just over 260 yards to the hole – way too far back to have any reasonable expectation of reaching the green. He had a beautiful black MacGregor three wood and he just hammered it.

The six of us – three players and three caddies – all looked on in awe at this ball heading straight at the green. And not the front but the middle. DJ did not urge the ball on – it was obvious it was flying all the way there. Same thing as Jonesy's shot – ask him about it and he'll remember.

I played the opening two rounds of the 1991 Australian Masters at Huntingdale with Ian Baker-Finch. He was at the top of his game, coming off a terrific season in 1990, including a fourth place at St Andrews in The Open. He was playing well when we came to Huntingdale's narrow, short par-four, eighth hole on Friday. The hole was (and still is) lined with ti-tree, pretty much a guarantee of an unplayable lie, and most of us played it sensibly with a one or two iron and a full wedge. There was no real need to hit the driver but Finchy did, hitting a perfect high, 5-yard draw up within 50 yards of the green.

He won't remember it, but it was obvious he was ready and more than competent enough to win something big. Three years later, it might have taken him one tee shot and then two provisionals to hit the same fairway. What happened? Who knows, but at least he had climbed the mountain – one from which very few have ever seen the view.

On the second afternoon of the 1980 Australian Open at The Lakes, a huge southerly wind came up from nowhere. Mark O'Meara was standing over a three iron at the 12th when his caddie told him to wait. Bemused he was, but wait he did, and a minute later he hit a seven iron onto the green. It was crazy. Hale Irwin hit a driver 158 yards at the par-three 18th (a 190-yard hole).

A couple of groups later Michael Gay came to the 18th. (My first interstate junior match was in Sydney in 1974 against Michael, who was older than me and a lot better. Clearly. He cleaned me up in 13 holes.) When Michael pulled out his one iron, the television commentators had a laugh. He ripped this thing hard and low through the wind and it flew 15 feet from the hole.

Michael and I hadn't seen each other for years when we ran into each other in Albury late in 2017 and he asked me if I remembered him.

'Remember you? Hell, you beat me seven and six in my first interstate match and then at The Lakes hit one of the most unbelievable one-irons I've ever seen.'

'You remember that shot?'

'Of course, you never forget shots like those.'

Greg Norman played the same 1974 interstate series at Ryde-Parramatta, losing three of the five matches but at the same time clearly showing he was the best player there. I went out to watch his match with Victoria's number one, Peter Sweeney, and the first shot I ever saw Greg hit was a drive at a par four late in the match, a match he lost.

He was using a Jack Nicklaus Slazenger driver with a head barely any bigger than a modern three wood and a 1.62-inch B51. It was a rocket ball (at Turnberry in 1994 Nicklaus called it 'the longest ball ever made') and Norman smashed his tee shot further than I'd ever seen anyone drive. It finished up in a willow tree through the fairway but it was an early glimpse into the future. Two and a half years later he won his first professional event, the West Lakes Classic in Adelaide, astounding the whole country with his power hitting. To most he was unknown – but not to any of us who had already seen him play.

The American player and coach Mac O'Grady competed in the Senior Australian Open at Royal Perth in 2010 and, as was his wont, he was teaching on the range after the round when an old member asked him if it was true he could hit left-handed as well as right. Mac has a great golf swing and an uncommon talent for both teaching and hitting shots. He won a couple of times on the US Tour – most would suggest it could have been more.

Mac confirmed to the old man he could indeed hit left-handed and asked what shot he'd like to see. 'High draw, high fade, whatever you want.'

'A high draw would be nice.'

Mac had more party tricks than anyone. He took the driver he was using (a right-handed persimmon 1990 Japanese Honma), turned it on the toe wrong-way around, made a left-handed swing identical to his right-handed swing and hit a perfect high draw 250 yards down the range.

'That,' said the old man, 'is the most incredible thing I have ever seen.'

There always has to be a Seve Ballesteros shot included in such a story.

We were playing Huntingdale in the 1983 Australian Masters and got to the 10th hole, a short par five playing into a fairly decent wind. Seve took out his Toney Penna three wood, the one he would use to hit the incredible bunker shot at the Ryder Cup eight months later. He burned the shot through the wind to 4 feet. He missed the putt and I suggested to his caddie, Manuel Ramos, a friend and former Portuguese Open champion, that his boss's putting wasn't so sharp.

'No, it's not but it will be by Augusta.' It was. He won the Masters by four in April and stood alone at the top of the game. What a player he was.

Wayne Grady once asked a fellow PGA Tour player ('I can't even remember who it was') who was the best player he'd ever seen on the Tour.

'I'll tell you one thing,' the player said. 'I've seen every bloke out here play badly – Nicklaus, Watson, all of them – with one exception. I never saw Bruce Lietzke play badly.'

– Mike Clayton

METAL CHOPSTICKS AND BONUS BURGERS

Se-ri Pak started a revolution in Korean women's golf two decades ago by blazing a trail on the LPGA Tour. Now, there are 20 Koreans on the main women's circuit, plus many more on a thriving domestic tour, and they're dominating. **Mike Clayton** speaks to two of their best players to discover the secret to their success.

For sure, they planned to make us the best players in the world.
— **So Yeon Ryu, on Korea's golf program**

'They've asked me this question about 200 times,' said 2011 US Open and 2017 ANA Inspiration champion So Yeon Ryu, without a hint of annoyance at me when I ask, 'How is it that Korean women have learned to play the game so well, dominating every tour they compete on, and playing at a level beyond the reach of most of their competitors?'

When Se-ri Pak won the US Women's Open in 1998, she was the lone Korean on the LPGA Tour. A decade later, there were more than 20. 'Definitely we should say thank you to Se-ri,' said So Yeon. 'She was the one who opened up the door for us.' And once open, hordes of Asian players stormed through it. The LPGA Tour became a global circuit, one strongly supported in Asia and by Asian companies.

Early in 2018, there were 20 Koreans ranked in the world's top 50 players – and 39 in the top 100. By contrast, there are a dozen Americans in the top 50 and 21 in the top 100. It has been an extraordinary transformation at the top of the women's game. In the decade since the start of 2008, Koreans have won 19 of the 45 major championships (The Evian Championship only became a major in 2013) while the Americans have 13.

Ryu is well placed to assess the phenomenon of the two-decade ascendancy of Korean women. She has been a top-10 player since her first full season on the LPGA in 2012, finishing in the top 10 in half of the 150-odd LPGA tournaments she has competed in since beating countrywoman Hee-kyung Seo in the 2011 US Open playoff.

Not only have Koreans dominated the rankings, they have raised the standard of play with superior technique and noticeably better ball striking. 'I think for sure the Koreans have the best-looking swings in the world – in general,' said Ryu.

The exception proving the rule is perhaps the best of them, Inbee Park, the champion of all five women's majors and the Olympic gold medal in Brazil. Her swing, with the unorthodox, head-turned-to-the-target-at-impact move, is no model to copy but she has a putter 'that has crippled more men than polio', as Gary Player once said of his blade.

In Seoul for the 2015 Hana Bank tournament, it took me just 15 minutes on the practice fairway observing one of the best fields of the season to understand why the Koreans are so dominant. It was simple: they had better, more repeatable, golf swings and they hit the ball better.

The range was lined end-to-end with impressive players. Americans Lexi Thompson and Brittany Lincicome rip the ball with great power but would you ever teach either method?

Michelle Wie once looked as though she would be the Tiger Woods of the women's game but she has won 'only' five times since finishing fourth as a 14-year-old amateur at the 2004 Kraft

Nabisco. Almost a decade and a half later, her swing looks a contorted contrivance – in stark contrast to the beautiful 'Ernie Els' move she had as a 15-year-old.

Others are more orthodox but don't hit with the same power. There are the one-dimensional players churning out one identical-looking shot after shot, but players such as Ryu, who have greater variety, are always likely to beat them.

The two most popular reasons put forward to explain the Koreans' success are their work ethic and how many of their best female athletes are being drawn to golf because it is seen as an important and aspirational game. I hear people say 'they work harder' almost in a derogatory way, as if working hard gives them an unfair advantage. They don't think Ben Hogan worked hard? Or Greg Norman? Or Tiger Woods?

Christina Kim, three times a winner on the LPGA Tour, was born of Korean parents but grew up in California, giving her a foot in both camps. 'Hard work,' she told me, 'is a cultural thing. It's part of the Korean identity.' Ryu agreed: 'Everybody in Korea works hard.'

Kim floated an interesting theory that related to Korean success at archery: 'If they don't sweep all the medals in archery, it's a failure, and there is one suggestion that their skill is to do with the use of metal chopsticks. All Asian countries use chopsticks and mostly they are wooden, but in Korea we have those really heavy round metal ones. They have been using them for thousands of years and many argue that the dexterity we have created in our fingertips is partly due to the use of those metal chopsticks. We are the only country that has been doing that – otherwise you starve. Try picking up a grain of rice with metal chopsticks – it's really hard.'

More specific to golf, Kim says, 'Koreans just hit every shot straight and they are so good around the greens – it's interesting in a nation where golfers are basically raised on five-tier driving ranges, often only 150 yards long and surrounded by nets. They are not necessarily taught to play the game or taught to create the artistry from tee to green but once you get them on the green it's absurd.'

Kim said the family structure in Korea, where the parents are obeyed and discipline is paramount, is also important. 'Korea is similar to a lot of European countries – it's a very family-orientated society and everything that is done is done with the entire family – there is a much tighter bond with the sense of family unity. And honestly some of it has to do with fear – parents are very strict and very demanding.'

Kim sees the Korean domination of the LPGA Tour as a continuation of a trend started by other non-Americans 20 years ago. 'The game itself has evolved so much. Thirty years ago, the LPGA Tour didn't have many players from other countries. It was an American tour. But the best four players in this generation – Karrie Webb, Lorena Ochoa, Annika Sörenstam and Inbee – have all been non-Americans.

'Inbee is the model Korean player. You are taught as a child not to let anything out, to let your clubs do the talking. You watch Inbee – it doesn't matter what tournament it is, her heart's pumping on the inside and she's nervous but she doesn't look it. You would put her in any situation – she would look the same, but deep inside it's still coursing through her veins.'

Ryu grew up in awe of Pak, the first great Korean player. As a result of Pak's trailblazing, Ryu said a new generation of young players emerged, 'and Korean companies were keen to support women's golf – so we always had the good support.

'People in Korea think, even ten years ago, that golf is a rich person's sport but my family wasn't that rich. When companies start to support women's golf they always make a team – they pick one or two really great players and a few okay players and have one or two amateurs – and I was one of the amateurs. Jiyai Shin [former world number one] was one of the amateurs also.

'But I really enjoyed it and couldn't wait to go to the driving range – but I cannot even call it a driving range. It's really just a cage only five yards long and I just keep hitting the ball in the net but it was just so much fun.

'When I was seven or eight, one of the famous snacks for us was the McDonald's hamburger. When we practised, there was a pocket in the net and who got the most balls in the pocket won the extra hamburger. That's the way I started to enjoy playing golf. My goal was to play golf and I accidentally became a national team member.

'I became a national team member when I was fifteen and we had the national camp in January with seventy players. We would wake up at six am and go running for ten kilometres, have breakfast, then either practise at a driving range or play golf and then have lunch. If we played in the morning it was practice in the afternoon. Then we would have another run before the dinner and then we studied about the golf rules.'

It sounds a little like a boot camp but the players obediently complied, understanding the intensive tuition and training would only help them improve.

Perhaps the work-life balance is skewed in Korea – and one wonders what happens to those who fall by the wayside – but the hours and the effort make it quite apparent why the country has produced so many great players.

'A private Korean company supported me to come to Australia to play golf,' said Ryu. 'I was fifteen when I went to Sydney with all the golf team – there were a few guys and a few girls. Because of all the support we didn't need to worry about the money. We were able to have quality practice and better golf lessons. It was good to be in Australia for practice because in Korea golf course is so expensive. There is the green fee and you have to pay the caddie one hundred dollars for the round. If you want to play eighteen holes you need two hundred and fifty.

'We learn to play on the driving range. We don't have the real grass practice fairway. Pretty much we practise on the mats with the shitty ball.

'When we came to Australia we were able to practise on the grass and play eighteen holes every day. We didn't play the best courses in Sydney but it didn't matter. Off the fake grass, we couldn't practise the flop shot – we just could not do it but we could play it in Australia.'

One of the accusations levelled at the Koreans is they forsake a normal childhood in an obsessive quest to be a golf champion.

'Maybe,' says Ryu, 'the difference between the "Korean work harder" and the "American work harder" is Koreans always want to do their best when we want to do something but, if I was to put it negatively, we just don't know how to have a good balance.

'So you see a lot of girls who come out onto the tour – if they win one or two times they just disappear because they burn out. There is pressure and all they've done for the last ten years is just golf, golf, golf – then they are just sick of it.

'The other kind of bad thing is so many Koreans come out on the tour and so many win tournaments. Winning is not an easy thing but Koreans think if you are professional golfer of course you have to win. So Koreans started to think it is really nothing – you achieve a really big thing but at home they don't see it as really big thing.

'From the American or European perspective they think we don't really know how to enjoy the life. They think the only thing Koreans do is just play golf, golf, golf and that is why they are great. But they think they know how to make a good balance between golf and their personal life and to play longer than Koreans – even though they might not win.

'But I cannot really tell what's right and what's wrong because it could be good to win the tournament and only play on tour for five years – it depends on how you want to live.'

While Pak was a pioneer and heroine to a new generation of Korean golfers, Ryu hinted that her legacy did have one downside. 'After Se-ri won the US Women's Open she said in a television interview: "I have been practising all day. I didn't go to school and if sometimes I failed my dad punished me. Like sometimes he just hit me or sometimes he just made me ... run for ten kilometres."

'Because of that,' Ryu said, 'Korean parents started to copy it. Se-ri really believed she was able to play well because of what her father did to her. So Korean parents push their children to always practise – just no studying.'

Fortunately for Ryu, she had a coach who was more worldly than most and understood the importance of an education. 'I started to play in elementary school and my golf coach was a friend of my father. He knew it was important to play golf and to study as well. He was always saying if you want to become professional golfer you have to study as well. You cannot just be dumb golfer. You better to know bigger world instead of just golf.

'He educated my parents pretty well also – and I am very independent. I always hated to do something if my parents forced me to do it – so my parents knew I am not going to do something if they force me to do it. They let me do what I want to do and I choose to study and practise – for a couple of hours but high quality.

'Still a lot of Korean players practise a crazy amount of time but the problem is you cannot give your best for ten hours. You cannot concentrate for that long. It's more a matter of quality time, instead of how many golf balls you hit.

'One thing the Korean Golf Association didn't do well was arrange for us to go to international tournaments like US Women's Amateur, Orange Bowl and US Junior. We are only experienced in Korea. I think because of that we don't really have the skill; we know how to hit straight but we don't know how to shape the ball. We know how to do normal chip shot but we don't know how to bump and run, how to make the spin.'

The antithesis of the Korean model is the environment of the Spanish caddie yards where genius of the like of Ballesteros was honed. As they waited for the members to come they would practise chipping, learning all the little shots. It's the mechanic-versus-artist debate. There is room for both and the contrasts are illuminating.

'If Koreans are learning golf they are always starting at the driving range – and they are always trying to make the pretty swing instead of just hitting well – so first thing they do is make a pretty swing and then next thing just hit it straight,' Ryu says. 'Always starting with the swing – not the chipping and the putting.'

Yet, strangely, few clubs allow non-members to practise on the course – even players as illustrious as Ryu and Inbee Park. 'It's still not easy at home,' Ryu says. 'They more care about the members. It's weird to see because people would expect they would allow us to do everything on the golf club.

'It's also easy to find a good coach now, but when I was young I had no idea who was a good coach or any idea about what's right swing and what's wrong swing. I had a Korean coach but before I started working with [Queenslander] Ian Triggs I didn't really know about my golf swing at all. He taught me how to hit a lot of different shots but it took me five years of good practice to be able to hit a fade.

'Since I have been working with Cam [Australian Cameron McCormick] I totally understand my golf swing and right now I can judge myself. If I only work with my Korean coach I have no chance to understand my swing.'

The growth in popularity of golf, and the attention that brings the top Korean players on the LPGA Tour, has produced a range of interesting side-effects, not all of them positive.

'The problem is women's golf is so popular it becomes so commercial now,' Ryu says. 'I would say people should judge the player by their performance not how they look, but because golfers become so famous they become like a celebrity and people start to judge a player by how they look.

'Because of that, a lot of Korean players started to lose weight and do a lot of plastic surgery. Selling the sexual thing may be helpful for growing the tour but it's not the main point and I feel like we are losing a bit of direction.'

Then Ryu addresses the issue many see as a difference between Korean golfers and their competitors: the mental game. Their outward stoicism is such that, birdie or bogey, it's hard to know how a Korean player is performing from just looking. There are no extravagant gestures, no histrionics. Outwardly at least, everything is a study of composure and equanimity.

'You have to learn to control your mind. You cannot swear in front of the people and you cannot hit the ground with your club in front of the people,' Ryu said.

'We naturally learn to control our mind because our parents don't let us carry on. Golf is a mind game where you have to control yourself.

'Maybe if you start screaming, maybe after that you could feel better – but we know how to make ourselves feel better without doing that. Maybe it's another thing why Koreans can play golf really well.'

A GOLFING EDUCATION

As an impressionable young Australian, **Mark Nelson**
studied for his Masters at Cambridge – which meant being
introduced to intervarsity golf, the annual Cambridge
Stymies v Oxford Divots grudge match, and the mandatory
drinking games that accompanied each and every fixture.

Don't we all love a surprise? Nothing quite beats the glow we get
from an unexpectedly positive outcome. Finding a crumpled $50
in a trouser pocket, oysters tasting so much better than they look –
or discovering the ridiculous fun of club golf in the UK. Forget the
clichéd stereotypes of buttoned-up, play-by-the-rules Englishmen.
The English club golfer treats his or her club as their personal
fiefdom, and manages to extract maximum enjoyment from their
membership, both on and off the course.

I made this surprising discovery as a youngster some years ago,
sent over to the UK, in a form of reverse transportation, to study
at Cambridge. Cricket season was over, I didn't have a clue about
rugby, so I thought I'd inveigle myself into the golf team as a means
of meeting a few people, and probably cadging a few free drinks
in the process.

The audition process was rigorous, and involved me convincing
the team hierarchy that my six handicap was a good enough
standard to make the team. (I was actually a 10 at that time,
but I assumed – correctly – that they were all bullshitting about
their own handicaps.) It also involved me buying drinks for them,

having a variety of drinks myself, and then buying the said team hierarchy even more drinks.

It all seemed to work, because it was decided that I'd be trialled in the second team the following week in a match against Royal West Norfolk GC up on the wild north-east Anglian coast. Quick note here for those not totally conversant with Oxbridge sporting matters. The first team in any major sport at Oxford or Cambridge is simply known as the Blue Team, or just The Blues. The second team always has a name. In cricket, the Cambridge Crusaders play against the Oxford Authentics. In rowing, the Cambridge second boat is called Goldie, and the Oxford second boat is called Isis (they might like to think about changing that one). And so it was that I found myself picked to play for the Cambridge Stymies in a club fixture that, if I proved that I was worth my place, would mean that I could eventually hope to play in the Varsity Match against our great rivals, the Oxford Divots.

I duly won my match against a charming elderly surgeon, and consequently became a competitor, a team member, a roving club golfer, and above all, a Stymie.

The golf 'season' was extraordinary. Friday night we would head off from Cambridge in a rented minibus, aiming to get to our opposing club in time for a drinks party, before being billeted out to the homes of various members. Most of these members were former Oxbridge inmates, with long memories of the state of a student's wallet, and were desperate to shower us with all manner of hospitality. Food, drink, comfortable beds; it got to the stage where I would often take along a bag of dirty laundry in the hope that it may miraculously end up clean by the end of the weekend.

The next day the golf match began in earnest, and always followed the same format, with straight foursomes in the morning, and singles matches in the afternoon. What transpired in between was the bit that required serious concentration, and usually meant that the Stymies quite often failed to trouble the scorers post-luncheon.

The day went a bit like this:

8.30 am: Begin foursomes match
11 am: Match over, four and three, or three and two
               (they were rarely close)
11.30 am: Head back to the locker room/bar

Then came the four stages of Imbibition. Firstly, a couple of pints of beer in the locker room while freshening up and dressing for lunch, followed by a move up to the club sitting room for a couple of pre-lunch gin and tonics while waiting for fellow team members to finish their matches (and their locker-room pints). Then lunch. A serious affair with the best food we were likely to have all week, accompanied by both red and white wine that came in bottles and that seemed to have been produced by real winemakers rather than chemical engineers.

Things would be getting rather fuzzy at this stage, but the coup de grace was still to be delivered. The draw for the singles matches having been made, and members notified as to who their opponents were, the inevitable hand on the shoulder would follow. 'Ah young fella, looks like you've got me this afternoon. Should be great fun. Now, before we head out, what are you having? Port or kummel?' They may as well have said: 'Do you prefer to be executed by firing squad or the electric chair?' You tentatively say 'Port', and a half-pint of port is delivered to you. You say 'Kummel', and, well ... Even Wikipedia describes kummel as 'a sweet, colourless liqueur flavoured with caraway seed, cumin, and fennel, and favoured by English golf clubs'. Favoured by Chemical Ali more likely. I rarely made the right choice, and just as rarely won a singles match after lunch. Pretty easy pickings, really, for the experienced English club golfer/luncher.

We ended up winning a few, and losing a few, but the Golfing Life Lessons were invaluable. There seemed to be an inverse correlation between the level of 'smartness' of the club and the post-match behaviour considered acceptable, or even 'normal'.

After finishing a match against one of the more desirable clubs (which shall remain nameless but rhymes with Funningdale), we were challenged by our opponents to an eight-man, eight-pint boat race in the club bar. Student form is good form, so we were quietly confident. The stewards neatly lined up the drinks, and we were awaiting the starter's gun when the opposition captain proudly informed us that 'at our club, a boat race always begins with a Le Mans start!' A degree of surprise on our part when we realised that rather than merely quaffing the pints sequentially in quick succession, one had to first run out of the bar, through the dining room, outon to the verandah, and then back to the bar before draining the glass. Nods of approval from many other members in the dining room as we completed the circuit, but no-one really raised an eyebrow. Quite nutty, but magnificent.

There were many such peculiarities throughout the season, but the common ground at all clubs was just how proud the members are of their own little slice of tee, green and fairway, and how hell-bent they were that visitors such as us should enjoy it to the maximum level.

The postscript to this induction into the ways of British club golf was that I managed to win enough matches during the season to be selected in the final team for the Stymies to play in the annual Varsity Match against Oxford. The overall golf team consisted of 22 players. The first 10 comprised the first team, the Blues as previously mentioned, and the bottom 10 made up the second team, the Stymies. Players 11 and 12 are the reserves for the Blues, but play in neither team. Instead they play the famous 'Dinner Match' of both foursomes and singles on the Thursday inbetween the Stymies and Blues matches, with the losing university expected to pick up the not insubstantial bill for the Varsity Match dinner on the Saturday evening. By all accounts, the pressure of playing the Dinner Match is unparalleled in global sport.

I was understandably quite nervous as I stood on the first tee to meet my Oxford opponent for my singles match. Not only had I already lost my foursomes but as my opponent strode towards me I could see that he was extremely well-dressed, a characteristic that never fails to unnerve me. Formal introductions were duly made and, having won the toss, I strode forward to the first tee intent on showing my sartorial adversary just what I thought of his colour-coordinated ensemble. Wanting to leave nothing in the sheds, I launched into my drive at full ramming speed, only to experience that sickening feeling on the follow through as I realised that I'd made the barest of contacts with the ball, and it now rested on the grass a full 6 inches in front of my still-implanted wooden tee.

The stony silence was punctuated by nervous coughing, and striped-tie adjustment from the many spectators, before the inevitable, smug request was delivered by my opponent: 'Excuse me old boy, would you mind marking that so I can play?' Complying, I made my way back through the throng, walked on to the tee, marked my ball then slunk away again.

Despite the embarrassing start, and a minor choke when I had him 'dormie three', I did manage to win the match, proving to myself at least that while the Battle of Waterloo may indeed have been won on the playing fields of Eton, the Varsity Match wasn't. The Stymies prevailed, and the celebrations were loud and long.

I left the Stymies a winner, with the added bonus of a Hawks Club tie (a most useful accessory at any major sporting venue in the UK), and considered myself extremely fortunate. I could now feel right at home on the heathlands, the linksland, and on the fens. I knew now that losing a match 7 and 6 was 'Dog Licence', that all my fellow golfers had been playing 'Spoof', since before I could count, and that the last player to three-putt always held 'The Snake'.

And if at the end of the game my reward was a pint of Adnams Ale in a solid silver tankard at Aldeburgh GC, or a superb lunch at New Zealand GC in Surrey, then it could be considered that all was indeed well with the world.

READ ON

Golf is a sport that has traditionally lent itself to fine writing, confirming the rule that the smaller the ball, the better the words. **Mike Clayton** lists his 12 best books written on the game.

If you are interested in golf there are any number of great books on all manner of the game's disciplines, from architecture to players, tournaments to instruction. For me all the instructions books aren't as good as a good relationship with a competent teacher, but that won't stop golfers trying to find a swing in a book or a magazine. Some of these books will be hard to find, but like out-of-the-way courses they are worth the search.

The Spirit of St. Andrews, by Alister MacKenzie

It is a remarkable thing about golf courses that nearly every man has an affection for the particular mud-heap on which he plays.

MacKenzie wrote *Golf Architecture* in 1920 and expanded on his thoughts in *The Spirit of St. Andrews*. He died unexpectedly in 1934, aged 63, a few months before the first US Masters at his Augusta, leaving behind the manuscript undiscovered until the early 1990s, when his stepson found it among a pile of family papers. The answers to many of golf's current problems lie within the covers of this book. MacKenzie worried about the ball going too far – way back then –

and understood 'there is no limit to science'. He writes too of the problems of the committee system and its inherent instability: 'The history of most golf clubs is that a committee is appointed, they make mistakes, and just as they are beginning to learn from these mistakes they resign office and are replaced by others who will make still greater mistakes, and so it goes on.' He argues the game's future and survival is dependent on interesting courses and explains why men grow bored with golf without understanding why.

The Confidential Guide to Golf Courses, by Tom Doak

Royal Melbourne, I think, is the course Augusta wants to be: wide enough for anybody, but brilliantly routed to make use of the topography and bunkered to reward bold play and bold decisions.

Doak's original early 1990s book is in the midst of a five-volume update with three co-authors to ensure they cover the world and see everything new worth seeing – or not. It began as a book for travelling friends, enabling them to make informed decisions about whether a course was worth the expenditure and effort to visit. Arguably this book is even more important now than it was in the early 1990s, given that green fees at famous courses have escalated to extraordinary sums. Rather than ranking courses in numerical order, Doak places them into 11 categories from zero to 10; it's a much better way to do it, making it more worthwhile than all the magazine lists put together. Of course there will be disagreement, but I've never seen a course more than a point from where I think it should be.

The World Atlas of Golf, edited by Mark Rowlinson

On paper, North Berwick seems like any other ancient links course – out along the water for two miles (three kilometres) or so and then back again to the clubhouse. Once a golfer gets on the ground, however, all preconceptions become misconceptions, and all certainties become ambiguities.

The original 1970s *World Atlas* must have been one of the biggest-selling golf books ever. While it was very safe and politically correct, covering all parts of the globe, it was hardly a collection of the best courses in the world. Despite that drawback, it was a tremendous book and the first introduction to many of the world's wondrous and exotic courses. It was of its time and pre-dated all the pretty picture books of the game's great courses. Editor Mark Rowlinson thought a new edition was in order more than another reprint was due and commissioned a group of writers to pick a representative collection of the best and most interesting courses in the world. Out went Singapore Island, Olgiata and Firestone; in came Kingston Heath, Morfontaine and Sand Hills. Each chapter has a beautifully drawn map showing the critical routing of the holes and a long essay on the historical and architectural significance of the course in question.

Hogan, by Curt Sampson

'Mr. Hogan, the President (Eisenhower) is on line two,'
Claribel (his secretary) said.
'I'm not playing with that goddam hack,' Hogan muttered.
Then he picked up the phone.

Sampson is one of the very best modern American golf writers and all of his books are more than worth seeking out. His biography of Hogan chronicles the golfer's life, uncovering the character and personality of the most private and mystical of the great champions. Apparently Mrs Hogan was not pleased with the book, disbelieving her husband swore, and authorised a biography by another author. Sampson says, 'He grew up in the caddie yard, he was in the army and he played the Tour. You think he didn't swear? He just never did in front of women.'

The Eternal Summer, by Curt Sampson

> Three eras came together on the final day ... The day
> embraced the last hurrah of Hogan, the confirmation of
> Palmer and the preview of a burly Ohio State undergraduate
> with terrifying length and frightening powers of
> concentration – Jack W Nicklaus.

Another by Sampson, *The Eternal Summer* is the story of the 1960 season and centres around arguably golf's greatest day, when the careers of Jack Nicklaus, Ben Hogan and Arnold Palmer intersected at Cherry Hills in the US Open. All three – the 20-year-old amateur Nicklaus, 30-year-old Palmer, then at the top of the game, and the older statesman, 48 years old but capable of hitting 52 consecutive greens in the Open – have a chance to win. If you could go back in time, it surely is the one day in golf's history to pick to witness – not least because there were 36 holes of it. A month later Palmer, the winner at Cherry Hills, would go to St Andrews in search of the third leg of the Grand Slam, only to be thwarted by a man playing in his third major championship, the former club pro at Pymble in New South Wales, Kel Nagle.

My Life in Golf, by Peter Thomson

> I learned to play the American game over there between
> 1951 and 1960 and it revolted me. I have always regarded the
> bounce of the ball as the third dimension in golf, but the ball
> is not allowed to bounce in America. It is sickening to see the
> game reduced to something like archery or darts.

I grew up reading Peter Thomson's columns in *The Age* in Melbourne. No player wrote more prolifically and he was not afraid to take on the most controversial of topics, writing what others dared not. He wrote a particularly scathing critique of the redesigned Australian course in Sydney after the 1977 Australian Open, in a column headlined 'Packer Money Wasted', likening water hazards by the greens to 'an American fad like fins on Cadillacs'. For years he seemingly wrote the foreword for each new golf book in Australia, and he often penned pieces on his approach to golf for books comprised of chapters by famous players. Still, he steadfastly refused to write a book of his own until Steve Perkin and publisher Geoff Slattery convinced him to do something resembling the structure of Harvey Penick's *Little Red Book*. Perkin sat a tape recorder in front of Thomson, asked the questions and the transcribed answers became the basis of the book. Included too were a wide collection of his best newspaper columns. The book itself sold decently in Australia, but British publishers declined to publish it because it 'wouldn't be of much interest over here'. A man who won The Open five times, the most articulate golfing writer ever, of no interest? Staggering.

The Future of Golf, by Geoff Shackelford

Actually tradition has been auctioned off in the name of the market-place. Golf is in serious danger of becoming just like too many other pastimes – controlled by a select few with only dollar signs in their hearts and minds. That perhaps would be tolerable if the sport was attracting new players, affordable for every day golfers, and preserving its most hallowed grounds.

Geoff Shackelford is a friend, an author and the keeper of geoffshackelford.com, the best blog in golf. Of his many books, this is perhaps the most important. 'As a golfer,' wrote Ben Crenshaw, 'open your mind when reading this treatise on the sport and its future. We all must consider where golf is headed and how best to protect the traditions of the game.' As with MacKenzie's *Spirit of St. Andrews*, the answers to many of the game's problems are to be found here. Published in 2004, it's more important than ever.

Masters of the Links, **edited by Geoff Shackelford**

> In this era of obscene power, the likes of which the game
> has never witnessed, why not strive to induce a little fun into
> the mix and at the same time present a true test of delicacy
> and accuracy?

So writes Ben Crenshaw in his essay on the short par three in this collection of essays by most of the best golf architects past and present, including Alister MacKenzie, AW Tillinghast, CB Macdonald, Bill Coore, Gil Hanse and Pete Dye. If you were thinking of sitting on the committee at your local club, this book is readable in one sitting and likely the best summary of everything you will need to understand.

Arnie, **by Tom Callahan**

> Throughout the years I watched him at many tournaments
> on both sides of the Atlantic Ocean. I was at Oakmont in
> Pennsylvania when, with six holes to play, Palmer was sure
> he was winning the US Open only to hear the thunder of
> Johnny Miller's 63 up ahead. I was at Medinah in Illinois
> when the vinegar between Arnold and Jack finally spilled
> out. I was at Muirfield Village when they reconciled. And
> I was at Augusta in Georgia on the Wednesday when they
> played their first practice round with 20-year-old amateur
> Tiger Woods.

Callahan is one of America's great sportswriters, having for decades covered many of his country's legendary sporting heroes for *Sports Illustrated*, including the famous 1974 Rope a Dope Foreman–Ali fight in Kinshasa. In the dressing room after the fight, which Ali won in the eighth round, Ali motioned to Callahan to come close and whispered, 'What you don't understand is black men scare white men a lot more than black men scare black men.' Callahan knew Palmer well and liked him. This book is storytelling at its best, covering for me the most interesting generations of professional golfers, who made the tour today what it is. Players can thank Tiger Woods all they like for the money they play for now, but it was Palmer before Woods who popularised the game.

The Story of American Golf, by Herbert Warren Wind

> There are three types of golf – golf, tournament golf and major championship golf. The difference between the three is one-tenth physiological and nine-tenths psychological.

If you are interested in the history of golf in the US this is the definitive book, beginning with the very origins of the game and running through all the way to 1975. It obviously pre-dates Tiger Woods and the then-unimaginable dominance of Korean women, but Wind writes beautifully and expansively on the development of the game in the US. And if you want to know anything about the first Australian-born winner of a major championship there is a chapter on Walter Travis – 'The Great Old Man'.

The Big Miss, by Hank Haney

> In retrospect, 2007 was when Tiger began to lose the joy of playing and began to look at his career as something he wanted to get over with sooner rather than later.

Hank Haney met a young golf pro on a range in Pinehurst struggling to keep his tour card with all he had left of a miserable game. It was the end of 1982 and Mark O'Meara barely survived the guillotine falling on the 126th man on the moneylist. In 1984, with a new swing crafted by Haney, O'Meara finished second on that list. O'Meara was a friend and mentor to Tiger Woods and years later Haney would take on the toughest teaching job in golf – not messing up Tiger Woods.

Some are critical of the job Haney did with Woods' swing, but from the beginning in March 2004 until May 2010 when they finished up, Woods won 38 tournaments. Not bad. The technical information is fascinating and any young, aspiring player should read it to glean an idea of just how hard Woods worked to achieve all he did.

Jenkins at the Majors, by Dan Jenkins

> In this episode at Sandwich along a gray, damp, mushy, blustery coast of Kent in the game's oldest professional championship, Norman played a round of golf in the 1993 British Open that has long been expected of him. Under gripping conditions against the best players in the world, he fired a 64 that is certain to be headed for a place in the Louvre or the British Museum.

A few years ago, Dan Jenkins chalked up his 52nd Masters. 'Can you imagine,' he said, 'spending a whole year of your life in Augusta, Georgia?' He's seen them all, from Hogan to Woods. Hogan was his man, because both lived in Fort Worth, Texas, and Jenkins was the newspaperman at the *Fort Worth Telegram* assigned to cover the great man's play. The book is a collection of his columns, the first covering Hogan's win at Oakland Hills in 1951, and the last Woods playoff win in the 2008 Open at Torrey Pines. There's a lot in between, all of it worth reading.

ABOUT THE AUTHORS

In 32 years as a journalist, **Charles Happell** has covered many of the world's leading sports events, including the Italia'90 World Cup, the Sydney Olympics and US Masters golf. At Melbourne's *Age* newspaper, he wrote about golf and covered 10 majors, including five Masters, before being appointed the paper's sports editor in 2002. He later became *Crikey*'s sports columnist and has authored two best-selling books as well as a short biography of Australian golfer Karrie Webb. A modestly performed batsman in his time, he has no trouble in racking up big scores on the golf course.

Mike Clayton is a modern golf renaissance man – a student of the game, as well as historian, course architect, former touring pro and journalist. Mike played on the Australasian Tour for 26 years, winning seven times, and also competed on the European Tour for 18 years, winning the 1984 Timex Open. For many years he wrote a golf column in *The Sunday Age*. He is now a course architect, partnering with 2006 US Open champion Geoff Ogilvy along with Mike Cocking and Ashley Mead in their Melbourne-based design business.

* * *

Peter Thomson is one of Australia's finest golfers, winning five British Opens between 1954 and 1965, and a host of other tournaments around the world. When he first began competing on the US Seniors

Tour, he won a then-record nine tournaments in the 1985 season. But he was much more than just a player, going on to become chairman of the Australian PGA for 32 years, an intelligent television and newspaper commentator, and also a noted golf-course designer, his Melbourne-based firm building or renovating 250 courses around the world.

Rob Sitch is an Australian director, screenwriter, actor, comedian and fair-to-middling golfer. In a midlife attempt at a drastically lower handicap, he ignored Ben Hogan's five fundamentals in favour of offset clubs, graphite shafts, YouTube videos, training aids, unsolicited tips and a variety of gut feelings. It's still early days but he now suspects Hogan might have been on to something.

Richard Allen has been playing golf for 50 years, during which time his wedge play has not improved. He spends most holidays wandering around looking for new courses to play. His four children are reluctant to take up the game, which is a source of much frustration. Richard has been writing about golf for 30 years, mainly for newspapers and magazines, both in Australia and overseas. He is the author of *The Spirit of Golf and How it Applies to Life: Inspirational Tales from the World's Greatest Game*.

Born in East Lothian, Scotland, **John Huggan** has been a freelance golf journalist for more than two decades. In a previous life he was, for eight years, the instruction editor at *Golf Digest* magazine in the United States; after returning to Scotland, he became the golf writer for *The Herald* newspaper. These days, he regularly contributes to two London-based dailies, *The Times* and the *Evening Standard*, as well as various publications around the world, including *Golf World* in the UK, *Golf Australia* and *New Zealand Golf*. He is also the European correspondent for *Golf Digest* and *Golf World* in the US.

Mark Nelson learned his golf on the sand scrapes of the Wimmera, where the stimpmeter runs at about 3, and still can't believe his luck that he is now allowed to play on grass. He is a member of several clubs including Royal Sydney and Royal Melbourne, but has accepted that his name is unlikely to ever adorn the honour boards at any of them. He graduated from Cambridge University in 1984 with a hard-fought 16–8 record for the Stymies, none of those wins, however, coming after lunch.

Born in east London to a non-golfing family, **Kathie Shearer** became acquainted with the game by chance – after meeting several Australian golfers, including her future husband, Bob, at work functions in London in the 1970s. A mother of two boys, and grandmother to another, she has been a mainstay on the Australasian golf scene for 30 years where she has run media centres at every major tournament – organising player interviews and looking after the golf scribes. She is also a marriage celebrant.

Andrew Thomson, a lawyer, is a former Australian MP and Minister for Sport. He attended university in Tokyo in the 1980s and currently lives in Fukuoka, Japan. As a student in Tokyo he caddied for foreign professionals playing the Japanese circuit and served as an interpreter at various ladies professional tournaments. These days he serves on the Foreign Affairs Committee of the Japan Golf Association and is one of Japan's most ardent hickory golfers. Andrew is the son of Peter Thomson, one of Australia's most accomplished professional golfers.

Steve Williams is the best-known, and most successful, caddie in golf. The straight-talking Kiwi toted the bag for Greg Norman, Raymond Floyd, Ian Baker-Finch and, most famously of all, Tiger Woods, with whom he won 13 major championships. Over those 40-odd years, which yielded more than 150 tournament wins, he was front and centre at some of the game's greatest moments. He recently wrote *Out of the Rough*, a memoir, and retired from caddying in 2018.

ACKNOWLEDGEMENTS

To the team at Hardie Grant, especially Pam, Mick and the ever-patient Emily, who drew the short straw and had to deal on a regular basis with two demanding golf writers and their many quirks and foibles. To Peter Thomson, Steve Williams and John Huggan, for their insights and helping to give the book a bit of extra gravitas. To the other contributors, Rob Sitch, Mark Nelson, Richie Allen and Andrew Thomson, who devoted their time to writing about a shared passion – and did so with enthusiasm, intelligence and humour. Mike and I thank you all for the contribution you've made in bringing this book to fruition and, hopefully, entertaining and informing a new generation of golfers about the game's rich history, great course design ... and eccentric cast of characters.

– Charles Happell, May 2018